BRICK, STONE & CONCRETE

TIME
LIFE
BOOKS ®

Other Publications:

THE TIME-LIFE GARDENER'S GUIDE

MYSTERIES OF THE UNKNOWN

TIME FRAME

FIX IT YOURSELF

FITNESS, HEALTH & NUTRITION

SUCCESSFUL PARENTING

HEALTHY HOME COOKING

UNDERSTANDING COMPUTERS

LIBRARY OF NATIONS

THE ENCHANTED WORLD

THE KODAK LIBRARY OF CREATIVE PHOTOGRAPHY

GREAT MEALS IN MINUTES

THE CIVIL WAR

PLANET EARTH

COLLECTOR'S LIBRARY OF THE CIVIL WAR

THE EPIC OF FLIGHT

THE GOOD COOK

WORLD WAR II

HOME REPAIR AND IMPROVEMENT

THE OLD WEST

BRICK, STONE & CONCRETE

TIME-LIFE BOOKS
ALEXANDRIA, VIRGINIA

Fix It Yourself was produced by
ST. REMY PRESS

MANAGING EDITOR	Kenneth Winchester
MANAGING ART DIRECTOR	Pierre Léveillé

Staff for *Brick, Stone & Concrete*

Series Editor	Brian Parsons
Editor	Dianne Thomas
Series Art Director	Diane Denoncourt
Art Director	Odette Sévigny
Research Editor	Michael Mouland
Designer	Nicolas Moumouris
Editorial Assistants	Cathleen Farrell, Donald Harman
Assistant Designer	Patrick J. Gordon
Contributing Writers	Edward Earle, James Fehr, Stewart Freed, Carol Halls
Electronic Designer	Maryse Doray
Contributing Illustrators	Gérard Mariscalchi, Jacques Proulx
Technical Illustrators	Nicolas Moumouris, Robert Paquet
Cover	Robert Monté
Index	Christine M. Jacobs
Administrator	Denise Rainville
Coordinator	Michelle Turbide
Systems Manager	Shirley Grynspan
Systems Analyst	Simon Lapierre
Studio Director	Maryo Proulx
Photographer	Julie Léger

Time-Life Books Inc. is a wholly owned subsidiary of
TIME INCORPORATED

FOUNDER	Henry R. Luce 1898-1967
Editor-in-Chief	Jason McManus
Chairman and Chief Executive Officer	J. Richard Munro
President and Chief Operating Officer	N. J. Nicholas Jr.
Editorial Director	Ray Cave
Executive Vice President, Books	Kelso F. Sutton
Vice President, Books	Paul V. Mc Laughlin

TIME-LIFE BOOKS INC.

EDITOR	George Constable
Executive Editor	Ellen Phillips
Director of Design	Louis Klein
Director of Editorial Resources	Phyllis K. Wise
Editorial Board	Russell B. Adams Jr., Dale M. Brown, Roberta Conlan, Thomas H. Flaherty, Lee Hassig, Donia Ann Steele, Rosalind Stubenberg
Director of Photography and Research	John Conrad Weiser
Asst. Director of Editorial Resources	Elise Ritter Gibson
PRESIDENT	Christopher T. Linen
Chief Operating Officer	John M. Fahey Jr.
Senior Vice Presidents	Robert M. DeSena, James L. Mercer, Paul R. Stewart
Vice Presidents	Stephen L. Bair, Ralph J. Cuomo, Neal Goff, Stephen L. Goldstein, Juanita T. James, Hallett Johnson III, Carol Kaplan, Susan J. Maruyama, Robert H. Smith, Joseph J. Ward
Director of Production Services	Robert J. Passantino
Supervisor of Quality Control	James King

Editorial Operations

Copy Chief	Diane Ullius
Production	Celia Beattie
Library	Louise D. Forstall
Correspondents	Elizabeth Kraemer-Singh (Bonn); Maria Vincenza Aloisi (Paris); Ann Natanson (Rome).

THE CONSULTANTS

Consulting Editor **David L. Harrison** served as an editor for several Time-Life Books do-it-yourself series, including *Home Repair and Improvement, The Encyclopedia of Gardening* and *The Art of Sewing.*

Monte Burch has written more than 50 books on subjects such as masonry and home repair. A regular contributor to national magazines, he is a member of the National Association of Home and Workshop Writers.

Richard Day, a do-it-yourself writer for a quarter century, is a founder of the National Association of Home and Workshop Writers and is the author of four books on concrete and masonry.

R. J. De Cristoforo has been a do-it-yourself writer for more than 40 years. He is a contributing editor of Popular Science magazine, and the author of 30 books on subjects ranging from leathercraft to stonework.

Jay Hedden, a former editor of Popular Mechanics and Workbench magazines, has written several books on home renovation and home repair.

Jim Mooney, of Waldo Bros. Company in Boston, Mass., a masonry and concrete supply company, has worked extensively with professional contractors and homeowners for 17 years.

Library of Congress Cataloging-in-Publication Data
Brick, stone & concrete.
   p. cm. – (Fix it yourself)
  Includes index.
  ISBN 0-8094-6264-8.
  ISBN 0-8094-6265-6 (lib. bdg.)
1. Masonry—Amateurs' manuals.
2. Dwellings—Maintenance and repair—Amateurs' manuals. I. Time-Life Books. II. Title: Brick, stone and concrete. III. Series.
TH5313.B75   1989
693' .1—dc19   88-39613
                    CIP

For information about any Time-Life book, please write:
Reader Information
Time-Life Customer Service
P.O. Box C-32068
Richmond, Virginia
23261-2068

CONTENTS

HOW TO USE THIS BOOK

Brick, Stone & Concrete is divided into three sections. The Emergency Guide on pages 8 to 13 provides information that can be indispensable, even lifesaving, in the event of a household emergency. Take the time to study this section *before* you need the important advice it contains.

The Repairs section — the heart of the book — is a comprehensive approach to troubleshooting and repairing brick, stone and concrete. Shown below are four sample pages from the chapter on stone, with captions describing the various features of the book and how they work.

For example, if the mortar joints in your stone retaining wall are crumbling, the Troubleshooting Guide on page 46 will suggest possible causes; if the problem is a blocked drainpipe, you will be directed to page 61 for instructions on how to clean it and maintain the retaining wall, and to page 59 for detailed steps on how to repair, or point, the joints. Or, if a stone surface is stained, the Troubleshooting Guide will refer you to the cleaning chart on page 49; there, you will be given information on a cleaning agent that is appropriate for the type of stone and the type of stain.

Introductory text
Describes the construction of brick, stone or concrete structures, their most common problems and basic repair approaches.

Anatomy diagrams
Locate and describe the various components of a brick, stone or concrete structure.

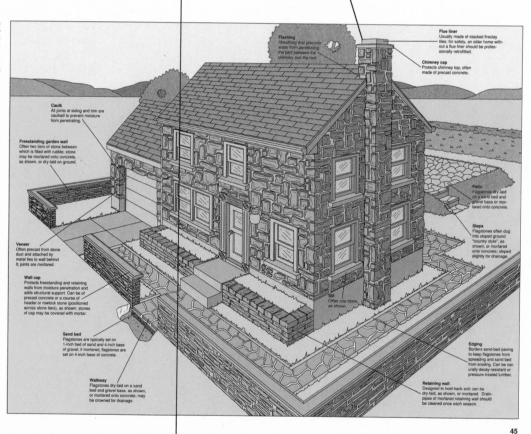

STONE

Many of the longest-lasting structures in the world are constructed of stone. Although stone can be more difficult to work with, and more expensive, than brick or concrete, it is strong, durable, and offers an incomparable beauty and range of effects—from the rustic grace of a dry-laid fieldstone wall to the fine elegance of an imported-marble floor. Usually less uniform than brick in its bonding pattern (the way that rows, or courses, are positioned), stone can be used for a variety of structures, including house walls, garden walls, retaining walls and chimneys, and also as paving for walkways, steps and patios. Common uses of stone are shown at right; refer to pages 47 and 48 for typical types and forms.

If stone is kept clean and in good repair, its beauty and charm can be enjoyed for centuries. Consult the appropriate section of the Troubleshooting Guide on page 46 for guidance in diagnosing problems. For specific information on cleaning up spills and removing stains, refer to the chart on page 49; in addition to the household cleaning agents listed there, many special products are now available on the market. Many stone problems begin at the mortar joints, which are especially vulnerable to expansion and contraction due to temperature changes and exposure to wind and precipitation. Climbing plants can also severely damage mortar joints over a period of time. Undertake repairs as soon as problems are detected to prevent moisture from entering and weakening the structure. Most of the tools, materials and supplies required for repairs are readily available at a building supply center. Refer to the Tools & Techniques chapter *(page 106)* for the proper use and cleaning of tools; be sure to follow all safety precautions when working on the roof *(page 114)*.

Once a year, inspect all stone structures around your home. Check mortar joints in house walls; repair damaged joints by removing the old mortar and replacing it with fresh mortar, a procedure known as pointing *(page 59)*; cracks that recur should be inspected by a professional. Check freestanding walls and retaining walls, especially the caps; replace loose or fallen dry-laid stones *(page 55)* or damaged mortared stones *(page 59)*, refit cap stones *(page 56)*, if necessary, and rebuild any damaged dry-laid *(page 57)* or mortared *(page 61)* wall sections. Frost heave and erosion can cause the paving stones of walkways, steps and patios to become uneven, unsightly and dangerous; maintain and repair sand-bed and mortar-bed paving as shown on pages 63 to 67. Also inspect your chimney; clean the flue at least once a year *(page 123)*. Check for leaks and repair damaged joints *(page 68)*. Pay special attention to the cap *(page 69)*, which often shows the first sign of a problem. If your house is an older one, the chimney may not be lined with rectangular or square fireclay tiles or round glazed tile; this can be a fire hazard and should be remedied by a professional.

Flashing
Sheathing that prevents water from penetrating the joint between the chimney and the roof.

Flue liner
Usually made of stacked fireclay tiles; for safety, an older home without a flue liner should be professionally retrofitted.

Chimney cap
Protects chimney top; often made of precast concrete.

Caulk
All joints at siding and trim are caulked to prevent moisture from penetrating.

Freestanding garden wall
Often two tiers of stone between which is filled with rubble; stone may be mortared onto concrete, as shown, or dry-laid on ground.

Patio
Flagstones dry-laid on a sand bed and gravel base or mortared onto concrete.

Steps
Flagstones often dug into sloped ground "country style", as shown, or mortared onto concrete; sloped slightly for drainage.

Veneer
Often precast from stone dust and attached by metal ties to wall behind it; joints are mortared.

Wall cap
Protects freestanding and retaining walls from moisture penetration and adds structural support. Can be of precast concrete or a course of header or rowlock stone (positioned across stone tiers), as shown; stones of cap may be covered with mortar.

Soil
Often one stone, as shown.

Sand bed
Flagstones are typically set on 1-inch bed of sand and 4-inch base of gravel; if mortared, flagstones are set on 4-inch base of concrete.

Edging
Borders sand-bed paving to keep flagstones from spreading and sand bed from eroding. Can be naturally decay-resistant or pressure-treated lumber.

Walkway
Flagstones dry-laid on a sand bed and gravel base, as shown, or mortared onto concrete; may be crowned for drainage.

Retaining wall
Designed to hold back soil; can be dry-laid, as shown, or mortared. Drainpipes of mortared retaining wall should be cleaned once each season.

STONE

44

45

Tools and techniques
General information on techniques for repairs to stone or concrete structures is covered in the Tools & Techniques section *(page 106)*. When a specific tool or method is required for a job, it is described within the step-by-step repair.

Each job has been rated by degree of difficulty and by the average time it will take for a do-it-yourselfer to complete. Keep in mind that this rating is only a suggestion. Before deciding whether you should attempt a repair, first read all the instructions carefully. Then be guided by your own confidence, and the tools and time available to you. For more complex or time-consuming repairs, such as rebuilding a large section of a mortared wall, you may wish to call for professional help. You will still have saved time and money by diagnosing the problem yourself. Most of the repairs in *Brick,* *Stone & Concrete* can be made with basic masonry tools such as hammers, chisels and trowels. Any special tool required is indicated in the Troubleshooting Guide. Basic tools — and the proper way to use them — along with information on masonry fasteners is presented in the Tools & Techniques section starting on page 106. If you are a novice at home repair, read this chapter first in preparation for a job. Repairing a brick, stone or concrete structure can be simple and worry-free if you work logically and systematically, and follow all safety tips and precautions.

Troubleshooting Guide
To use this chart, locate the symptom that most closely resembles your brick, stone or concrete problem, review the possible causes in column 2, then follow the recommended procedures in column 3. Simple fixes may be explained on the chart; in most cases you will be directed to an illustrated, step-by-step repair sequence.

Name of repair
You will be referred by the Troubleshooting Guide to the first page of a specific repair job.

Step-by-step procedures
Bold lead-ins summarize each step or highlight the key action pictured. Follow the numbered repair sequence carefully. Depending on the result of each step, you may be directed to a later step, or to another part of the book, to complete the repair.

STONE

TROUBLESHOOTING GUIDE

SYMPTOM	POSSIBLE CAUSE	PROCEDURE
HOUSE, RETAINING AND FREESTANDING WALLS		
Surface dirty or stained	Weather, wear and pollution	Clean surfaces (p. 49) □●
Efflorescence (white, powdery deposits of dissolved salts)	High humidity or poor air circulation	Clean surfaces (p. 49) □●; indoors, install dehumidifier or increase ventilation
	Moisture penetrating mortar joint or stone damaged by climbing plant	Destroy climbing plant (p. 50) □●; point mortar joint (p. 59) ■● or replace stone (p. 59) ■● or stone veneer (p. 62) ■●
	Moisture penetrating door or window trim	Recaulk exterior trim (p. 52) ■●
	Moisture buildup behind retaining wall due to blocked drainpipe	Maintain retaining wall (p. 61) ■●
	Insufficient drainage or leak in roof or plumbing	Inspect gutters, downspouts and soil grading (p. 110) □○; if necessary, consult a professional
Mortar joint loose or crumbling	Damage caused by climbing plant	Destroy climbing plant (p. 50) □●; point mortar joint (p. 59) ■●
	Moisture penetrating door or window trim	Recaulk exterior trim (p. 52) ■●; point mortar joint (p. 59) ■●
	Retaining wall drainpipe blocked	Maintain retaining wall (p. 61) ■●; point mortar joint (p. 59) ■●
	Insufficient drainage or leak in roof or plumbing	Inspect gutters, downspouts and soil grading (p. 110) □○; if necessary, consult a professional
Water damage around door or window	Caulk at joint between stone and trim loose or damaged	Recaulk exterior trim (p. 52) ■●
Stone loose, fallen, cracked or crumbling	Structure settlement; weather and traffic	Replace stone (p. 59) ■○, mortared stone (p. 59) ■●, stone veneer (p. 62) ■● or cap stone (p. 56) ■●
Wall leaning, buckling or sagging	Structure settlement; weather and traffic	Rebuild dry-laid section (p. 57) ■● or corner (p. 58) ■●, or rebuild mortared section (p. 61) ■●; maintain retaining wall (p. 61) ■●
	Damaged foundation or footing	Consult a professional
Decorative stone edge chipped, cracked or broken	Weather; blow by heavy object	Repair decorative stone edge (p. 70) ■●
PAVING AND STEPS		
Surface weedy	Windblown seeds and pods rooted in sand bed or damaged mortar joints	Pull out weeds by roots and apply herbicide such as glyphosate; repair mortared step (p. 63) ■●
Surface dirty or stained	Weather, wear and pollution; spills	Clean surfaces (p. 49) □●
Stone loose, cracked or crumbling	Weather and traffic	Relay sand-bed stone (p. 65) ■○, repair dry-laid step (p. 64) ■○; replace mortar-bed stone (p. 65) ■●, repair mortared step (p. 63) ■●
Paving stones sunken or heaved, or spreading or crooked	Weather and traffic	Relay sand-bed stone (p. 65) ■● or remake sand bed (p. 66) ■●; replace mortar-bed stone (p. 65) ■● or consult a professional to replace mortar bed
	Edging misaligned or damaged; no edging	Realign wood edging (p. 36) ■○, realign railroad-tie edging (p. 37) ■● or install wood edging (p. 38) ■●
Step stones sunken or heaved	Erosion; weather and traffic	Repair dry-laid step (p. 64) ■○ or repair mortared step (p. 63) ■●
CHIMNEYS		
Surface dirty or stained	Smoke, weather and pollution	Clean surfaces (p. 49) □●
	Chimney leaks due to damaged mortar	Locate leaks and point joints (p. 68) ■●
Water leaking in attic, from ceiling or along wall near chimney	Flashing at joint between chimney and roof damaged or caulk along joint between chimney and siding damaged	Repair flashing (p. 40) ■●; recaulk exterior trim (p. 52) ■●
	Chimney leaks due to damaged mortar	Locate leaks and point joints (p. 68) ■●
	Chimney cap damaged	Repair (p. 40) ■● or replace (p. 69) ■● concrete cap; for stone cap, consult a professional
	Insufficient drainage or leak in roof or plumbing	Inspect gutters, downspouts and soil grading (p. 110) □○; if necessary, consult a professional
Chimney cap loose, cracked or crumbling	Weather	Repair (p. 40) ■● or replace (p. 69) ■● concrete cap; for stone cap, consult a professional
Chimney leaning	Structure settlement or damaged foundation	Consult a professional

DEGREE OF DIFFICULTY: □ Easy ■ Moderate ■ Complex
ESTIMATED TIME: ○ Less than 1 hour ● 1 to 3 hours ● Over 3 hours

46

STONE

REPLACING STONE VENEER

1 **Chipping out the damaged stone veneer.** Wearing work gloves and goggles, use a cold chisel and a ball-peen hammer to cut away the mortar joints around the loose or damaged stone. If necessary, drag a mortar hook along the interior of the cut-back joints to scrape off mortar that is hard to reach. Fit a pry bar into the cleaned-out joint below the damaged stone *(above)* and work it back and forth to free the damaged stone. If you expose a metal tie holding the stone in position, chip the mortar off it and leave it in place.

2 **Cleaning the wall cavity.** Wearing work gloves and goggles, use the blade of a cold chisel to carefully scrape mortar off the back and sides of the wall cavity *(above)*; if necessary, chip off stubborn mortar by tapping the chisel lightly with a ball-peen hammer. Clean out loose particles with a stiff fiber brush. If the backing material behind the stone is damaged, consult a professional. Otherwise, buy replacement stone veneer and seal it, if necessary *(step 3)*.

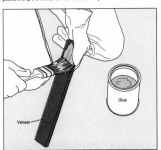

3 **Sealing the replacement stone.** Buy replacement stone veneer *(page 47)*, mason's glue and spacers at a building supply center or a stone dealer. Prepare and mortar the stone following the label instructions; for example, some precast types require sealing with mason's glue to prevent the leaching of moisture from fresh mortar. If the stone requires sealing with glue, wear rubber gloves and use a paintbrush to apply an even coat on the back of the stone *(above)*; allow the glue to set according to the label instructions. If the stone does not require sealing with glue, soak it with clean water.

4 **Mortaring the new stone.** Wearing work gloves, mix a batch of mortar *(page 48)* and add a little mason's glue to it—about 1 tablespoon or according to the label instructions. Wet the cavity with clean water. Use a pointing trowel to spread a 1-inch layer of mortar on the bed joint and sides of the cavity; also, butter the back of the stone *(inset)*. Sit spacers into the bed joint to support the stone as the mortar sets and push the stone straight into the cavity, in position on them *(above)*; align the face of the stone with the face of adjoining stones. Pack mortar into the joints around the stone using the trowel and scrape off excess with the edge of the trowel blade. Wipe mortar off the face of the stones using a damp piece of burlap or rough cloth.

62

Degree of difficulty and time
Rate the complexity of each repair and how much time the job should take for a homeowner with average do-it-yourself skills.

Cross-references
Direct you to important information elsewhere in the book, including alternative techniques and disassembly steps.

Insets
Provide close-up views of specific steps and illustrate variations in techniques.

EMERGENCY GUIDE

Preventing problems with brick, stone and concrete. When working with masonry, proper work habits are the key to preventing problems. The weight of some materials used is considerable; avoid back injury by following the correct procedure for lifting heavy objects *(page 111)*. Have a helper aid in lifting stones, concrete slabs and other heavy objects; wear steel-toed work boots to protect your feet. Use power tools only in dry conditions; consult the Tools & Techniques chapter *(page 106)* for the correct use of tools. Remember that breaking up concrete mechanically *(page 81)* can lead to hearing loss; wear ear protection.

Be sure you know the dangers of every substance you use. In addition to acids, solvents and chemical cleaners, the lime in mortar and concrete is caustic; some products used to preserve wood are toxic. When working with any of these substances, avoid contact with your skin and eyes: Wear eye protection, work gloves and a long-sleeved shirt. Should accidental contact with skin or eyes occur, flush the affected area immediately with water from a garden hose or nearby faucet *(page 12)*. When in doubt about the seriousness of any injury, seek medical attention as soon as possible. When disposing of substances, keep in mind their impact on the environment. See page 116 for information on the disposal of hazardous substances; consult your fire department or local environmental agency with questions about the correct disposal of toxic products in your community.

Before beginning a repair that requires working on the roof, a ladder or scaffolding, consult the Tools & Techniques chapter for safety guidelines. The safety tips at right offer important information for specific repairs. Keep a fire extinguisher handy to help snuff household fires *(page 11)*. **Caution:** Do not attempt to fight any fire that seems out of control; in the unlikely event of a chimney fire, leave the house immediately and call the fire department from a neighbor's telephone. The Troubleshooting Guide on page 9 puts emergency procedures at your fingertips, and refers you to pages 10 through 13 for quick-action steps to take.

When in doubt about your ability to handle an emergency, do not hesitate to call for help. Post numbers for the fire department; the water, gas and power companies; and the poison control center near the telephone. Even in non-emergency situations, their professionals can answer questions concerning the safe use of tools and materials.

SAFETY TIPS

1. Before beginning any repair in this book, read the entire procedure. Familiarize yourself with the specific safety information presented in each chapter.

2. Before using any acid, solvent or cleaner, read the product label carefully. Follow the manufacturer's instructions and safety precautions to prevent injury to yourself and the structure being repaired.

3. When mixing acid and water, always add the acid to the water; never add water to acid.

4. Wear the proper protective gear for any job. Use safety goggles and rubber gloves when handling acids, solvents and cleaners. Wear work gloves when handling concrete and mortar, and safety goggles when chiseling masonry.

5. To prevent foot injuries, wear steel-toed work boots when working with heavy masonry units such as stones.

6. Prolonged contact with concrete or mortar can burn the skin; rinse off splashes immediately with clean water. Wear long pants and a shirt with snug-fitting long sleeves when working with concrete, mortar, or chemicals. Change after leaving the work area and launder work clothes separately.

7. Take all safety precautions when working on a roof *(page 114)*, ladder *(page 112)* or scaffolding *(page 114)*. Never do anything on the roof that can be done as easily and more safely on the ground.

8. Use the proper technique when lifting heavy objects to prevent back injury *(page 111)*.

9. When using acids, solvents or cleaners—especially indoors—make sure the work area is well ventilated. If you feel faint or sick, leave the work area immediately and get fresh air *(page 12)*, then improve ventilation before continuing work.

10. Take periodic breaks from your work to rest and inspect what you have done. Never work when you are fatigued.

11. When working with flammable chemicals or with power tools, have on hand a fire extinguisher rated ABC; know how to use it before you begin work *(page 11)*.

12. Hang any rags soaked with paint, acid, solvent, or cleaner outdoors so that they dry thoroughly or seal them in airtight metal or glass containers. Store chemical products away from all sources of heat and sunlight.

13. Keep children and pets away from the work area. When you take a break or finish work for the day, put all tools and materials safely away.

14. Do not pour acids, solvents, or cleaners down a house drain or into a septic system. When disposing of empty chemical containers or old chemicals, put them out for municipal pick-up on designated Household Hazardous Waste Clean-up Days. (Call your local Department of Public Works or the Mayor's Office for specific information.) Should such a service not exist in your community, package substances separately and seal all containers securely before putting them out for regular trash collection.

15. Post the numbers of your fire department, hospital and local poison control center near the telephone.

TROUBLESHOOTING GUIDE

SYMPTOM	PROCEDURE
Paint spilled on masonry	Soak up paint with rag or paper towel; scrub surface with scouring powder and rinse *(p. 10)*
Oil spilled on masonry	Soak up oil with rag or paper towel; spread absorbent material on surface to absorb stain *(p. 10)*
	Use commercial cleaner containing a solvent and an absorbent material
Acid spilled on masonry	Neutralize acid by adding baking soda and flush surface thoroughly with water *(p. 10)*
Fire in paint or solvent, or power tool or outlet	Use a fire extinguisher rated ABC *(p. 11)*
	If fire spreads, leave house and call fire department immediately
Fire in chimney or on roof	Leave house immediately and call fire department
Fire caused by spark from fireplace	Use a fire extinguisher rated ABC *(p. 11)*; soak burning home furnishings with water to douse flames, then take them outside
	If fire spreads, leave house and call fire department immediately
Masonry wall buckling	Keep people and pets away from area; call a professional immediately
Cut or scratch	Apply pressure to stop bleeding *(p. 11)*; if bleeding does not stop, seek medical attention
Bruise	Apply ice pack to reduce swelling *(p. 11)*; if pain does not diminish or swelling persists, seek medical attention for possible fracture
Blood blister caused by hammer blow	Have blister treated by physician
Splinter	Use sterilized needle and tweezers to remove splinter *(p. 11)*; if splinter is lodged deeply or wound becomes infected, seek medical attention
Strained back	Apply ice pack immediately; treat old injuries with heating pad *(p. 12)*; if pain does not diminish, seek medical attention
Acid or solvent splashed onto skin	Flush skin thoroughly with water *(p. 12)*; wash affected clothing before rewearing it
	Seek medical attention for chemical burns. **Caution:** Never apply ointment to burns
Concrete, mortar, hydraulic cement, or cementitious paint splashed onto skin	Flush skin thoroughly with water *(p. 12)*; wash affected clothing before rewearing it
Foreign particle in eye	Do not rub eye; remove particle with moistened corner of clean cloth *(p. 12)*; if particle cannot be removed, bandage both eyes and seek medical attention
Acid, solvent, concrete splashed in eye	Flush eye with water *(p. 12)*; cover eye with bandage and seek medical attention immediately
Faintness, dizziness, nausea, or blurred vision when working with acid, solvent or cleaner	Leave room immediately to get fresh air, and have helper cover chemical containers and ventilate work area *(p. 12)*
	Read instructions on container labels and seek medical attention, if necessary
Acid, solvent or cleaner ingested	Call local poison control center, emergency room, or physician immediately
	Follow emergency instructions on label; take container when you seek medical attention
Fall from roof, ladder or scaffolding	Call an ambulance immediately; cover victim with blankets to treat for possible shock *(p. 13)*
	Unless absolutely necessary to prevent further injury, do not move victim until qualified medical help arrives and determines extent of injuries
Electrical shock	If person is immobilized by live current from a power tool, knock tool loose using a non-conducting object such as a wooden broom handle *(p. 13)*
	Check whether victim is breathing and has pulse. If not, begin artificial respiration or cardiopulmonary resuscitation (CPR) if you are qualified. Otherwise, place victim in recovery position *(p. 13)* and call for help
Electrical burn	Seek medical attention immediately. **Caution:** Never apply ointment to burns

CLEANING UP PAINT AND OIL SPILLS

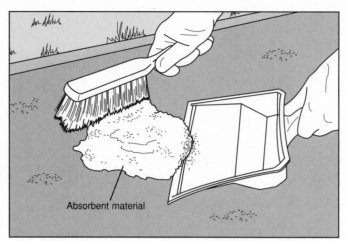

Preventing a paint stain. Immediately after a paint spill, wear rubber gloves and absorb the paint with a clean rag *(above)* or paper towel. Use a stiff fiber brush to scrub out any remaining paint with scouring powder and water. Rinse the surface and repeat the procedure, if necessary. Do not use paint remover or solvents on paint spills; masonry will absorb thinned paint.

Removing an oil stain. As soon as possible after an oil spill, sprinkle a layer of absorbent material such as sodium bicarbonate (baking soda), talc or kitty litter on the surface. Moisten the absorbent material with water and leave it for 24 hours to pull the stain from the masonry. Use a whisk broom and dust pan to sweep up the absorbent material *(above)*. Repeat the procedure, if necessary.

CLEANING UP ACID SPILLS

Neutralizing a fresh spill. Caution: Avoid acid contact with skin and clothing; flush immediately with water if contact occurs *(page 12)*. Wearing rubber gloves, pour a 1-inch layer of sodium bicarbonate (baking soda) on the freshly spilled acid to prevent it from etching the surface *(above, left)*. Wait 15 minutes to allow the acid to neutralize, then flush away the mixture with water from a garden hose *(above, right)* or splash a bucket of water on the surface.

EXTINGUISHING A FIRE

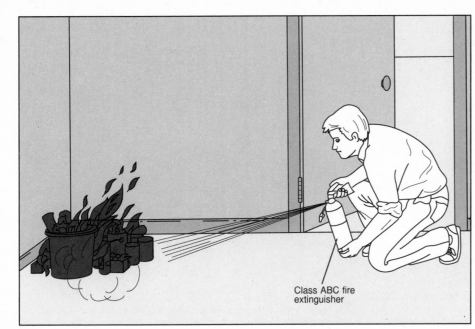

Class ABC fire extinguisher

Fighting a fire. Call the fire department immediately. If the fire is inside the house or chimney and there are flames or smoke coming from the walls or ceiling, evacuate the house; go to a neighbor's house to call for help. To extinguish a small fire in paints or solvents, in a power tool or outlet, or in furnishings near a fireplace, use a dry-chemical fire extinguisher rated ABC. Note the nearest exit and position yourself 6 to 10 feet from the fire. Holding the extinguisher upright, pull the lock pin out of the handle and aim the nozzle at the base of the flames. Squeeze the handle and spray in a quick side-to-side motion *(left)* until the fire is completely out. Watch for "flashback," or rekindling, and be prepared to spray again. If the fire spreads, leave the house. Dispose of any burned waste by following the advice of your local fire department. Have your extinguisher recharged professionally after every use or dispose of it if it is non-rechargeable.

PROVIDING MINOR FIRST AID

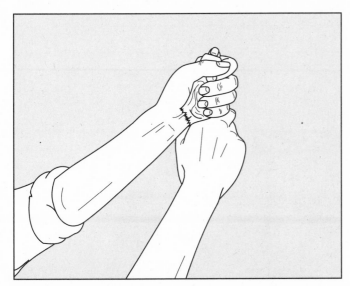

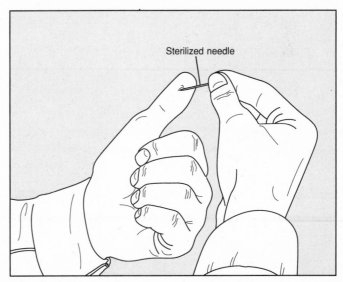

Sterilized needle

Treating cuts, scratches and bruises. To stop bleeding, wrap a clean cloth around the wound and apply direct pressure with your hand, elevating the limb *(above)*. If the cloth becomes blood-soaked, add a second cloth over the first one; continue applying pressure and elevating the limb until the bleeding stops. Wash a minor wound with soap and water, then bandage it. Seek medical attention if bleeding persists or if the wound is deep or gaping. Treat a fresh bruise with an ice pack to reduce swelling. If there is any doubt about the severity of an injury, seek medical attention.

Treating splinters. Wash your hands and the area around the wound with soap and water. A metal splinter may require treatment for tetanus; seek medical attention. For other types of splinters, use the point of a needle that has been sterilized in a flame or with alcohol to loosen the splinter from the skin *(above)*; pry up the splinter until you can pull it out with tweezers. Wash the area again with soap and water to prevent infection, then bandage it. If the splinter is lodged too deeply for removal, seek medical attention.

PROVIDING MINOR FIRST AID (continued)

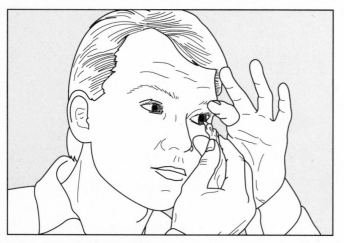

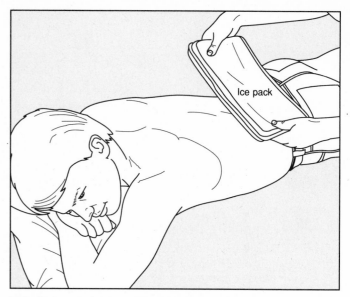

Removing a foreign particle from the eye. Looking in a mirror, examine the eye. Pull down the lower lid and lift back the upper lid to locate the particle. If the particle is on either lid, remove it by brushing the lid lightly with the corner of a clean, moistened cloth *(above)*. Brush lightly away from the nose and toward the side of the face. If the particle is on the eyeball, flush out the eye with water *(step below, right)*. If the particle remains lodged in the eye, cover both eyes with a clean, dry bandage to prevent eye movement and seek medical attention immediately.

Treating a strained back. Lie down on a flat surface and apply an ice pack to the sore area to reduce swelling and soothe pulled muscles *(above)*. After 24 hours, a heating pad may be used to lessen pain and speed healing. If the pain does not decrease after several days, seek medical attention.

TREATING CHEMICAL EXPOSURE

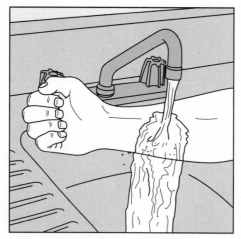

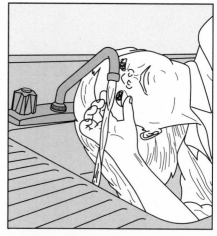

Escaping toxic vapors. Leave the work area to get fresh air. Remove clothing splashed by chemicals; loosen clothing at the waist, chest and neck. If you feel faint, sit with your head lowered between your knees *(above)*. Have someone ventilate the work area and close all containers. Call the local poison control center for medical advice.

Flushing chemicals from the skin. Rinse off chemicals immediately to prevent severe burns or "degreasing" (dissolving of the skin's protective oils). Remove affected clothing and flush the skin thoroughly with clean, cold water *(above)* for at least five minutes; relieve a burn's pain by soaking it in cold water. If there is any doubt about the seriousness of a burn, seek medical attention.

Flushing chemicals from the eye. Immediately hold the eyelids apart and position the injured eye under a gentle flow of cool water. Tilt your head to prevent the chemical from washing into the uninjured eye *(above)*. Flush the eye for 10 minutes, then cover it with a sterile gauze bandage and seek medical attention immediately.

TREATING A VICTIM OF ELECTRICAL SHOCK

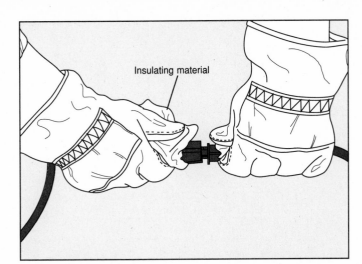

Insulating material

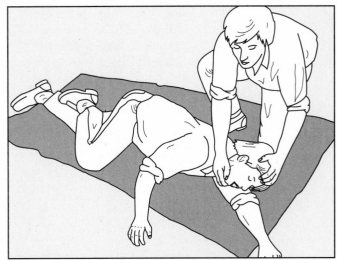

1 **Freeing someone from a live current.** Usually a person who contacts live current is thrown back from the source but sometimes muscles can contract involuntarily around a power tool or its cord. Do not touch the victim or the tool. Use a wooden broom handle or other non-conducting object to separate the victim from the source of current or—in a dry area only—insulate your hands with heavy work gloves or thick pieces of cloth and unplug the power tool or extension cord *(above)*. Tingling or numbness may indicate an internal injury; seek medical attention immediately.

2 **Handling a victim of electrical shock.** Call for help immediately. Check the victim's breathing and heartbeat. If there is no breathing or heartbeat, give mouth-to-mouth resuscitation or cardiopulmonary resuscitation (CPR) if you are qualified. If the victim is breathing and has not sustained neck or back injuries, place him in the recovery position *(above)*. Tilt the head back with the face to one side and the tongue forward to maintain an open airway. Keep the victim calm and comfortable.

TREATING THE VICTIM OF A FALL

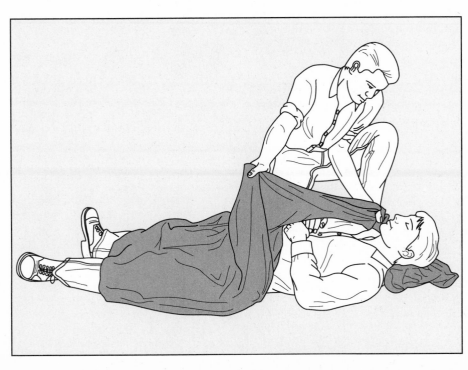

Treating the victim of a fall. Call an ambulance immediately, then cover the victim to regulate the body temperature in case of shock *(left)*. **Caution:** The victim of a fall should not be moved until qualified medical help arrives, especially if there is pain in the areas of the neck or back, or if clear spinal fluid can be seen flowing from the ears or nose. Help the victim to stay calm and keep others from crowding around. When qualified medical help arrives, make sure that they are advised of possible spinal cord injury.

BRICK AND BLOCK

For at least 5,000 years, bricks have been popular for their strength, durability and beauty. Although traditionally made of natural clay, which is heated in a kiln at high temperatures, many bricks today are made from compressed concrete, and come in a wide variety of shapes and colors. Bricks can be used for a variety of structures, including house walls, garden walls, retaining walls, chimneys and fireplaces, and also as pavers for driveways, walkways and patios. Concrete blocks offer a different kind of symmetry; although standard blocks are typically used for house foundations, decorative blocks make strong garden or retaining walls. Common uses of bricks and blocks are shown at right; refer to page 19 for typical ways that rows, or courses, of bricks and blocks can be positioned — known as their bond pattern.

The beauty of bricks and blocks is ageless, provided they are kept clean and in good repair. Consult the appropriate section of the Troubleshooting Guide on pages 16 and 17 for guidance in diagnosing problems. For specific information on cleaning up spills and removing stains, refer to the chart on page 20; in addition to the household cleaning agents listed there, many special products are now available on the market. Most brick and block problems begin at the mortar joints, which are especially vulnerable to expansion and contraction due to temperature changes and exposure to wind and precipitation. Climbing plants and deicing salt used in cold climates can also severely damage mortar joints over a period of time. Undertake repairs as soon as problems are detected to prevent moisture from entering and weakening the structure. Most of the tools, materials and supplies required for repairs are readily available at a building supply center. Refer to the Tools & Techniques chapter *(page 106)* for the proper use and cleaning of tools; be sure to follow all safety precautions when working on the roof *(page 114)*.

Once a year, inspect all brick and block structures around your home. Check mortar joints in the house walls; repair damaged joints by removing the old mortar and replacing it with fresh mortar, a procedure known as pointing *(page 22)*. Look for cracks in foundation blocks and plug them *(pages 27 and 28)*; cracks that recur should be inspected by a professional. Clean the weep holes at the base of exterior brick walls *(page 30)*; these holes provide drainage for moisture. Inspect freestanding walls and retaining walls, especially the caps; repair any damage *(page 30)* and ensure that drainpipes at the base of retaining walls are kept clear *(page 31)*. Frost heave and erosion take their toll on patios, walkways and driveways, causing pavers and edging to become uneven and unsightly. Maintain and repair sand-bed and mortar-bed paving as shown on pages 32 to 39. Also inspect your chimney; clean the flue at least once a year *(page 123)*. Check for leaks and point any damaged joints *(page 39)*. Pay special attention to the cap and top *(pages 40 to 42)*, which usually show the first signs of a problem. If your house is an older one, the chimney may not be lined with rectangular or square fireclay tiles or round glazed tile; this can be a fire hazard and should be remedied by a professional.

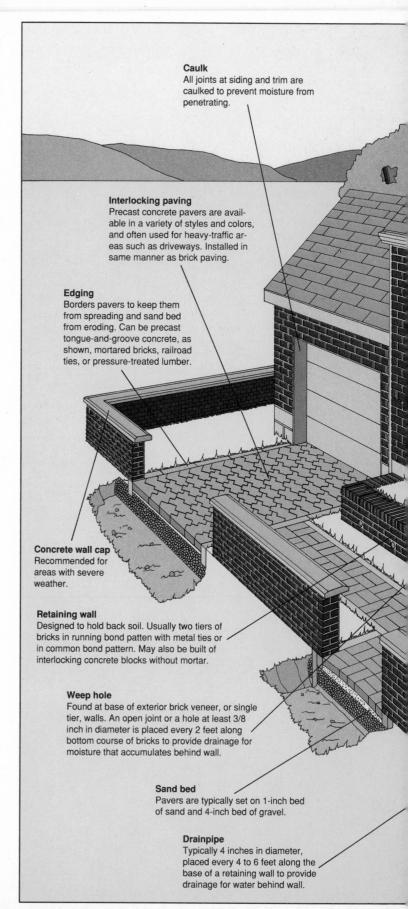

Caulk
All joints at siding and trim are caulked to prevent moisture from penetrating.

Interlocking paving
Precast concrete pavers are available in a variety of styles and colors, and often used for heavy-traffic areas such as driveways. Installed in same manner as brick paving.

Edging
Borders pavers to keep them from spreading and sand bed from eroding. Can be precast tongue-and-groove concrete, as shown, mortared bricks, railroad ties, or pressure-treated lumber.

Concrete wall cap
Recommended for areas with severe weather.

Retaining wall
Designed to hold back soil. Usually two tiers of bricks in running bond patten with metal ties or in common bond pattern. May also be built of interlocking concrete blocks without mortar.

Weep hole
Found at base of exterior brick veneer, or single tier, walls. An open joint or a hole at least 3/8 inch in diameter is placed every 2 feet along bottom course of bricks to provide drainage for moisture that accumulates behind wall.

Sand bed
Pavers are typically set on 1-inch bed of sand and 4-inch bed of gravel.

Drainpipe
Typically 4 inches in diameter, placed every 4 to 6 feet along the base of a retaining wall to provide drainage for water behind wall.

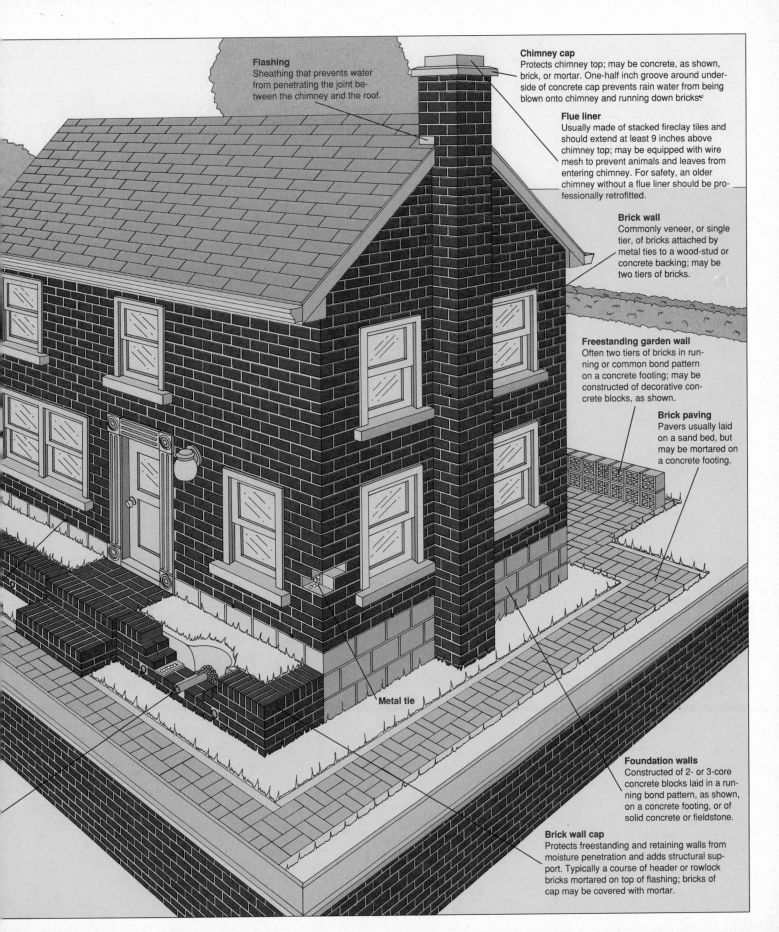

Flashing
Sheathing that prevents water from penetrating the joint between the chimney and the roof.

Chimney cap
Protects chimney top; may be concrete, as shown, brick, or mortar. One-half inch groove around underside of concrete cap prevents rain water from being blown onto chimney and running down bricks.

Flue liner
Usually made of stacked fireclay tiles and should extend at least 9 inches above chimney top; may be equipped with wire mesh to prevent animals and leaves from entering chimney. For safety, an older chimney without a flue liner should be professionally retrofitted.

Brick wall
Commonly veneer, or single tier, of bricks attached by metal ties to a wood-stud or concrete backing; may be two tiers of bricks.

Freestanding garden wall
Often two tiers of bricks in running or common bond pattern on a concrete footing; may be constructed of decorative concrete blocks, as shown.

Brick paving
Pavers usually laid on a sand bed, but may be mortared on a concrete footing.

Metal tie

Foundation walls
Constructed of 2- or 3-core concrete blocks laid in a running bond pattern, as shown, on a concrete footing, or of solid concrete or fieldstone.

Brick wall cap
Protects freestanding and retaining walls from moisture penetration and adds structural support. Typically a course of header or rowlock bricks mortared on top of flashing; bricks of cap may be covered with mortar.

TROUBLESHOOTING GUIDE

SYMPTOM	POSSIBLE CAUSE	PROCEDURE
HOUSE, RETAINING AND FREESTANDING WALLS		
Brick or block surface dirty or stained	Weather, wear and pollution	Clean surfaces (p. 20) □●
Brick or block surface efflorescence (white, powdery deposits of dissolved salts)	High humidity or poor air circulation	Clean surfaces (p. 20) □●; indoors, damp-proof wall (p. 29) □●, install dehumidifier or increase ventilation
	Moisture penetrating mortar joint, brick or block damaged by climbing plant	Destroy climbing plant (p. 21) □●; point (p. 22) □● or repair (p. 23) ▣● mortar joints; repair (p. 24) ▣● or replace (p. 25) ●● brick; repair dry crack (p. 27) ▣● or plug leaking crack (p. 28) ▣● in block or replace block face (p. 28) ▣●; or repair brick wall cap (p. 30) ▣●
	Moisture penetrating door or window trim	Recaulk exterior trim (p. 21) ▣●
	Moisture buildup behind house wall due to clogged weep hole or behind retaining wall due to blocked drainpipe	Clean house wall weep holes (p. 30) □○ or clean retaining wall drainpipes (p. 31) ▣●
	Insufficient drainage or leak in roof or plumbing	Inspect gutters, downspouts and soil grading (p. 110) □○; if necessary, consult a professional
Mortar joint loose or crumbling	Erosion and moisture penetration caused by climbing plant	Destroy climbing plant (p. 21) □●; point (p. 22) □● or repair (p. 23) ▣● mortar joints
	Moisture penetrating door or window trim	Recaulk exterior trim (p. 21) ▣●; point (p. 22) □● or repair (p. 23) ▣● mortar joints
	Moisture buildup behind house wall due to clogged weep hole or behind retaining wall due to blocked drainpipe	Clean house wall weep holes (p. 30) □○ or clean retaining wall drainpipes (p. 31) ▣●; point (p. 22) □● or repair (p. 23) ▣● mortar joints
	Insufficient drainage or leak in roof or plumbing	Inspect gutters, downspouts and soil grading (p. 110) □○; if necessary, consult a professional
Mortar joint cracked	Structure settlement	Repair joints (p. 23) ▣●; if cracks recur, consult a professional
Water damage around door or window	Caulk at joint between brick or block and trim loose or damaged	Recaulk exterior trim (p. 21) ▣●
	Clogged weep hole	Clean weep holes (page 30) □○
Brick loose, cracked or crumbling	Mortar or brick damaged by climbing plant	Destroy climbing plant (p. 21) □●; point (p. 22) □● or repair (p. 23) ▣● mortar joints; repair (p. 24) ▣● or replace (p. 25) ●● brick or repair brick wall cap (p. 30) ▣●
	Moisture penetrating door or window trim	Recaulk exterior trim (p. 21) ▣●
	Moisture buildup behind house wall due to clogged weep hole or behind retaining wall due to blocked drainpipe	Clean house wall weep holes (p. 30) □○ or clean retaining wall drainpipes (p. 31) ▣●
	Insufficient drainage or leak in roof or plumbing	Inspect gutters, downspouts and soil grading (p. 110) □○; if necessary, consult a professional
Block loose, cracked or crumbling	Mortar or block damaged by climbing plant	Destroy climbing plant (p. 21) □●; point (p. 22) □● or repair (p. 23) ▣● mortar joints; repair dry crack (p. 27) ▣● or plug leaking crack (p. 28) ▣● or replace block face (p. 28) ▣●
Foundation wall block cracked; no leak	Structure settlement	Repair dry cracks (p. 27) ▣● or replace block face (p. 28) ▣●; if cracks recur, consult a professional
Foundation wall block cracked and leaking	Structure settlement	Plug leaking cracks (p. 28) ▣●
	Moisture buildup behind house wall due to clogged weep hole	Clean house wall weep holes (p. 30) □○
	Insufficient drainage or leak in roof or plumbing	Inspect gutters, downspouts and soil grading (p. 110) □○; if necessary, consult a professional
Water at base of wall	Moisture penetrating mortar joint, brick or block damaged by climbing plant	Destroy climbing plant (p. 21) □●; point (p. 22) □● or repair (p. 23) ▣● mortar joints; repair (p. 24) ▣● or replace (p. 25) ●● brick; repair dry crack (p. 27) ▣● or plug leaking crack (p. 28) ▣● in block or replace block face (p. 28) ▣●; or repair brick wall cap (p. 30) ▣●

DEGREE OF DIFFICULTY: □ Easy ▣ Moderate ■ Complex
ESTIMATED TIME: ○ Less than 1 hour ● 1 to 3 hours ● Over 3 hours

SYMPTOM	POSSIBLE CAUSE	PROCEDURE
Water at base of wall (cont.)	Moisture penetrating door or window trim	Recaulk exterior trim (p. 21) ▣◗
	Moisture buildup behind house wall due to clogged weep hole or behind retaining wall due to blocked drainpipe	Clean house wall weep holes (p. 30) □○ or clean retaining wall drainpipes (p. 31) ▣●
	Insufficient drainage or leak in roof or plumbing	Inspect gutters, downspouts and soil grading (p. 110) □○; if necessary, consult a professional
Wall leaning	Structure settlement or damaged foundation or footing	Consult a professional
PAVING		
Paver surface weedy	Windblown seeds and pods rooted between sand-bed pavers	Clean sand-bed paving joints (p. 32) □●
Paver surface dirty or stained	Weather, traffic and pollution; oil, grease or paint spills	Remove surface stains (p. 33) □●; apply sealer (p. 33) □●
Pavers loose, cracked or crumbling	Weather and traffic; shrub or tree roots or deicing salts	Replace mortar-bed pavers (p. 33) ▣● or relay sand-bed pavers (p. 34) ▣◗; have tree roots removed and limit use of deicing salts
Pavers sunken or heaved, or spreading or crooked	Weather and traffic	Replace mortar-bed pavers (p. 33) ▣● or relay sand-bed pavers (p. 34) ▣◗; if necessary, remake sand bed (p. 35) ▣● or recrown sand bed (p. 35) ■●
	Edging misaligned or damaged; no edging	Realign wood edging (p. 36) ▣◗, realign railroad-tie edging (p. 37) ▣◗ or repair brick edging (p. 37) ▣◗; install wood edging (p. 38) ▣● or precast concrete edging (p. 39) ▣●
Edging loose, sunken or heaved	Weather and traffic	Realign wood edging (p. 36) ▣◗, realign railroad-tie edging (p. 37) ▣◗ or repair brick edging (p. 37) ▣◗; install wood edging (p. 38) ▣● or precast concrete edging (p. 39) ▣●
Water does not drain from walkway pavers	Bed eroded or improperly crowned	Recrown sand-bed walkway (p. 35) ▣●; for a mortar-bed walkway, consult a professional
CHIMNEYS AND FIREPLACES		
Surface dirty or stained	Smoke, weather and pollution	Clean surface (p. 20) □●
	Chimney leaks due to damaged mortar	Locate leaks and point joints (p. 39) ▣●
Water leaking in attic, from ceiling or along wall near chimney	Flashing at joint between chimney and roof damaged or caulk along joint between chimney and siding damaged	Reseal chimney joints (p. 40) ▣◗
	Chimney leaks due to damaged flue liner	Check for leaks (p. 39) ▣●; consult a professional
	Chimney cap damaged	Repair (p. 40) ▣● or replace (p. 41) ■● chimney cap
	Chimney top damaged	Rebuild chimney top (p. 42) ■●
	Insufficient drainage or leak in roof or plumbing	Inspect gutters and downspouts (p. 110) □○; if necessary, consult a professional
Chimney cap loose, cracked or crumbling	Weather	Repair (p. 40) ▣● or replace (p. 41) ■● chimney cap
	Chimney top damaged	Rebuild chimney top (p. 42) ■●
Chimney bricks loose, cracked or crumbling	Weather; structure settlement	Rebuild chimney top (p. 42) ■●; otherwise, consult a professional
Chimney leaning	Structure settlement or damaged foundation	Consult a professional
Firebrick mortar joint loose, cracked or crumbling	Age and temperature extremes	Point firebricks (p. 43) ▣◗
Firebricks loose, cracked or crumbling	Age and temperature extremes	Point (p. 43) ▣◗ or replace firebricks (p. 43) ▣◗

DEGREE OF DIFFICULTY: □ Easy ▣ Moderate ■ Complex
ESTIMATED TIME: ○ Less than 1 hour ◗ 1 to 3 hours ● Over 3 hours

TYPES OF BRICKS AND BLOCKS

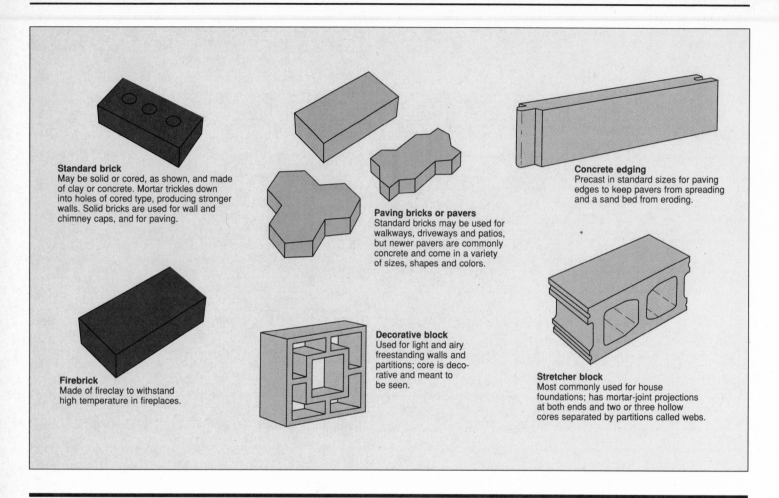

Standard brick
May be solid or cored, as shown, and made of clay or concrete. Mortar trickles down into holes of cored type, producing stronger walls. Solid bricks are used for wall and chimney caps, and for paving.

Firebrick
Made of fireclay to withstand high temperature in fireplaces.

Paving bricks or pavers
Standard bricks may be used for walkways, driveways and patios, but newer pavers are commonly concrete and come in a variety of sizes, shapes and colors.

Decorative block
Used for light and airy freestanding walls and partitions; core is decorative and meant to be seen.

Concrete edging
Precast in standard sizes for paving edges to keep pavers from spreading and a sand bed from eroding.

Stretcher block
Most commonly used for house foundations; has mortar-joint projections at both ends and two or three hollow cores separated by partitions called webs.

MIXING MORTAR

Mortar is the basic bonding material that holds bricks and blocks together; it must be properly mixed in the right proportions for a sound repair. For most jobs, you can produce workable mortar using one of the recipes below. (Different proportions may be required, especially in colder climates; check your local building code, or consult your local builders association or masonry distributor.) Use one of two types of cement: Portland cement, a bonding agent, must be mixed with hydrated lime which gives the mixture workability; masonry cement is a portland cement and lime mixture. All recipes use finely-graded building sand and clean water (preferably with low mineral content to prevent efflorescence). For small repairs, premixed mortar is affordable; simply add water. Because the exact amount of water required for mortar depends on the humidity, the temperature and the moisture in the sand, there is no recommended water ratio. Page 117 tells you how to judge the correct amount of water to add and the proper technique for mixing it. Depending on the size of the batch, mix the mortar by hand on a mason's hawk or in a mortar box or wheelbarrow. Be sure to mix only as much mortar as you can use before it hardens--which is about 2 1/2 hours. The ratios given in each recipe for cement, lime and sand remain constant, whatever the size of the batch.

MORTAR	USES	DRY INGREDIENTS
TYPE N	Used for outdoor, above-ground masonry subjected to severe weathering	1 part portland cement, 1 part hydrated lime and 6 parts sand
		1 part type II masonry cement and 3 parts sand
TYPE M	Used for below-ground masonry in contact with soil, e.g. foundations, retaining walls, walkways	1 part portland cement, 1/4 part hydrated lime and 3 parts sand
		1 part portland cement, 1 part type II masonry cement and 6 parts sand
TYPE S	Used for masonry subjected to lateral force, e.g. walls designed to resist winds	1 part portland cement, 1/2 part hydrated lime and 4 1/2 parts sand
		1/2 part portland cement, 1 part type II masonry cement and 4 1/2 parts sand
FIRECLAY	Used for interior fireplace work where resistance to heat is required	1 part fireclay mortar (available premixed) and 3 parts sand

IDENTIFYING BOND PATTERNS

Common wall bond patterns. The common bond pattern *(above, left)* is a double-thickness brick wall that uses lengthwise, or stretcher, courses with an end, or header, course every 4th, 5th, or 6th course to tie the two tiers of bricks together. The running bond pattern *(above, right)* is widely used for brick veneer walls; using metal ties, a single tier of bricks is tied to a backing of wood or steel studs or, less commonly, concrete blocks.

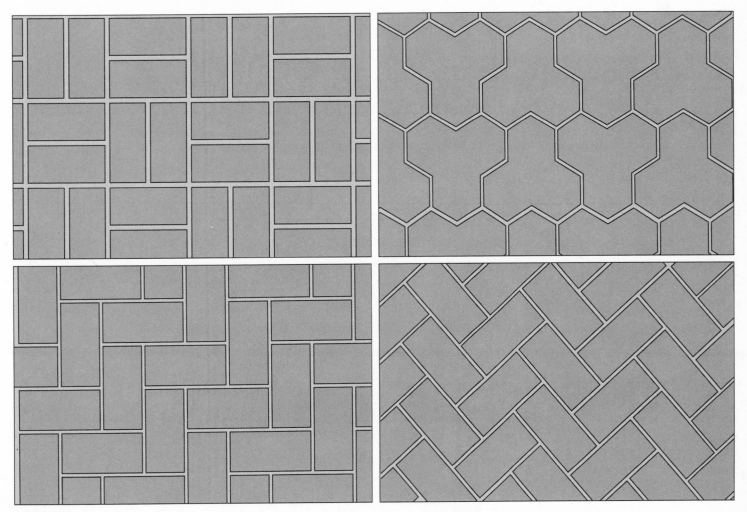

Common paving bond patterns. Basketweave *(top, left)* uses pairs of bricks set at right angles to each other. Munich *(top, right)* is an example of the popular interlocking concrete pavers now available. Herringbone, a zig-zag pattern, can be installed at a 90-degree angle *(bottom, left)* or a 45-degree angle *(bottom, right)*. Also common for paving is the running bond pattern *(step above)*.

MAINTAINING BRICKS AND BLOCKS

PROBLEM	CLEANING AGENT	PROCEDURE
Efflorescence (white, powdery deposits)	On concrete or light-colored bricks and blocks and on colored mortar, use water	Scrub with stiff fiber brush and rinse
	On clay bricks, use muriatic acid*	Wearing rubber gloves and goggles, mix 1 part acid to 12 parts water *(page 116)*. **Caution:** Add acid to water. Presoak surface with water, use stiff fiber brush to scrub surface with acid solution and rinse surface
Fresh mortar spots	Water	Chip off mortar chunks with trowel edge. Scrub off mortar streaks with water and stiff fiber brush
Old mortar spots	On concrete bricks and blocks, use commercial cleaner*	Rub off mortar chunks with a piece of brick or block. Wearing rubber gloves and goggles, apply cleaner according to label instructions
	On clay bricks, use muriatic acid*	Rub off mortar chunks with a piece of brick or block. Wearing rubber gloves and goggles, mix 1 part acid to 9 parts water *(page 116)*. **Caution:** Add acid to water. Presoak surface with water, use stiff fiber brush to scrub surface with acid solution and rinse surface
Paint	Commercial paint remover*	Wearing rubber gloves and goggles, apply paint remover according to label instructions; use putty knife, scraper or wire brush to remove it
Rust	Oxalic acid crystals*	Wearing rubber gloves and goggles, mix 1 pound of oxalic acid to 1 gallon of water in a plastic or glass container. **Caution:** Add acid to water. Presoak surface with water, use stiff fiber brush to scrub surface with acid solution and rinse surface
Oil	Trisodium phosphate (TSP)*, thickener (talcum powder*** or fuller's earth***) and water	Wearing rubber gloves and goggles, add 1 pound of TSP to 1 gallon of water and mix in thickener until pasty; apply poultice *(below)*
Grease	Oil-dissolving solvent* and thickener (talcum powder*** or fuller's earth***)	Scrape off excess grease with putty knife. Wearing rubber gloves and goggles, mix solvent and thickener until pasty; apply poultice *(below)*
Tar	Kerosene and thickener (talcum powder*** or fuller's earth***)	Scrape off excess tar with putty knife; wearing work gloves, apply dry ice to make globs brittle. Wearing rubber gloves and goggles, mix kerosene and thickener until pasty; apply poultice *(below)*
Climbing plant	Ammonium sulphate paste** or herbicide**	Cut plant near ground level; wearing rubber gloves and goggles, apply paste or herbicide on plant stems and remaining plant growth *(page 21)*
Moss or algae	Herbicide**	Wearing rubber gloves and goggles, apply herbicide
Dirt, grime, smoke or general discoloration	Household scouring powder	Wearing rubber gloves and goggles, apply powder *(page 21)*
	Trisodium phosphate (TSP)***, household detergent and water	Wearing rubber gloves and goggles, add 1/2 cup of TSP and 1/2 cup of detergent to 1 gallon of water; apply solution *(page 21)*

* Available at a building supply center   ** Available at a garden center   *** Available at a drug store

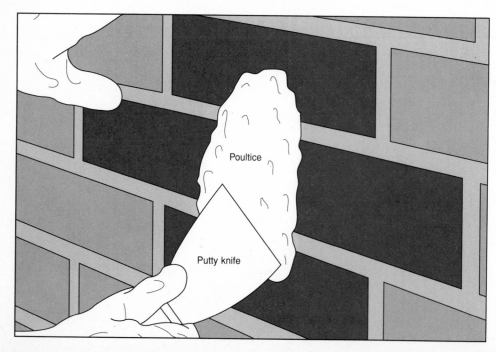

Applying a poultice. Working in a temperature between 60 and 80 degrees fahrenheit, prepare a poultice into a stiff, smooth paste *(chart, above)*. **Caution:** Work in a well-ventilated area, wearing rubber gloves and goggles. Wet the stained surface thoroughly with clean water and use a putty knife to apply a 1/2 inch layer of the poultice *(left)*. Cover the surface with plastic, taping it in place with duct tape. Allow the poultice to sit for 24 hours. Remove the plastic and use a putty knife to scrape off the poultice. Wash the surface with water and a stiff fiber brush.

Destroying a climbing plant with ammonium sulphate or herbicide. Cut the plant stems about 6 inches above ground level using pruning shears. Wearing rubber gloves and goggles, use a narrow paintbrush to apply ammonium sulphate paste or herbicide on the cut stems *(above)*, according to label instructions. When the plant withers, remove it; wherever plant growth remains, repaint it with the paste or herbicide. When the plant stems stop growing, use a spade to dig up the roots.

Cleaning with scouring powder or trisodium phosphate (TSP) solution. Scrub off dirt and grime using household scouring powder or a mixture of 1/2 cup of TSP and 1/2 cup of household detergent in one gallon of clean water *(chart, page 20)*; wear rubber gloves and goggles. Wet the surface thoroughly and apply the powder or solution, scrubbing vigorously with a stiff fiber brush *(above)*. Rinse off the surface and repeat the procedure, if necessary.

RECAULKING EXTERIOR TRIM

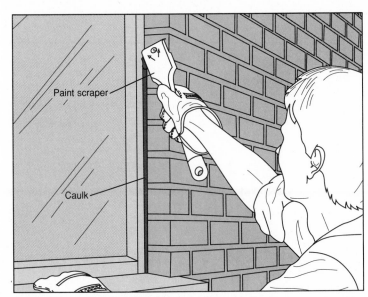

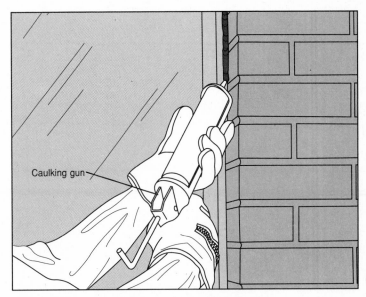

1 **Removing old caulk.** Starting at one end of a joint, pry out the damaged caulk using the corner of a paint scraper *(above)* or a putty knife. Using a stiff fiber brush, scrub the joint and clean the outer edge of the trim with a solution of mild detergent and clean water. Rinse the joint and let it dry; if the finish of wood trim is damaged, touch it up with finish or preservative.

2 **Applying new caulk.** Buy a tube of exterior silicone or acrylic caulk at a building supply center. Load the tube into a caulking gun. Following the label instructions, use a utility knife to cut the tip of the tube at a 45-degree angle, providing an opening for a 1/4-inch bead. Use a long nail or an awl to break the tube seal. Holding the gun at a 45-degree angle to the joint, squeeze the gun trigger to lay a continuous bead of caulk along the joint *(above)*. Wearing a rubber glove, run a wet finger along the caulk to press it into the joint, smoothing and shaping it.

POINTING BRICK AND BLOCK JOINTS

1 **Removing the old mortar.** Wearing work gloves and goggles, use a cold chisel and a ball-peen hammer or small sledgehammer to cut back the joints 1/2 to 3/4 inch *(above)*, usually far enough to be able to remove the damaged surface mortar. Work carefully to avoid damaging any bricks or blocks.

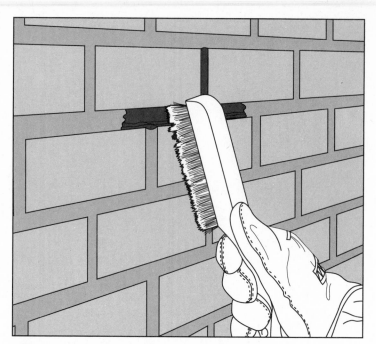

2 **Brushing out the joints.** Use a stiff fiber brush or a vacuum cleaner to clean all loose mortar particles out of the cut-back joints *(above)*. Do not use a wire brush for cleaning; any wire particles left behind by the brush may react with moisture and cause rust stains in the bricks or blocks and the new mortar.

3 **Soaking the joints.** To prevent the bricks or blocks from leaching moisture out of fresh mortar, soak the surface thoroughly with clean water. Apply enough water to penetrate the joints completely, using the fine spray of a garden hose or working the water into the joints with a large paintbrush *(above)*.

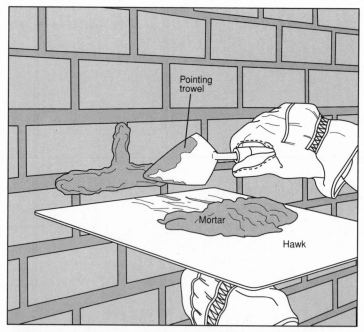

4 **Tuck-pointing the joints.** Wearing work gloves, mix a batch of mortar *(page 18)* on a mason's hawk. Hold the hawk just below the joints to catch any mortar that is accidentally dropped. Use a pointing trowel to tuck-point, or work mortar into the joints. Fill the joints completely, packing them as tightly as possible with mortar *(above)*. Scrape off excess mortar with the flat edge of the trowel blade.

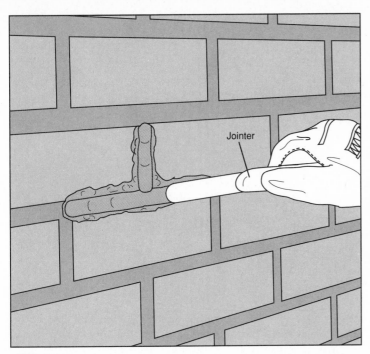

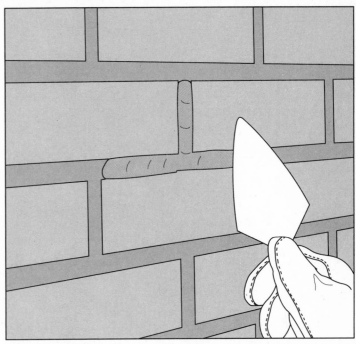

5 **Striking the joints.** Wait 30 minutes or until the mortar has set enough to hold a thumbprint. Using a jointer with a shape that matches the original joints *(page 119)*, strike the joints, or press them to form a watertight seal. For the neatest appearance, strike the vertical joints first, then the horizontal joints. Wet the jointer with clean water and drag it smoothly along the joints, leaving a concave impression in the mortar *(above)*.

6 **Smoothing the joints.** Use the edge of a pointing trowel to scrape off excess mortar forced out of the joints by the pressure of the jointer *(above)*. Using a wet piece of burlap or rough cloth, wipe mortar off the brick or block faces. Allow the new mortar to cure, keeping it damp for at least 3 days: Mist the surface occasionally with a garden hose or, in hot weather, use duct tape to hang a wet cloth on the surface and moisten the cloth periodically.

REPAIRING CRACKED BRICK AND BLOCK JOINTS

Cutting back mortar cracks. Structural shifting and settling can cause continuous cracks in the mortar joints of a brick or block wall; repair minor cracks immediately, before they cause major problems. Wearing work gloves and goggles, cut back the joints using a cold chisel and a ball-peen hammer *(left)* or small sledgehammer; cut back each joint to a depth of at least 2 inches or until solid mortar is reached. Mix a batch of mortar *(page 18)*. Soak and tuck-point the joints *(page 22)*, then strike *(step 5, above)* and smooth *(step 6, above)* the joints. If the cracks recur, there may be a serious structural problem; have the wall inspected by a professional.

REPAIRING A LOOSE BRICK

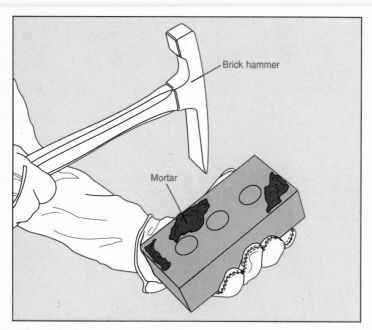

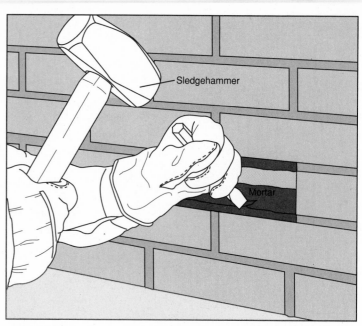

1 **Chipping old mortar off the brick.** When mortar joints crack, bricks and blocks can loosen in a wall. A loose brick is usually easy to work out of the wall; use a pry bar or the end of a cold chisel, being careful not to damage any bricks. Wearing work gloves and goggles, hold the brick in one hand and use the curved, chisel-like end of a brick hammer to chip off the old mortar from each brick face *(above)*. When all the mortar is removed, place the brick in a bucket of clean water to wash and soak it.

2 **Cleaning old mortar out of the cavity.** Using a cold chisel and a ball-peen hammer or small sledgehammer, chip old mortar out of the brick cavity *(above)*; work carefully to avoid damaging the bricks around the cavity. Use a stiff fiber brush to clean loose mortar particles out of the cavity.

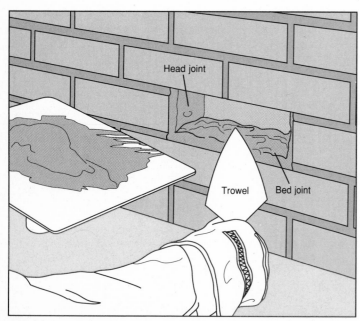

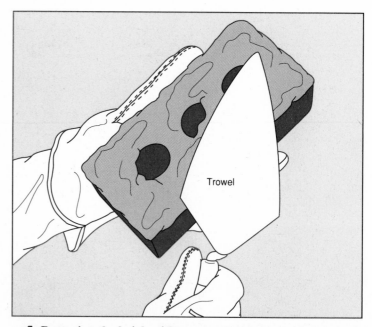

3 **Spreading new mortar in the cavity.** Wet the cavity thoroughly with clean water, applying it with a paintbrush or the fine spray of a garden hose; this will prevent the old masonry from leaching moisture out of fresh mortar. Wearing work gloves, mix a batch of mortar *(page 18)* and use a pointing trowel to spread a 3/4-inch layer of mortar on the bed joint *(above)* and each head joint of the cavity.

4 **Buttering the brick with mortar.** Remove the brick from the bucket of water and shake off excess water. Scoop up mortar onto the top surface of a mason's trowel and flip it onto the top of the brick *(above)*; repeat the procedure until the brick is covered with a 3/4-inch layer of mortar. Use the bottom surface of the trowel to smooth the mortar on the brick.

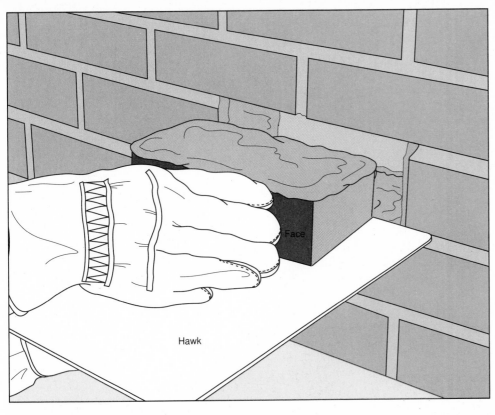

5 **Inserting the brick into the cavity.**
Place the brick on a mason's hawk and position the hawk level with the bottom of the cavity. Slide the brick forward into the cavity *(left)* until the brick face is flush with adjacent bricks; if necessary, tap the brick into position using the trowel handle. If mortar does not squeeze out around the brick, the joint is too thin; remove the brick, add mortar to the cavity and the brick *(page 24)* and reinsert the brick. When the brick is in position and the joints are filled, scrape off excess mortar with the flat edge of the trowel blade; then, strike and smooth the joints *(page 23)*.

REPLACING A DAMAGED BRICK

Chipping out a stretcher brick. Identify the type of bond pattern *(page 19)*. If the brick is a header, cut it back *(step right)*. If the brick is a stretcher, wear work gloves and goggles to remove it. Chip the brick out of the wall using a cold chisel and a small sledgehammer *(above)* or ball-peen hammer. First break the mortar around the brick, then break the brick into pieces small enough to be removed with a pry bar or the end of the chisel. Buy a replacement brick at a building supply center; if necessary, take a piece of the old brick to match it. Install the new brick *(pages 24 and 25, steps 2 to 5)*.

Cutting back a header brick. Identify the type of bond pattern *(page 19)*. If the brick is a stretcher, remove it *(step left)*. If the brick is a header, replace the outer face. Wearing work gloves and goggles, use a cold chisel and a small sledgehammer or ball-peen hammer to first break the mortar joints, then cut back the brick at least 4 inches *(above)*. Buy replacement bricks at a building supply center; if necessary, take a piece of the old brick to match it. Rough- or fine-cut the new brick to fit the cavity *(page 26)* and install it *(page 27)*.

ROUGH-CUTTING A BRICK

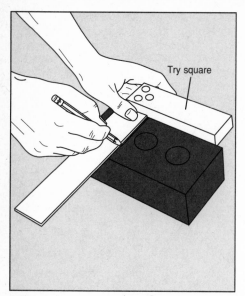

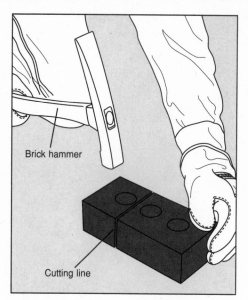

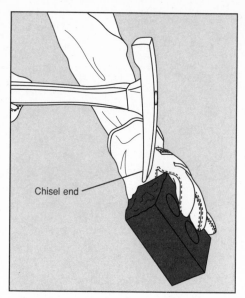

1 Marking the brick. Cutting a brick properly takes practice; have several extra bricks on hand. Measure the dimensions of the cavity to be filled with a tape measure and use a try square and a pencil to scribe a cutting line on all four sides of the brick *(above)*; allow about 1/2 inch at the cut end of the brick for mortar. If you have experience cutting bricks, try making a fine cut *(step below)*.

2 Scoring and cutting the brick. Wearing work gloves and goggles, tap lightly along the cutting line with the chisel end of a brick hammer, scoring each side of the brick. Using the hammer end of the brick hammer, strike the waste side of the brick near the scored line with one sharp blow *(above)*. The brick should break at the scored line; if not mark a new brick *(step 1)* and repeat the procedure.

3 Trimming the cut end of the brick. If the break in the brick is not even, use the chisel end of a brick hammer to chip off projecting bits of brick on the cut end *(above)*. Dry-fit the brick in the cavity and retrim the cut end of it, if necessary; then, install the brick *(page 27)*.

FINE-CUTTING A BRICK

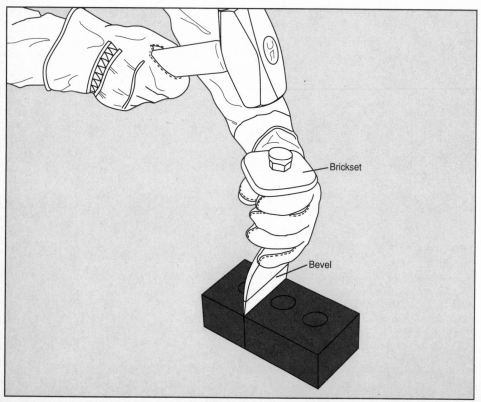

Cutting the brick. When the technique is mastered, fine-cutting a brick produces finer and faster results than rough-cutting. However, since fine-cutting a brick requires practice and rarely works the first time, have several extra bricks on hand. Mark the brick *(step 1, above)*. Wearing work gloves and goggles, score each side of the brick along the marked line by tapping lightly using a brickset and a small sledgehammer. Position the brickset on the scored line at about a 30-degree angle, with the beveled edge of its blade against the waste side of the brick; strike the brickset once sharply with the sledgehammer *(left)*. The brick should break cleanly along the scored line; if not, repeat the procedure. Trim the cut end of the brick, if necessary *(step 3, above)*; then, install the brick *(page 27)*.

INSTALLING A CUT BRICK

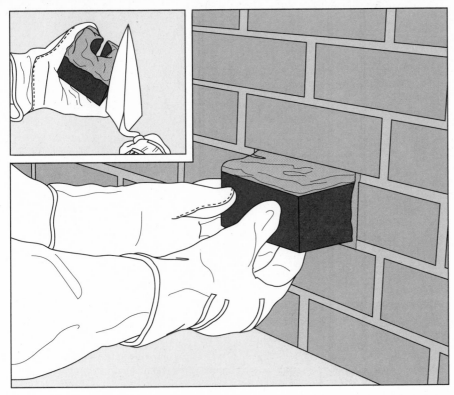

Inserting the brick into the cavity. Mix a batch of mortar *(page 18)*. To prevent the leaching of moisture from the fresh mortar, soak the brick in a bucket of clean water and wet the cavity thoroughly, applying water with a paintbrush or the fine spray of a garden hose. Remove the brick from the bucket and shake off excess water. Using a pointing trowel, spread a 3/4-inch layer of mortar on the bed, or bottom, and the head, or side, joints of the cavity; force some extra mortar into the back of the cavity to ensure a good bond. Butter the top of the brick with a 3/4-inch layer of mortar using a mason's trowel: Scoop up mortar on the top surface of the trowel, flip it onto the brick and use the bottom surface of the trowel to smooth the mortar on the brick *(inset)*. Slide the brick into the cavity *(left)* until it is flush with adjacent bricks; if necessary, tap it into position using the trowel handle. Strike and smooth the joints *(page 23)*.

REPAIRING A DRY CRACK IN A BLOCK WALL

1 Preparing the crack. Wearing work gloves and goggles, undercut the edges of the crack in a dovetail shape *(inset)* using a cold chisel and a small sledgehammer *(above)* or ball-peen hammer. Clean out loose particles using a stiff fiber brush. If the crack is large, fill the interior core of the block with fiberglass insulation, creating a backing for a patch.

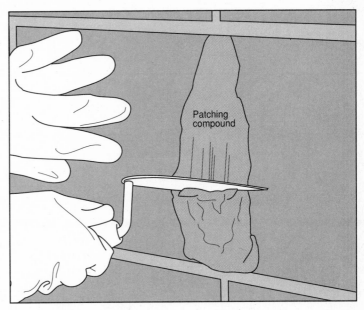

Patching compound

2 Patching the crack. For a patch, buy concrete patching compound at a building supply center. Wearing work gloves, mix the patching compound, following the label instructions; a thick mix will help avoid sagging. Using a paintbrush dipped in water, wet the crack to prevent the leaching of moisture from the fresh patching compound. Use a pointing trowel to work patching compound into the crack. Scrape off excess patching compound, smoothing the surface, with the edge of the trowel *(above)*. Allow the patching compound to cure according to the label instructions; until it cures, use a plant sprayer to mist it with water whenever it begins to lighten around the patch edges.

PLUGGING A LEAKING CRACK IN A BLOCK WALL

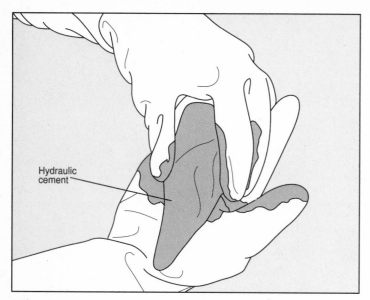

Hydraulic cement

Plug

1 **Making the plug.** Prepare the crack *(page 27)* and flush it with clean water to wash off any dirt. For a patch, buy quick-set hydraulic cement at a building supply center. Wearing rubber gloves, prepare the cement according to the label instructions; mix only as much cement as you can use in 3 minutes. Working the cement into a plug with your hands *(above)*, add just enough water to give it the consistency of putty.

2 **Inserting the plug.** Wearing rubber gloves, begin at the top of the crack and work downward, pressing the cement into the crack with your fingers *(above)*. At the bottom of the crack, hold the cement in place until it sets--about 3 minutes. Use a trowel to smooth the patch flush with the wall. Allow the cement plug to damp-cure for at least 15 minutes or according to the label instructions. If necessary, apply a sealer *(page 29)*.

REPLACING A DAMAGED BLOCK FACE

Web

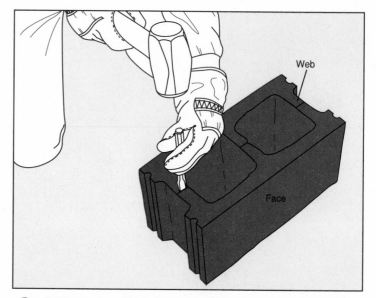

Web

Face

1 **Chipping off the block face.** When a block is too badly damaged to patch, it is often easiest to replace only the face. Wearing work gloves and goggles, use a cold chisel and a small sledgehammer to cut back the mortar joints around the damaged block face. Use the sledgehammer to break away the block face, exposing the interior webs *(above)*. Chip back the webs about 2 inches with the cold chisel and sledgehammer. Clean loose mortar particles out of the block core using a stiff fiber brush. Buy a replacement block at a building sup-ply center; have the face cut for you, then butter and insert it *(page 29)* or cut the face yourself *(step 2)*.

2 **Cutting a new block face.** Some standard two-core concrete blocks have cutting lines or perforations scored on the top surface of the webs to make cutting them in half easier. Wearing work gloves and goggles, cut the block by tapping the cutting lines with a cold chisel and a small sledgehammer *(above)*; score a cutting line first if the block does not have one. If the block does not break uniformly, it is still usable if there is enough of the webs remaining for the face to be inserted into the cavity.

REPLACING A DAMAGED BLOCK FACE (continued)

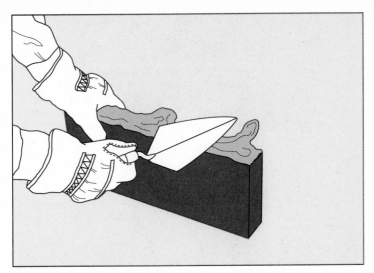

3 **Buttering the new block face.** Dry-fit the new block face to be sure that it fits the cavity; if necessary, trim the webs using a cold chisel and a small sledgehammer or ball-peen hammer, allowing about 1/2 inch at the cut ends of the webs for mortar. To prevent the leaching of moisture from fresh mortar, wet the cavity thoroughly with clean water using a paintbrush and soak the block face. Wearing work gloves, mix a batch of mortar *(page 18)*. Use a pointing trowel to spread a 1-inch layer of mortar on the bottom, sides and webs of the cavity. Shake excess water off the block face and butter the top of it with a 1-inch layer of mortar using a mason's trowel *(above)*.

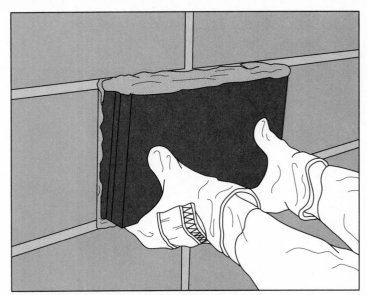

4 **Inserting the new block face.** Slide the block face into the cavity *(above)*, pushing it flush with adjacent blocks; if necessary, tap it into position using the handle of a trowel. Because the blocks are hollow, some of the mortar will be lost as it falls into the cores of the blocks below. If necessary, use the pointing trowel or a margin trowel to work more mortar into the joints after the block face is in position. Scrape off excess mortar with the flat edge of the trowel blade, then strike and smooth the joints *(page 23)*.

DAMP-PROOFING A BLOCK WALL

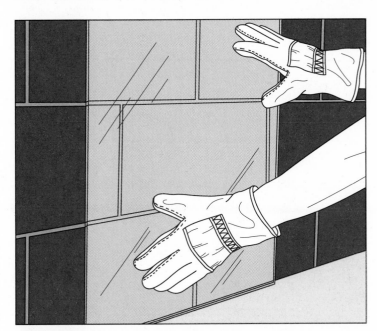

1 **Determining the extent of the problem.** Place a large piece of glass against the interior foundation wall *(above)*; if necessary, hold it in position with duct tape. Or, tape plastic onto the wall. Leave the glass or plastic in position overnight. If in the morning, there is condensation or moisture on the side of the glass or plastic against the wall, and not on the other side, damp-proof the wall *(step 2)*.

2 **Applying a sealer.** Buy cementitious paint, available in a variety of colors, at a building supply center and follow the label instructions to apply it; a primer is usually required. Wearing rubber gloves, use a paintbrush *(above)*, or a medium- or long-nap roller to apply the primer and at least two thick coats of the paint; using different colors for the coats will help you judge if coverage is complete. Work the primer and the paint thoroughly into the block pores and be sure to coat all joints. Keep the finish coat damp for at least 48 hours by misting it periodically with a plant sprayer or, if the basement is hot, by hanging a wet blanket from the ceiling.

CLEANING WEEP HOLES

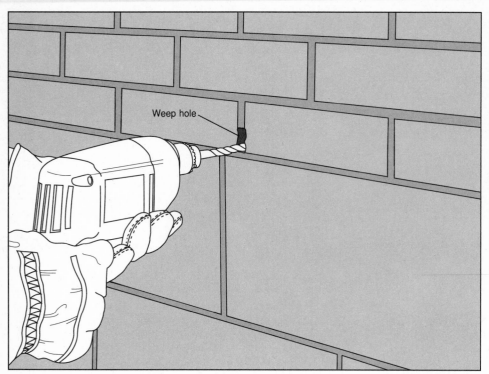

Opening clogged weep holes. Clogged weep holes can cause water damage, especially around basement windows. To clean a clogged weep hole, use a star drill and a ball-peen hammer, or a power drill with a carbide-tipped masonry bit that is 1/16 inch narrower than the hole and long enough to reach the wall cavity behind the bricks; usually a bit at least 4 inches long is required. Remember that a weep hole is designed to channel water out of the wall; it is angled and often backed by flashing. Wearing work gloves and goggles, fit the star drill into the hole, following its angle, and strike the star drill with the hammer; or, insert the drill bit into the hole *(left)*, adjust the drill to follow the hole angle, and drill slowly to avoid damaging any flashing. Using the same procedure, clean out all the weep holes.

REPAIRING A BRICK WALL CAP

1 Removing damaged cap bricks. When the cap on a freestanding or retaining wall is damaged, repair it before moisture penetration causes structural problems. Identify the brick bond pattern *(page 19)*; usually the cap on a brick wall is a course of header or rowlock bricks, mortared on a top course of stretcher bricks, as shown. If the cap bricks are loose, lift them off the wall. If the cap brick joints are cracked, use a cold chisel and a small sledgehammer or ball-peen hammer to chip out the mortar around the bricks *(above)* and remove the bricks; wear work gloves and goggles. Chip old mortar off the bricks *(page 24)* and reuse them or purchase replacement bricks at a building supply center.

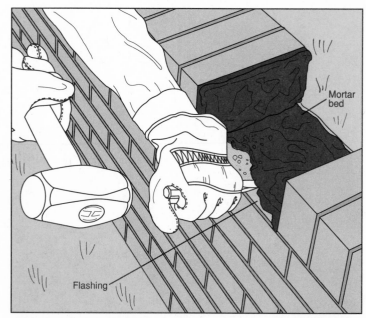

2 Removing the old mortar bed. Before mortaring the cap bricks, soak them thoroughly in clean water. Wearing work gloves and goggles, chip the old mortar off the top of the wall and any bricks bordering the damaged area using a cold chisel and a small sledgehammer *(above)* or ball-peen hammer; work carefully to avoid damaging any bricks. If you uncover a metal tie holding two tiers of bricks together, chip off any damaged mortar around it. If there is flashing under the mortar and it is damaged, repair it *(step 3)*; if it is undamaged or if there is no flashing under the mortar, mortar the cap bricks *(step 4)*.

REPAIRING A WALL CAP (continued)

Roofing cement

Tin snips

Patch

3 **Patching the flashing.** Over time, flashing can become corroded from exposure to moisture; purchase replacement flashing and roofing cement at a building supply center. Wearing work gloves, use tin snips to cut a flashing patch to the size required *(inset)*; be sure it covers any holes in the old flashing. **Caution:** Handle flashing careful-ly; cut edges, in particular, can be very sharp. Use a piece of scrap wood to apply a layer of cement on the old flashing *(above)*, filling in any holes. Position the patch and press it down firmly on the cement until it sticks securely.

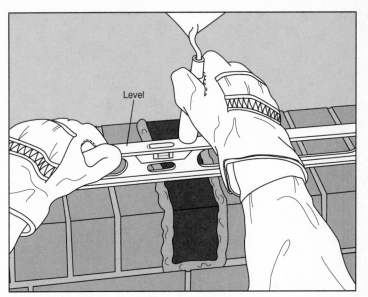

Level

4 **Mortaring the cap bricks.** Wearing work gloves, mix a batch of mortar *(page 18)*. Use a cloth or paintbrush dipped in clean water to wet the old bricks wherever fresh mortar will be applied; do not, however, wet any flashing. Using a mason's trowel, apply a 3/4-inch bed of mortar on the top of the wall and furrow the mortar *(page 118)*. To install a new cap brick, shake excess water off it and butter each side that adjoins another brick already on the wall with a 3/4-inch layer of mortar. Position the brick and use the trowel handle to tap it into the bed and, if possible, against each adjoining brick, until the joints around it are about 3/8-inch wide. Scrape off excess mortar with the edge of the trowel. To check the position of the bricks, use a car-penter's level; if necessary, tap lightly on the top of it with the trowel handle to adjust the bricks *(above)*. Finish the joints *(page 119)*. Keep the repair damp until the mortar cures for at least 3 days.

CLEANING A RETAINING WALL DRAINPIPE

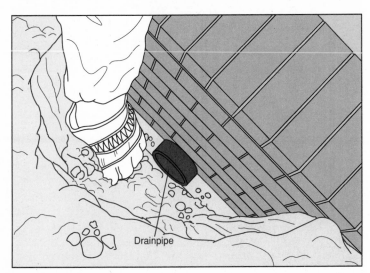

Drainpipe

1 **Uncovering a drainpipe.** Locate the drainpipe opening on one side of the wall and dig a hole on the other side of the wall, ex-posing the other end of the drainpipe. Wearing work gloves, use a spade to cut and remove any sod, then carefully dig up the soil until the end of the drainpipe is visible. Clear away the soil in and around the drainpipe opening using your hand *(above)* .

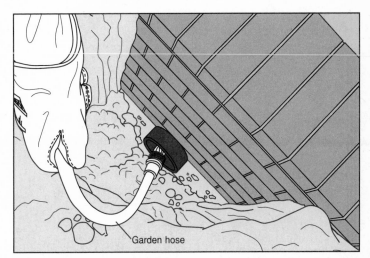

Garden hose

2 **Flushing out a drainpipe.** To flush out a drainpipe, insert a gar-den hose into the opening and turn on the water *(above)*. If the opening is too small for the hose to fit, clean out the drainpipe by pushing a wadded-up rag on the end of a broom handle through it from the other side of the wall. To prevent a drainpipe from clogging again, install a filter and backfill around the drainpipe with gravel *(step 3)*. Otherwise, refill the hole with soil *(step 4)*.

CLEANING A RETAINING WALL DRAINPIPE (continued)

Retaining wall

3 **Installing a filter.** Purchase 1/4-inch mesh screen or hardware cloth, also called filter fabric, and gravel at a building supply center. Use a spade to dig a drainage area about 4 inches deep and 1 foot square directly below the drainpipe opening; fill the drainage area with gravel. Wearing work gloves, use wire cutters or cutting pliers to cut a filter about 8 inches square. Bend the filter so it covers the drainpipe opening and lies flat on the gravel, then add about 4 inches of gravel on the filter *(above)*. As an added measure, surround the gravel with the same material as the filter.

4 **Refilling the hole.** Use a spade to refill the hole with soil to a height at least 2 feet above the filter; tamp the soil with your feet after each 6-inch layer is added. Refill the hole with soil until it is slightly higher than ground level to compensate for the settling that is likely to occur. Replace any sod removed and tamp again.

MAINTAINING SAND-BED AND MORTAR-BED PAVING

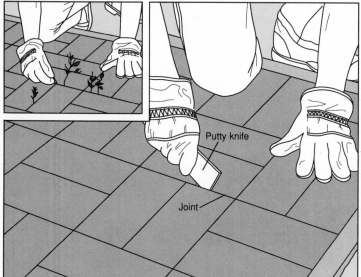

Putty knife

Joint

Cleaning out sand-bed paving joints. Dirt that accumulates in sand-bed joints spoils the paving appearance and allows windblown seeds and pods to root. Wearing work gloves, pull up any seedlings by hand *(inset)*, taking out as much of their roots as possible. To prevent seedlings from growing back, buy a herbicide such as glyphosate at a garden center and apply it according to label instructions. **Caution:** Spray herbicide only on a calm day, never when it is windy. Scrape dirt out of the joints with the edge of a putty knife *(above, left)* and use a stiff broom to sweep away loosened particles.

Using a hoe and a wheelbarrow or mortar box, mix a dry grout of 1 part masonry cement and 4 parts fine sand; mix about 80 pounds of grout for each 100 square feet of paving. Spread the grout on the paving surface with a bucket, applying one bucketful at a time, and work it into the joints with a stiff broom *(above, right)*. Sweep off any excess grout. When all the joints are filled with grout, water the surface with the fine spray of a garden hose to settle the grout in the joints. After the grout has dried, check that the joints are level with the paving. If necessary, use the same procedure to add more grout.

MAINTAINING SAND-BED AND MORTAR-BED PAVING (continued)

Removing stains from paving. Depending on the type of stain, there are a number of ways to clean paving; for guidance, refer to the chart on page 20 for an appropriate cleaning agent and procedure to try on a particular stain. Wearing rubber gloves and goggles, apply the cleaning agent according to the label instructions. To scrub the surface, use a stiff fiber brush or, to avoid bending, a push-broom *(above)*. When the stain is removed, rinse the surface thoroughly with clean water. To prevent stains, consider applying a sealer *(step right)*.

Applying a sealer on paving. To protect paving from staining or restore an original paving gloss, you may apply a sealer; consult your paving manufacturer or local building supply center, however, since applying a sealer can be controversial. If the surface is rough, use an acrylic or silicone sealer; if the surface is smooth, a sealer is usually not advised since it may make the paving dangerously slippery. When shopping for a sealer, keep in mind that some types are recommended only for paving that is at least a year old. **Caution:** Read the label instructions carefully and follow all safety precautions; apply a sealer only once every 3 years. Remove any stains from the paving *(step left)* and allow the surface to dry. Apply the sealer using a paint roller fitted with an extension *(above)*; a paintbrush is not recommended on sand-bed paving since it tends to pull sand from the joints and mar the finish.

REPLACING MORTAR-BED PAVING

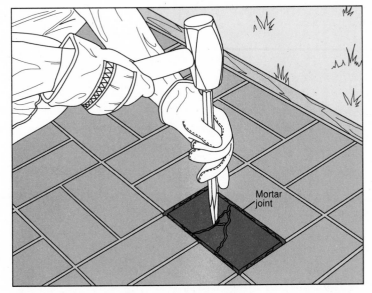

1 **Chiseling out sunken or cracked pavers.** To remove a paver, use a cold chisel and a small sledgehammer or ball-peen hammer to chip out the mortar around it; wear work gloves and goggles. If the paver is not damaged, try working it loose and lifting it out using an old screwdriver or a pry bar. If the paver is damaged or cannot be lifted out, break it up into pieces using the chisel and hammer *(above)* and remove it. Chisel old mortar off the bed and sides of the cavity. Clean out loose particles using a stiff fiber brush and a vacuum cleaner. Chip old mortar off a paver if it can be reinstalled *(page 24)*.

2 **Mortaring new pavers.** Buy replacement pavers at a building supply center; if necessary, take a piece of a paver to match it. If required, have pavers specially cut to fit; or, if paving with bricks, cut them yourself *(page 26)*. Mix a batch of mortar *(page 18)*. Use clean water to soak replacement pavers and wet the surfaces around the cavity. To install a new paver, shake excess water off it and use a pointing trowel to apply a 3/4-inch layer of mortar on the bottom and sides of it or the cavity. Position the paver and press it into place *(above)*. Scrape off excess mortar with the trowel edge. Use a carpenter's level to check the position of pavers; if necessary, lift out a paver to add mortar. Finish the joints flush with the paving surface *(page 119)*. Keep the repair damp until the mortar cures for at least 3 days.

RELAYING SAND-BED PAVING

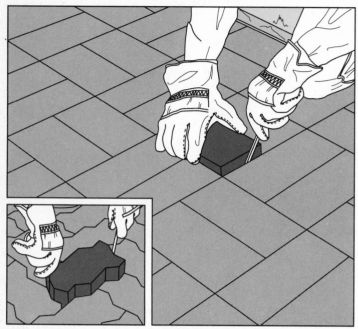

1 **Removing sunken or cracked pavers.** To remove a standard, square-cornered paver, lift up one side using an old flat-tipped screwdriver *(above)* or a pry bar and pull it out. To remove an interlocking paver, lift it straight up using two screwdrivers *(inset)* or pry bars. If removing a section of paving, note the position of any cut pavers on the bottom with a permanent marker. If a paver is damaged, replace it.

2 **Building up the sand bed.** Buy replacement pavers and fine sand for the bed at a building supply center; if necessary, take a damaged paver with you to match it. If required, have pavers specially cut to fit; or, if paving with bricks, cut them yourself *(page 26)*. Use a spade to add sand on the bed *(above)*, raising it to the bottom of adjoining pavers.

3 **Smoothing and tamping the sand bed.** If relaying a small section of paving, smooth the bed with a gloved hand; if relaying a large section of paving, strike off the bed using a screed *(page 35)*. Tamp the bed using the end of a 2-by-4; if the bed is large enough, make a tamper *(page 121)* and use it *(above)*. Continue building up the sand bed *(step 2)*, smoothing or striking off and tamping until the bed is level with the bottom of adjoining pavers.

4 **Installing and leveling new pavers.** Position new pavers one at a time, wiggling each one back and forth to work it into the bed until it is about 1/16 inch higher than and 1/8 inch away from adjoining pavers. Use a carpenter's level to check the position of the paver and tap it into place with the handle of a trowel *(above)* or a rubber mallet. If necessary, lift up the paver and add or remove sand. After positioning and leveling the pavers, spread a thin layer of sand on them with a spade; using a stiff broom, work the sand into the joints and sweep excess off the pavers. Use the fine spray of a garden hose to dampen the joints and refill them, if necessary, after the sand has dried and settled.

REMAKING A SAND BED

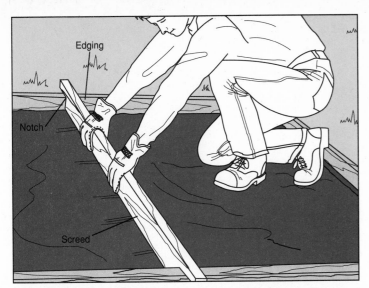

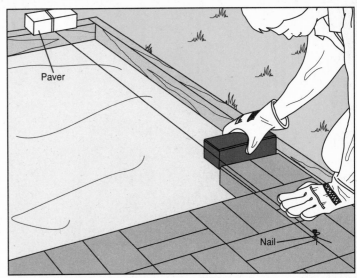

1 **Striking off the sand bed using a screed.** Identify the paving bond pattern *(page 19)* and remove all the pavers *(page 34, step 1)*; if necessary, build up the sand bed *(page 34, step 2)*. Use a 2-by-4 to make a leveling tool or screed about 6 inches longer than the width of the paving; cut a notch at each end to fit over the edging *(page 121)*. Starting at one end of the bed, drag the screed across the sand to level the bed *(above)*, filling in your footprints as you go. Smooth and tamp the bed *(page 34, step 3)* and strike off again, adding more sand, if necessary.

2 **Relaying the pavers.** Use a string as a guide to make sure that paving joints are straight. Position two pavers about 1/8 inch apart at one corner of the bed and check that they are level using a carpenter's level; tap them into place with a trowel handle or a rubber mallet. Align the string with the inner sides of the pavers just positioned and secure the ends of the string with pavers or nails. Using the string as a guide, install and level the rest of the first course of pavers *(page 34, step 4)*. Repeat the procedure to lay the other courses of pavers, using the string as a guide along the length *(above)* or width of the bed.

RECROWNING A SAND-BED PAVING WALKWAY

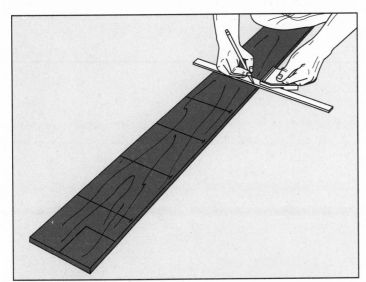

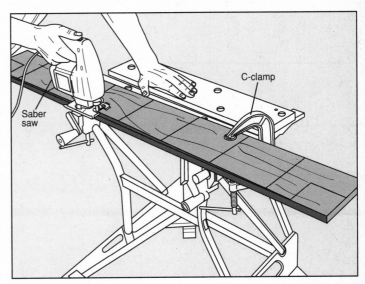

1 **Measuring and marking a screed.** For drainage, crown a walkway, sloping it slightly away from the center with a screed. Identify the paving bond pattern *(page 19)* and remove all the pavers *(page 34)*. Make the screed from a straight 1-by-6 that is 6 inches longer than the bed width. At each end, mark a notch to fit on the edging that is 3 inches long and equal in width to the thickness of a paver. Mark the center and, working from it toward each end, draw a line every 6 inches across the width *(above)*. Working from each end toward the center, mark a point on each line that is 1/8 inch farther from the same edge as the point before it. Join the points to form a rough curve.

2 **Cutting the screed curve and notches.** Secure the screed on a workbench using C-clamps, as shown, making sure that each cutting mark on the screed overhangs the workbench by at least 1 inch. Wearing goggles, use a saber saw *(page 120)* to cut the curve along the length of the screed *(above)* and the notch at each end of the screed *(page 121)*.

RECROWNING A SAND-BED PAVING WALKWAY (continued)

3 **Striking off the sand bed using the screed.** Build up the sand bed, if necessary *(page 34)*, and strike off using the screed to crown it. Starting at one end of the bed, fit the screed on the edging and drag it across the sand *(above)*, filling in your footprints as you go. Tamp the bed with a tamper *(page 121)* and strike off again, adding more sand, if necessary.

4 **Relaying the pavers.** Work from one end of the walkway to the other to relay the pavers. Wiggle each paver into position on the sand bed, about 1/8 inch away from other pavers *(above)*. Use a carpenter's level to check the position of the paver, resting one end on it and the other end on pavers already installed; tap the paver into place with the handle of a trowel or a rubber mallet. If necessary, lift up the paver and add or remove sand. After positioning and leveling the pavers, spread a thin layer of sand on the top of them with a spade; using a stiff broom, work the sand into the joints and sweep any excess off the pavers. Use the fine spray of a garden hose to dampen the joints and refill them, if necessary, after the sand has dried and settled.

REALIGNING WOOD EDGING

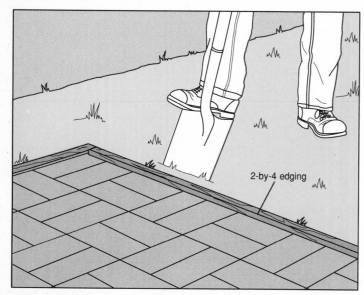

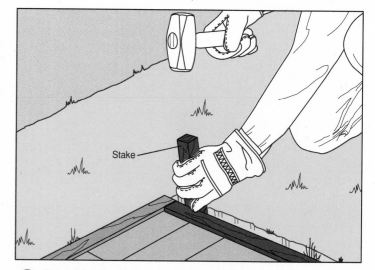

1 **Digging beside the edging.** Wearing work gloves, use a spade to cut and remove any sod within 4 inches of the edging *(above)*, then carefully dig a trench along the edging, exposing the stakes supporting it. If the edging is rotted, remove it using a crowbar and install new wood edging *(page 38)* or precast concrete edging *(page 39)*. If the edging is not damaged, work the stakes off the edging using a hammer or a pry bar and pull them out of the ground; if a stake is rotted, cut a new one *(page 120)* 12 to 18 inches long.

2 **Repositioning the edging and installing stakes.** Reposition the edging flush with the pavers; if necessary, have one or more helpers support it in place. Install stakes every 2 feet along the length of the edging. Using a small sledgehammer, drive each stake into the ground *(above)* until the top of it is about 1 inch below the top of the edging; cushion the hammer blows with a wood block to keep the stake from splitting, if necessary. Drive at least two 2-inch galvanized nails through each stake into the edging using a hammer. Use a spade to fill in the trench, grading the soil slightly away from the edging. Tamp the soil with your feet, put back any sod removed and tamp again.

REALIGNING RAILROAD TIE EDGING

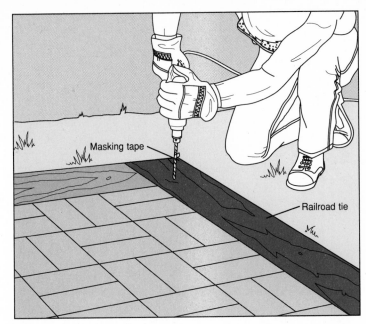

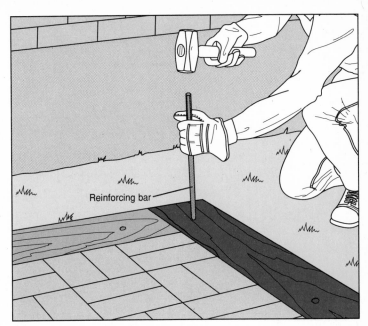

1 **Boring holes in the edging.** Reposition the edging flush with the pavers; if necessary, use a spade to cut and remove any sod within 4 inches of the edging and dig a trench along it. To support the edging in place, install reinforcing bars. Use a power drill with a 3/8-inch extension wood bit to bore holes for the bars; to avoid boring into the ground, mark the edging thickness on the bit with masking tape. Wearing goggles, bore a hole through the center of the edging every 2 feet along it, starting and stopping 6 inches from the end *(above)*.

2 **Installing reinforcing bars.** Purchase 1/4-inch reinforcing bars about 3 feet long at a building supply center. Wearing work gloves and goggles, use a small sledgehammer to drive a bar through each hole in the edging into the ground *(above)*; cushion the hammer blows with a wood block to protect the edging when the top of a bar reaches it. Use a spade to fill in any trench made, grading the soil slightly away from the edging, and tamp the soil with your feet; put back any sod removed and tamp again.

REPAIRING BRICK EDGING

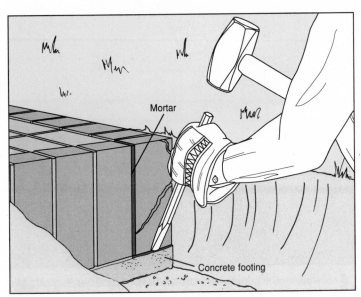

1 **Removing a damaged brick.** Wearing work gloves, use a spade to cut and remove any sod within 4 inches of the damaged edging and dig a trench along it deep enough to expose the concrete footing under it. Wearing goggles, chip off the mortar around the damaged brick using a cold chisel and a small sledgehammer *(above)* or ball-peen hammer and remove the brick. Chip the old mortar off the footing and the bricks adjoining the opening. Buy a replacement brick at a building supply center.

2 **Installing a new brick.** Mix a batch of mortar *(page 18)*; to prevent the leaching of moisture from it, use clean water to soak the new brick and wet the footing and sides of the opening. Use a pointing trowel to spread a 3/4-inch layer of mortar on the footing and sides of the opening. Shake excess water off the new brick and position it; tap it into the mortar using the trowel handle *(above)* until it is flush with the adjoining bricks. Scrape off excess mortar using the edge of the trowel blade and finish the joints *(page 119)*. Use a spade to fill in the trench, grading the soil slightly away from the edging. Tamp the soil with your feet, put back any sod removed and tamp again.

RESEALING CHIMNEY ROOF AND SIDING JOINTS

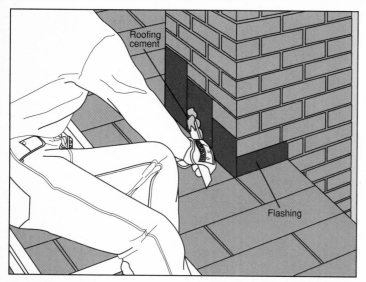

Cementing chimney roof flashing. Caution: Prepare to work safely on the roof *(page 114)*. With age, chimney flashing often begins to corrode at the point where it joins the chimney. If there are a number of large holes in the flashing, have it replaced by a professional. To patch small holes in the flashing, buy roofing cement at a building supply center. Following the label instructions, wear gloves and use a scrap piece of wood to apply a thick coat of cement, filling in the holes completely *(above)*.

Caulking chimney and siding joints. Caution: Prepare to work safely on a ladder *(page 112)* or scaffolding *(page 114)*. Local building codes specify the size of the gap required between the chimney and the siding on your home. If the caulking in this gap is loose or cracked, pry it out with the corner of a paint scraper or a putty knife and scrub the joint with a stiff fiber brush. Buy a tube of latex or silicone caulk at a building supply center and load it into a caulking gun; for a large job, buy a container of caulk and apply it with a putty knife. Following the label instructions, fill the gap with caulk *(above)*, pressing it firmly into the joint.

REPAIRING A CHIMNEY CAP

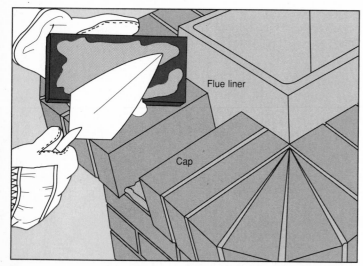

Replacing a cap brick. Caution: Prepare to work safely on the roof *(page 114)*. If a brick or the mortar around it is damaged, chip off the mortar using a cold chisel and a small sledgehammer or ball-peen hammer and remove the brick; wear work gloves and goggles. Chisel the mortar off the cavity bed and sides. Brush off particles using a stiff fiber brush. Buy a replacement brick at a building supply center; if necessary, have it cut to size. Mix a batch of mortar *(page 18)*. Use clean water to soak the new brick and wet the cavity. Use a mason's trowel to apply a 3/4-inch layer of mortar on the brick sides *(above)* and cavity bed. Position the brick and tap it into place using the trowel handle; preserve the cap slope. Finish the joints *(page 119)*.

Patching a concrete cap. Caution: Prepare to work safely on the roof *(page 114)*. To repair a crack in a concrete cap, use a cold chisel and a small sledgehammer or ball-peen hammer to enlarge and undercut the crack edges; wear work gloves and goggles. Clean out the crack with a stiff fiber brush. For a patch, buy concrete patching compound at a building supply center. Wearing work gloves, mix a small amount of the patching compound, following the label instructions. Dampen the crack with a cloth or a paintbrush dipped in clean water and use a pointing trowel to apply the patching compound *(above)*. Smooth the patch surface with the trowel edge. Until the patch cures, tape plastic over it with duct tape; do not use the fireplace until the plastic is removed.

REPLACING A CONCRETE CHIMNEY CAP

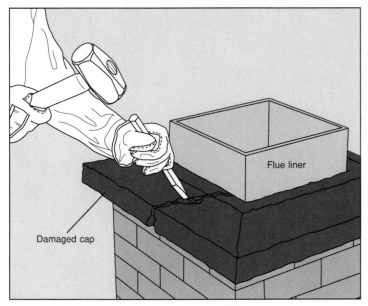

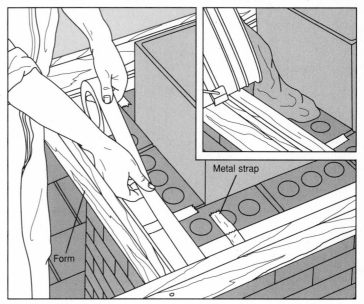

1 **Chiseling off the old cap. Caution:** Prepare to work safely on the roof *(page 114)*. Replace the chimney cap if it is badly damaged or a repaired crack recurs; take the cap measurements before removing it. To remove the old cap, break it into pieces small enough to take off by hand using a cold chisel and a small sledge-hammer *(above)* or ball-peen hammer; wear work gloves and goggles. Buy a precast cap at a building supply center or have a cap custom made and install it *(page 42)*, or make a concrete cap yourself *(step 2)*.

2 **Positioning the cap form and placing concrete.** Build a chimney cap form *(page 121)*. With one or more helpers, hoist the form onto the roof and carefully position it on the chimney top; check its position using a carpenter's level and adjust it, if necessary. Use 2-inch wide masking tape to cover the bolts for the metal straps, preventing concrete from adhering to them *(above)* and position the reinforcing bars. Wearing work gloves, mix a batch of concrete *(page 86)* and pass it up to the roof one bucketful at a time. Place concrete into the form and against the flue liner *(inset)*, distributing it evenly.

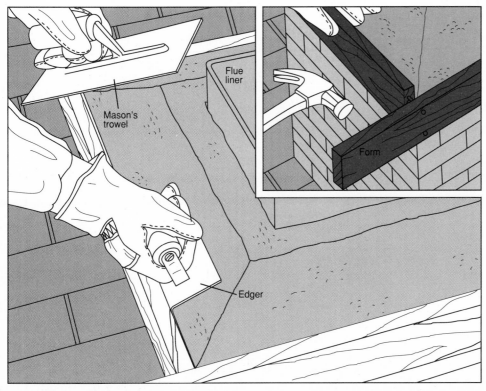

3 **Finishing the cap.** Add concrete to fill the form and use a wooden float to shape the cap for drainage, sloping it away from the flue liner; the cap should be 1/2 inch higher at its inside edge against the flue liner than at its outside edge. Avoid using metal tools for shaping; they draw moisture to the top of the concrete, weakening it. After the cap is shaped, smooth the surface using a rectangular trowel and curve the outside edge with an edger *(left)*; work with two hands, as shown. Cover the cap with plastic and tape the edges with duct tape. Allow the concrete to cure for 3 days before removing the plastic and the form; do not use the fireplace. **Caution:** Keep people away from the house when removing the form. To take apart the form, hammer on the inside edge of the extended sides *(inset)*. Remove the bolts from the bottom of the form and use pliers to pry the metal straps out of the cap.

REBUILDING A CHIMNEY TOP

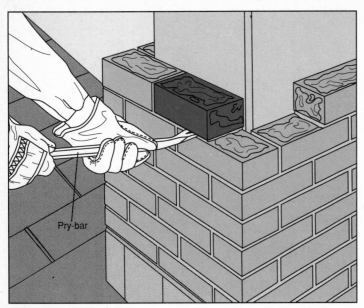

1 Removing the damaged section. Caution: Prepare to work safely on the roof *(page 114)*. If a concrete cap is damaged, chisel it off the chimney top *(page 41)*. If a concrete cap is undamaged, chip off enough of the first course of bricks to lift it off the chimney top. To chip off a brick cap and a top course of bricks, use a cold chisel and a small sledgehammer or ball-peen hammer; wear work gloves and goggles. Break the mortar around a brick, then break the brick into pieces small enough to remove by hand. Working one course at a time, use the same procedure to remove each brick or try lifting up the bricks from the bottom using a pry bar *(above)*. As each brick is removed, place it in a bucket; when the bucket is full, carefully lower it to the ground. Continue until all the damaged bricks and mortar are removed. Chip old mortar off surfaces where new mortar will be applied and off bricks that can be reused *(page 24)*. Buy replacement bricks at a building supply center; if necessary, take an old brick to match it.

2 Relaying the bricks. Wearing work gloves, mix a batch of mortar *(page 18)* and hoist it onto the roof one bucketful at a time. To prevent the leaching of moisture from the fresh mortar, soak replacement bricks in a bucket of clean water *(inset)* and dampen surfaces where fresh mortar is to be applied using a cloth or a paintbrush. Using a mason's trowel, apply a 3/4-inch bed of mortar on the top course of old bricks and furrow the mortar *(page 118)*. To install each brick, shake off excess moisture, butter its ends with a 3/4-inch layer of mortar, and position it on the bed; tap it into place using the trowel handle. To check the position of a brick, use a carpenter's level; if necessary, remove the brick and add mortar *(above)*. Scrape off excess mortar with the flat edge of the trowel blade. Use the same procedure to install each course of bricks, striking and smoothing the joints as you go *(page 23)*. Tape plastic over the repaired section using duct tape and allow the mortar to cure for 3 days; do not use the fireplace.

3 Installing a chimney cap. To install a new chimney cap, position a cap form, place concrete and finish the cap *(page 41)*, purchase a precast concrete cap at a building supply center, or have a concrete cap custom made. Make sure the chimney cap overhangs the chimney top by at least 3 inches. To put on a precast chimney cap, work with at least one helper. Wearing work gloves, mix a batch of mortar *(page 18)*; use a stiff mix to prevent the mortar from oozing out when the cap is positioned. Using a mason's trowel, spread a 1-inch bed of the mortar on the top course of chimney bricks and furrow the bed *(page 118)*. Working with a helper, carefully lower the cap over the flue liner and into position on the chimney top *(left)*. Fill the joint between the cap and the flue liner with mortar, sloping it slightly away from the liner. Use the flat edge of the trowel blade to scrape off any excess mortar, then strike and smooth the joints *(page 23)*. Tape plastic over the cap using duct tape until the mortar cures for 24 hours; do not use the fireplace until the plastic is removed.

POINTING FIREBRICKS

Hawk

1 **Cutting back mortar joints.** Wearing work gloves and goggles, cut back a damaged mortar joint until you reach solid mortar using a cold chisel and a small sledgehammer *(above)* or ball-peen hammer. Work carefully to avoid damaging any bricks. Clean loose particles out of the cut-back joints using a stiff fiber brush and, if necessary, a vacuum cleaner.

2 **Tuck-pointing the joints.** Wearing work gloves, mix a batch of fireclay mortar *(page 18)* on a mason's hawk. Using a cloth or a paintbrush dipped in clean water, dampen the damaged surfaces to prevent the leaching of moisture from the fresh mortar. Use a pointing trowel to tuck-point, or work mortar into the joints *(above)*, packing them as tightly as possible. If working on the wall, position the hawk as shown to catch any mortar that is accidently dropped. Scrape off excess mortar with the flat edge of the trowel blade. Strike and smooth the joints *(page 23)*.

REPLACING FIREBRICKS

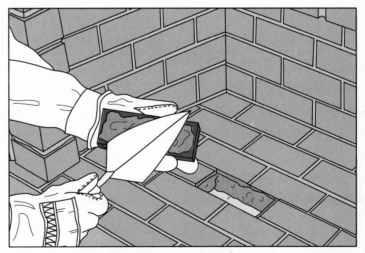

1 **Removing a damaged brick.** Wearing work gloves and goggles, chip out the brick using a cold chisel and a small sledgehammer or ball-peen hammer. First break the mortar around the brick, then break the brick *(above)* into pieces small enough to remove with a pry bar or the end of the chisel. Chip the old mortar off the sides and the bottom or back of the cavity. Clean loose particles out of the cavity using a stiff fiber brush and, if necessary, a vacuum cleaner. Buy a replacement brick at a building supply center; if necessary take a piece of the damaged brick to match it. **Caution:** Be sure that the new brick is made to withstand the high temperatures of a fireplace.

2 **Installing a new brick.** To install the new brick, wear work gloves to mix a batch of fireclay mortar *(page 18)*. Dampen the cavity with a cloth or a paintbrush dipped in clean water and soak the replacement brick to prevent the leaching of moisture from the fresh mortar. Use a pointing trowel to apply a 3/4-inch layer of mortar on the bottom or back and the sides of the cavity; if it is easier, also butter one or more sides of the brick with mortar *(above)*. Position the brick in the cavity, tapping it into place with the trowel handle until it is flush with the adjoining bricks. Scrape off excess mortar with the flat edge of the trowel blade. Strike and smooth the joints *(page 23)*.

STONE

Many of the longest-lasting structures in the world are constructed of stone. Although stone can be more difficult to work with, and more expensive, than brick or concrete, it is strong, durable, and offers an incomparable beauty and range of effects—from the rustic grace of a dry-laid fieldstone wall to the fine elegance of an imported-marble floor. Usually less uniform than brick in its bonding pattern (the way that rows, or courses, are positioned), stone can be used for a variety of structures, including house walls, garden walls, retaining walls and chimneys, and also as paving for walkways, steps and patios. Common uses of stone are shown at right; refer to pages 47 and 48 for typical types and forms.

If stone is kept clean and in good repair, its beauty and charm can be enjoyed for centuries. Consult the appropriate section of the Troubleshooting Guide on page 46 for guidance in diagnosing problems. For specific information on cleaning up spills and removing stains, refer to the chart on page 49; in addition to the household cleaning agents listed there, many special products are now available on the market. Many stone problems begin at the mortar joints, which are especially vulnerable to expansion and contraction due to temperature changes and exposure to wind and precipitation. Climbing plants can also severely damage mortar joints over a period of time. Undertake repairs as soon as problems are detected to prevent moisture from entering and weakening the structure. Most of the tools, materials and supplies required for repairs are readily available at a building supply center. Refer to the Tools & Techniques chapter *(page 106)* for the proper use and cleaning of tools; be sure to follow all safety precautions when working on the roof *(page 114)*.

Once a year, inspect all stone structures around your home. Check mortar joints in house walls; repair damaged joints by removing the old mortar and replacing it with fresh mortar, a procedure known as pointing *(page 59)*; cracks that recur should be inspected by a professional. Check freestanding walls and retaining walls, especially the caps; replace loose or fallen dry-laid stones *(page 55)* or damaged mortared stones *(page 59)*, refit cap stones *(page 56)*, if necessary, and rebuild any damaged dry-laid *(page 57)* or mortared *(page 61)* wall sections. Frost heave and erosion can cause the paving stones of walkways, steps and patios to become uneven, unsightly and dangerous; maintain and repair sand-bed and mortar-bed paving as shown on pages 63 to 67. Also inspect your chimney; clean the flue at least once a year *(page 123)*. Check for leaks and repair damaged joints *(page 68)*. Pay special attention to the cap *(page 69)*, which often shows the first sign of a problem. If your house is an older one, the chimney may not be lined with rectangular or square fireclay tiles or round glazed tile; this can be a fire hazard and should be remedied by a professional.

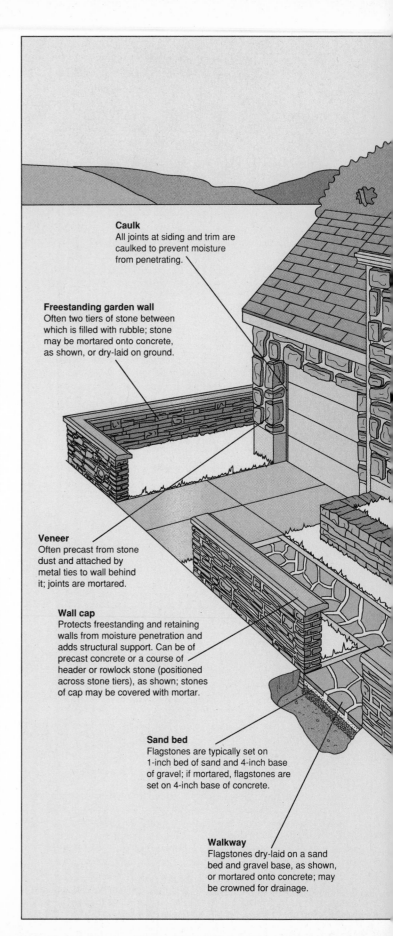

Caulk
All joints at siding and trim are caulked to prevent moisture from penetrating.

Freestanding garden wall
Often two tiers of stone between which is filled with rubble; stone may be mortared onto concrete, as shown, or dry-laid on ground.

Veneer
Often precast from stone dust and attached by metal ties to wall behind it; joints are mortared.

Wall cap
Protects freestanding and retaining walls from moisture penetration and adds structural support. Can be of precast concrete or a course of header or rowlock stone (positioned across stone tiers), as shown; stones of cap may be covered with mortar.

Sand bed
Flagstones are typically set on 1-inch bed of sand and 4-inch base of gravel; if mortared, flagstones are set on 4-inch base of concrete.

Walkway
Flagstones dry-laid on a sand bed and gravel base, as shown, or mortared onto concrete; may be crowned for drainage.

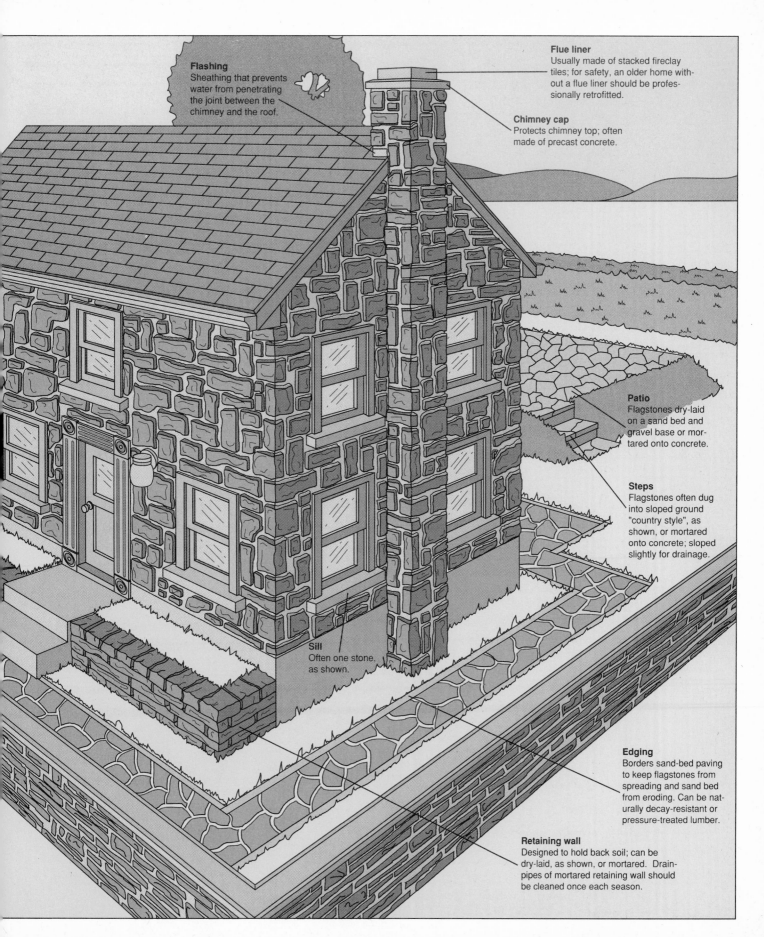

Flashing
Sheathing that prevents water from penetrating the joint between the chimney and the roof.

Flue liner
Usually made of stacked fireclay tiles; for safety, an older home without a flue liner should be professionally retrofitted.

Chimney cap
Protects chimney top; often made of precast concrete.

Patio
Flagstones dry-laid on a sand bed and gravel base or mortared onto concrete.

Steps
Flagstones often dug into sloped ground "country style", as shown, or mortared onto concrete; sloped slightly for drainage.

Sill
Often one stone, as shown.

Edging
Borders sand-bed paving to keep flagstones from spreading and sand bed from eroding. Can be naturally decay-resistant or pressure-treated lumber.

Retaining wall
Designed to hold back soil; can be dry-laid, as shown, or mortared. Drainpipes of mortared retaining wall should be cleaned once each season.

TROUBLESHOOTING GUIDE

SYMPTOM	POSSIBLE CAUSE	PROCEDURE
HOUSE, RETAINING AND FREESTANDING WALLS		
Surface dirty or stained	Weather, wear and pollution	Clean surfaces *(p. 49)* □●
Efflorescence (white, powdery deposits of dissolved salts)	High humidity or poor air circulation	Clean surfaces *(p. 49)* □●; indoors, install dehumidifier or increase ventilation
	Moisture penetrating mortar joint or stone damaged by climbing plant	Destroy climbing plant *(p. 50)* □◒; point mortar joint *(p. 59)* ▨◒ or replace stone *(p. 59)* ■◒ or stone veneer *(p. 62)* ▨◒
	Moisture penetrating door or window trim	Recaulk exterior trim *(p. 52)* ▨◒
	Moisture buildup behind retaining wall due to blocked drainpipe	Maintain retaining wall *(p. 61)* ▨●
	Insufficient drainage or leak in roof or plumbing	Inspect gutters, downspouts and soil grading *(p. 110)* □○; if necessary, consult a professional
Mortar joint loose or crumbling	Damage caused by climbing plant	Destroy climbing plant *(p. 50)* □◒; point mortar joint *(p. 59)* ▨◒
	Moisture penetrating door or window trim	Recaulk exterior trim *(p. 52)* ▨◒; point mortar joint *(p. 59)* ▨◒
	Retaining wall drainpipe blocked	Maintain retaining wall *(p. 61)* ▨●; point mortar joint *(p. 59)* ▨◒
	Insufficient drainage or leak in roof or plumbing	Inspect gutters, downspouts and soil grading *(p. 110)* □○; if necessary, consult a professional
Water damage around door or window	Caulk at joint between stone and trim loose or damaged	Recaulk exterior trim *(p. 52)* ▨◒
Stone loose, fallen, cracked or crumbling	Structure settlement; weather and traffic	Replace dry-laid stone *(p. 55)* ▨○, mortared stone *(p. 59)* ■◒, stone veneer *(p. 62)* ▨◒ or cap stone *(p. 56)* ▨◒
Wall leaning, buckling or sagging	Structure settlement; weather and traffic	Rebuild dry-laid section *(p. 57)* ■● or corner *(p. 58)* ■●, or rebuild mortared section *(p. 61)* ■●; maintain retaining wall *(p. 61)* ▨●
	Damaged foundation or footing	Consult a professional
Decorative stone edge chipped, cracked or broken	Weather; blow by heavy object	Repair decorative stone edge *(p. 70)* ▨◒
PAVING AND STEPS		
Surface weedy	Windblown seeds and pods rooted in sand bed or damaged mortar joints	Pull out weeds by roots and apply herbicide such as glyphosate; repair mortar-bed paving *(p. 65)* ▨◒ or mortared step *(p. 63)* ▨◒
Surface dirty or stained	Weather, wear and pollution; spills	Clean surfaces *(p. 49)* □●
Stone loose, cracked or crumbling	Weather and traffic	Relay sand-bed stone *(p. 65)* ▨○, repair dry-laid step *(p. 64)* ▨○; replace mortar-bed stone *(p. 65)* ▨◒, repair mortared step *(p. 63)* ▨◒
Paving stones sunken or heaved, or spreading or crooked	Weather and traffic	Relay sand-bed stone *(p. 65)* ▨○ or remake sand bed *(p. 66)* ▨●; replace mortar-bed stone *(p. 65)* ▨◒ or consult a professional to replace mortar bed
	Edging misaligned or damaged; no edging	Realign wood edging *(p. 36)* ▨◒, realign railroad-tie edging *(p. 37)* ▨◒ or install wood edging *(p. 38)* ▨●
Step stones sunken or heaved	Erosion; weather and traffic	Repair dry-laid step *(p. 64)* ▨○ or repair mortared step *(p. 63)* ▨◒
CHIMNEYS		
Surface dirty or stained	Smoke, weather and pollution	Clean surfaces *(p. 49)* □●
	Chimney leaks due to damaged mortar	Locate leaks and point joints *(p. 68)* ▨●
Water leaking in attic, from ceiling or along wall near chimney	Flashing at joint between chimney and roof damaged or caulk along joint between chimney and siding damaged	Repair flashing *(p. 40)* ▨◒; recaulk exterior trim *(p. 52)* ▨◒
	Chimney leaks due to damaged mortar	Locate leaks and point joints *(p. 68)* ▨●
	Chimney cap damaged	Repair *(p. 40)* ▨● or replace *(p. 69)* ■● concrete cap; for stone cap, consult a professional
	Insufficient drainage or leak in roof or plumbing	Inspect gutters, downspouts and soil grading *(p. 110)* □○; if necessary, consult a professional
Chimney cap loose, cracked or crumbling	Weather	Repair *(p. 40)* ▨● or replace *(p. 69)* ■● concrete cap; for stone cap, consult a professional
Chimney leaning	Structure settlement or damaged foundation	Consult a professional

DEGREE OF DIFFICULTY: □ Easy ▨ Moderate ■ Complex
ESTIMATED TIME: ○ Less than 1 hour ◒ 1 to 3 hours ● Over 3 hours

IDENTIFYING TYPES OF STONE

Since no two stones in nature are ever exactly alike, no two stones you find or buy will ever be identical in size, shape or color. However, use replacement stone that matches the original as closely as possible in type and form. To identify common types of stone, refer to the chart below; for usual forms of stone, see page 48. Keep in mind that the same type of stone can vary considerably, especially in strength, depending on the region it comes from. Stone of the proper form is easiest to fit

snugly—the secret of handsome stonework. You may find stone in a nearby field or the site of an old building about to be demolished. Otherwise, consult a building supply center or your local stone dealer. When hunting for or buying replacement stone, take a piece of original stone with you to ensure a match. Depending on the stone type and form, you can, if necessary, choose to face it *(page 53)*, cut it *(page 53)* or split it *(page 54)* yourself, or, have it prepared professionally.

TYPE OF STONE	COMMON USES	CHARACTERISTICS	WORKABILITY
Granite	Foundation walls, retaining walls, walkways, steps and patios.	Usually gray, often mixed with brown, black, white, pink or red. Surface sparkles. Non-porous.	Heavy (170 pounds per cubic foot). High strength and durability. Difficult to work and expensive. Can be polished.
Sandstone	Walls (other than foundations) and sills in dry, no-frost areas.	Can be buff, cream, brown, grayish pink, red, or blue; reddish hues depend on iron content. Rough, sandy surface. Porous; areas exposed to rain require most frequent cleaning to prevent embedded crusts of dirt from forming.	Moderately heavy (150 pounds per cubic foot). Strength and durability depend on hardness; soft seams that can be picked out with a nail indicate poor quality. Easy to work. Hardest and finest-grained can be polished.
Limestone	Walls (other than fire-resistant), rock gardens, walkways, steps and patios.	Typically buff, cream, ivory, brown or green. Chalky surface, often embedded with small fossils. Porous; described as "self-cleaning" (areas exposed to rain are cleanest). Sensitive to pollution; over time, may crumble due to sulphur dioxides in acid rain.	Heavy (170 pounds per cubic foot). Low to moderate strength and high durability. Easy to work.
Slate	Roofing, walkways, steps and patios.	Can be black, gray, green, blue or bluish gray. Surface skid-resistant. Non-porous; dense and brittle.	Very heavy (175 pounds per cubic foot). High strength and moderate durability; should always be set flat, not on edge. Easy to work.
Marble	Veneer, lintels (load-bearing pieces above a door or a window), keystones (wedge-shaped pieces at top of arch that lock other pieces in place) and interior floors and countertops.	Purest when white, but can be other colors; often has visible stripes. Crystalline; surface similar in appearance to sugar. Non-porous.	Heavy (170 pounds per cubic foot); hardness varies. Moderate to high strength and high durability. Difficult to work and expensive. Almost always polished.

FORMS OF STONE

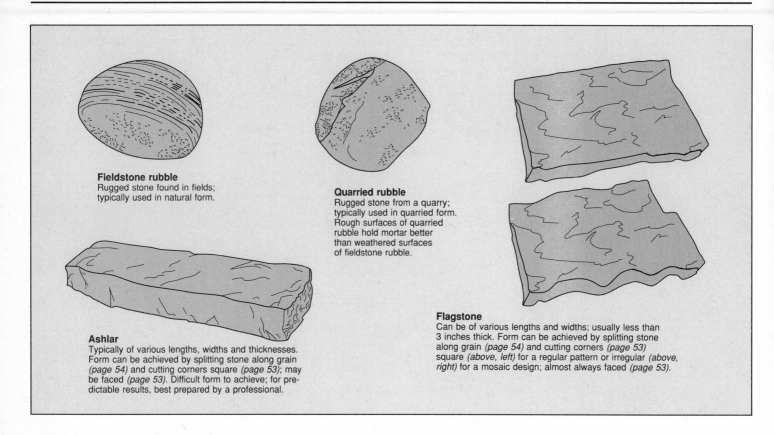

Fieldstone rubble
Rugged stone found in fields;
typically used in natural form.

Quarried rubble
Rugged stone from a quarry;
typically used in quarried form.
Rough surfaces of quarried
rubble hold mortar better
than weathered surfaces
of fieldstone rubble.

Ashlar
Typically of various lengths, widths and thicknesses.
Form can be achieved by splitting stone along grain
(page 54) and cutting corners square *(page 53)*; may
be faced *(page 53)*. Difficult form to achieve; for pre-
dictable results, best prepared by a professional.

Flagstone
Can be of various lengths and widths; usually less than
3 inches thick. Form can be achieved by splitting stone
along grain *(page 54)* and cutting corners *(page 53)*
square *(above, left)* for a regular pattern or irregular *(above,
right)* for a mosaic design; almost always faced *(page 53)*.

MIXING MORTAR

Mortar is the basic bonding material that holds stones together—unless
they are dry-laid, or not mortared. Mortar must be properly mixed in the
right proportions for a sound repair. For most jobs, you can produce
workable mortar using one of the recipes below. (Different proportions
may be required, especially in colder climates; check your local building
code, or consult your local builders association or masonry distributor.)
Use one of two types of cement: Portland cement, a bonding agent,
must be mixed with hydrated lime which gives the mixture workability;
masonry cement is a portland cement and lime mixture. All recipes use
finely-graded building sand and clean water (preferably with low mineral
content to prevent efflorescence). For small repairs, premixed mortar
is affordable; simply add water. Because the exact amount of water required for mortar depends on the humidity, the temperature and the
moisture in the sand, there is no recommended water ratio. Page 117
tells you how to judge the correct amount of water to add and the
proper technique for mixing it. Depending on the size of the batch, mix
the mortar by hand on a mason's hawk or in a mortar box or wheelbarrow. Be sure to mix only as much mortar as you can use before it hardens—which is about 2 1/2 hours. The ratios given in each recipe for
cement, lime and sand remain constant, whatever the size of the batch.

MORTAR	USES	DRY INGREDIENTS
TYPE N	Used for outdoor, above-ground masonry subjected to severe weathering	1 part portland cement*, 1 part hydrated lime and 6 parts sand
		1 part type II masonry cement and 3 parts sand
TYPE M	Used for general masonry and below-ground masonry in contact with soil, e.g. foundations, retaining walls, walkways	1 part portlant cement*, 1/4 part hydrated lime and 3 parts sand
		1 part portland cement*, 1 part type II masonry cement and 6 parts sand
TYPE S	Used for masonry subjected to lateral force, e.g. walls designed to resist strong winds	1 part portland cement*, 1/2 part hydrated lime and 4 1/2 parts sand
		1/2 part portland cement*, 1 part type II masonry cement and 4 1/2 parts sand
FIRECLAY	Used for interior fireplace work where resistance to heat is required	1 part fireclay mortar (available premixed) and 3 parts sand

*White portland cement is recommended, especially for light and colored mortar.

MAINTAINING STONE

No masonry is more handsome than stone—when it is well maintained. And stone requires little maintenance. Every few years, water-soak the surface *(page 50)* to clean off accumulated dirt and grime, as well as unsightly efflorescence—white, powdery deposits of dissolved salts. Take action to remove stains as soon as they occur. For guidance, refer to the chart below; in addition to the common cleaning agents listed, many special products are now available on the market. Always begin by trying the mildest cleaning agent possible; do not underestimate the effectiveness of household detergent and water *(page 50)*.

If you must resort to more powerful cleaning agents, be sure to read the label instructions carefully and follow all safety precautions. Keep in mind that a cleaning agent can have different effects on different types of stone—and on different stones of the same type. Marble, in general, requires more gentle cleaning than other stone. Polish marble (and some other types of stone) to restore its gloss *(page 51)*. Before applying a cleaning agent on a stain, test it on a small, inconspicuous surface to determine if it has any damaging side-effects. When you have finished cleaning, safely dispose of all leftover products *(page 116)*.

PROBLEM	CLEANING AGENT	PROCEDURE (Test first on inconspicuous surface)
GRANITE, SANDSTONE, LIMESTONE AND SLATE		
Efflorescence (white, powdery deposits)	Water	Water-soak surface and scrub with stiff fiber brush (p. 50)
Mortar	On fresh spot, use water; on old spot, use commercial cleaner*	Scrub fresh spot with stiff fiber brush and rinse. Rub off old mortar chunks with piece of stone; wearing rubber gloves and goggles, apply cleaner according to label instructions
Oil or grease	Cat litter; benzene* and thickener (talcum powder*** or fuller's earth***)	Soak up fresh oil or grease by applying cat litter—do not rub; sweep off after oil or grease absorbed. Wearing rubber gloves and goggles, mix benzene and thickener until pasty; apply poultice (p. 51)
Tar	Benzene* and thickener (talcum powder*** or fuller's earth***)	Scrape off excess tar with putty knife; wearing work gloves, apply dry ice to make globs brittle. Wearing rubber gloves and goggles, mix benzene and thickener until pasty; apply poultice (p. 51)
Organic stain (including food, coffee, tea, leaves, fungus, bird droppings)	Household detergent, household bleach and water	Wearing rubber gloves and goggles, add 1 cup of detergent and 1/2 cup of bleach to 1 gallon of water; apply solution (p. 50)
	Household scouring powder—except on polished stone	Wearing rubber gloves and goggles, apply powder (p. 50)
Climbing plant	Ammonium sulphate paste** or herbicide**	Cut plant near ground level; wearing rubber gloves and goggles, apply paste or herbicide on plant stems and remaining plant growth (p. 50)
Moss or algae	Herbicide**	Wearing rubber gloves and goggles, apply herbicide according to label instructions
Dirt, grime or smoke	Water	Water-soak surface and scrub with stiff fiber brush (p. 50)
	Household detergent, household bleach and water	Wearing rubber gloves and goggles, add 1 cup of detergent and 1/2 cup of bleach to 1 gallon of water; apply solution (p. 50)
	Trisodium phosphate (TSP)***, household detergent and water	Wearing rubber gloves and goggles, add 1/2 cup of TSP and 1/2 cup of detergent to 1 gallon of water; apply solution (p. 50)
	Household scouring powder; except on polished stone	Wearing rubber gloves and goggles, apply powder (p. 50)
Paint, rust or copper		Call for professional cleaning
MARBLE		
Oil or grease (including milk, cooking oil, cosmetics, mustard)	Acetone* and thickener (talcum powder*** or fuller's earth***)	Wearing rubber gloves and goggles, mix acetone and thickener until pasty; apply poultice (p. 51). If necessary, polish surface (p. 51)
Organic stain (including food, coffee, tea, leaves, fungus, bird droppings)	6% hydrogen peroxide solution*** and thickener (talcum powder*** or fuller's earth***)	Wearing rubber gloves and goggles, mix peroxide and thickener until pasty; apply poultice (p. 51). If necessary, polish surface (p. 51)
Dirt, grime or smoke	Household liquid detergent and water	Add 1/2 cup of detergent to 1 gallon of water; apply solution (p. 50). If necessary, polish surface (p. 51)
	Household bleach and thickener (talcum powder*** or fuller's earth***)	Wearing rubber gloves and goggles, mix bleach and thickener until pasty; apply poultice (p. 51). If necessary, polish surface (p. 51)
Paint, rust or copper		Call for professional cleaning

* Available at a building supply center   ** Available at a garden center   *** Available at a drug store

MAINTAINING STONE (continued)

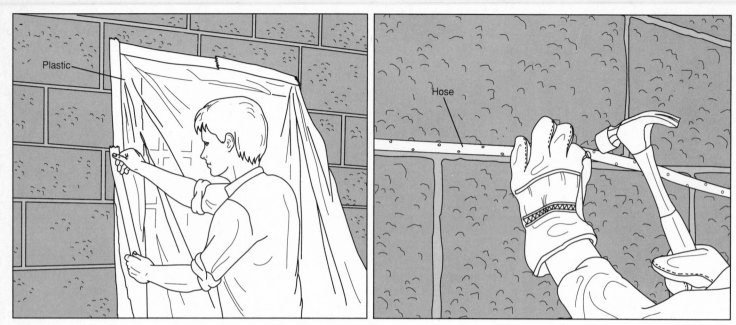

Water-soaking the surface. A constant flow of water is an effective way to clean accumulated dirt and grime off stone—without damaging it. Work only, however, when there is no risk of frost. Seal off any windows, doors, vents and other openings near the surface to be cleaned with plastic and duct tape *(above, left)*; be sure to overlap the tape ends at each joint. Set up a garden sprinkler to spray the entire surface steadily or, especially for a high wall, use a perforated garden hose equipped with a plastic coupling. (A copper coupling may stain the stone.) Support the hose against the surface to be cleaned by driving galvanized nails under it into the mortar joints around the stone *(above, right)* or by taping it. Allow water to run uninterrupted over the surface for at least 24 hours. If necessary, use a stiff fiber brush to scrub off stubborn spots and rinse thoroughly. Leave the nails in place for the next cleaning or remove them and point the mortar joints *(page 59)*.

Destroying a climbing plant with ammonium sulphate or herbicide. Cut the plant stems about 6 inches above ground level using pruning shears. Wearing rubber gloves and goggles, use a narrow paintbrush to apply ammonium sulphate paste or herbicide on the cut stems *(above)* according to label instructions. When the plant withers, remove it; wherever plant growth remains, repaint it with the paste or herbicide. When the plant stems stop growing, use a spade to dig up the roots.

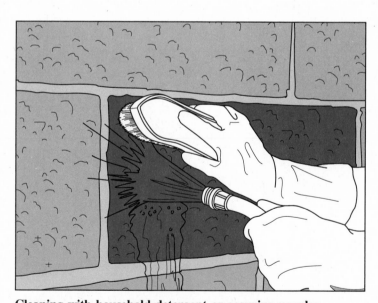

Cleaning with household detergent or scouring powder. Presoak the stone with clean water from a garden hose. Mix a solution of household detergent and water in a bucket, following the proportions given in the chart on page 49; add bleach or other cleaning agent, if necessary, wearing rubber gloves and goggles. If you are cleaning a wall, apply the solution working upward from the bottom, scrubbing in a circular motion with a stiff fiber brush and rinsing at the same time *(above)*. If you are cleaning paving, apply the solution using a push-broom to avoid bending. On stubborn dirt and grime, and on common stains, scrub gently with a little scouring powder. Rinse the surface thoroughly and allow it to dry. If necessary, repeat the procedure.

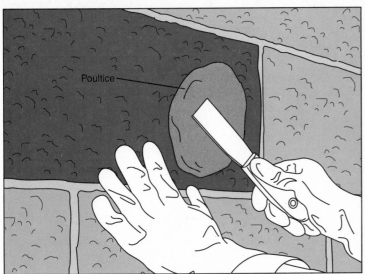 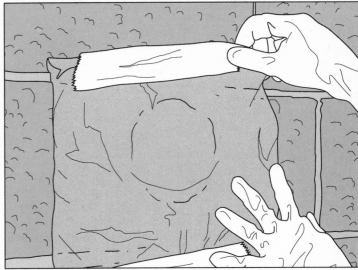

Applying a poultice. Working in a temperature betwen 60 and 80 degrees fahrenheit, prepare a poultice into a stiff, smooth paste *(chart, page 49)*. **Caution:** Work in a well-ventilated area, wearing rubber gloves and goggles. Wet the stained surface thoroughly with clean water and use a putty knife to apply a 1/2-inch layer of the poultice *(above, left)*. Cover the surface with plastic, taping it in place with duct tape *(above, right)*. Allow the poultice to sit for 24 hours or until it dries and falls away from the surface. Remove the plastic and wash off the surface using clean water, scrubbing with a stiff fiber brush. Rinse the surface thoroughly and allow it to dry. If necessary, repeat the procedure.

POLISHING STONE

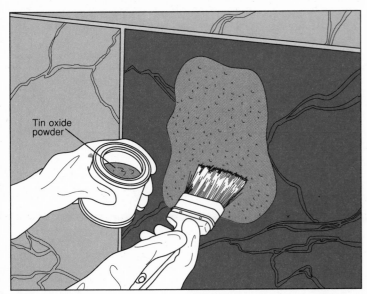 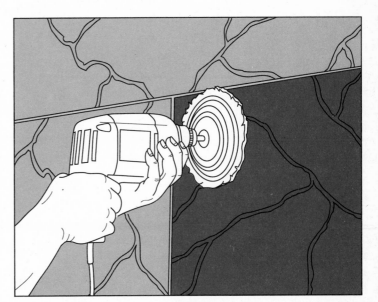

1 Applying tin oxide powder. To disguise shallow scratches and restore a gloss to marble, granite and certain varieties of sandstone, buy tin oxide powder at a building supply center. Wet the surface with clean water. Wearing rubber gloves and goggles, load the bristles of a dry paintbrush with powder and gently spatter it onto the surface *(above)*, without touching the bristles to the stone. Repeat the procedure until the entire surface is finely spattered.

2 Buffing the stone. Fit a lamb's wool pad onto a power drill to buff the surface. Applying light pressure, guide the pad slowly over the surface in a circular motion *(above)*. Continue until the entire surface is well buffed. Mix a solution of 1/2 cup of household liquid detergent per gallon of water in a bucket. Wash off the surface with the solution using a clean cloth. Rinse the surface thoroughly and, if necessary, reapply tin oxide powder *(step 1)* and repeat the procedure.

RECAULKING EXTERIOR TRIM

1 **Removing the old caulk.** Starting at one end of a joint, pry out the damaged caulk using the corner of a paint scraper *(above)* or a putty knife. Using a stiff fiber brush, scrub the joint and clean the outer edge of the trim with a solution of mild detergent and clean water. Rinse the joint and let it dry; if the finish of wood trim is damaged, touch it up with finish or preservative.

2 **Applying the new caulk.** Buy a tube of exterior silicone or acrylic caulk at a building supply center. Load the tube into a caulking gun. Following the label instructions, use a utility knife to cut the tip of the tube at a 45-degree angle, providing an opening for a 1/4-inch bead. Use a long nail or an awl to break the tube seal. Holding the gun at a 45-degree angle to the joint, squeeze the gun trigger to lay a continuous bead of caulk along the joint *(above)*. Wearing a rubber glove, run a wet finger along the caulk to press it into the joint, smoothing and shaping it.

WORKING SAFELY WITH STONE

Preventing injury. Proper handling of stone is critical in order for repairs to be performed safely, especially because it is extremely heavy and rarely uniform. Most stones weigh well over 150 pounds per cubic foot, with the weight often distributed unevenly in its mass. Wear work gloves and steel-toed work boots whenever handling a stone. When lifting a stone, for example, minimize the use of your back muscles: Always bend your knees and keep your back straight *(left)*, relying on the muscles in your legs for strength. Transport stones using a wheelbarrow *(page 112)* rather than carrying them by hand. Take periodic breaks to avoid tiring or straining yourself. If you must work at a height above your head, follow recommended practices on a ladder *(page 112)* or scaffolding *(page 114)*. Do not, however, attempt to remove and replace any stone that you cannot reach from the ground; instead, consult a professional.

FACING A STONE

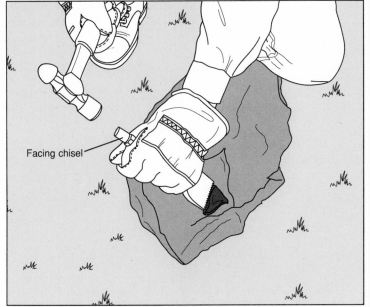

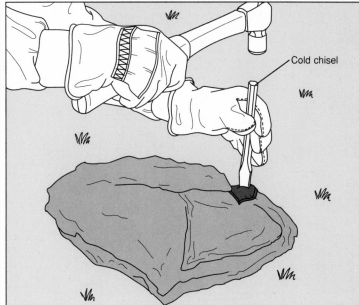

Facing chisel

Cold chisel

Chipping off protrusions. Protrusions on a stone can be dangerous: On a flagstone for a patio, bumps can cause falls; on ashlar or another stone form for a wall, sharp edges can cause scratches and cuts. Wearing work gloves and goggles, chip protrusions off a stone, or face it, using a facing chisel or a cold chisel and a ball-peen hammer. With either chisel, keep yourself positioned well away from the cutting edge. To use a facing chisel, hold the blade at a 45-degree angle against the base of the protrusion and rap sharply on the top of the chisel with the hammer *(above, left)*. To use a cold chisel, hold the blade at almost a 90-degree angle against the base of the protrusion and follow the same procedure *(above, right)*. Continue until all bumps and sharp edges are chipped off the stone face.

CUTTING A STONE

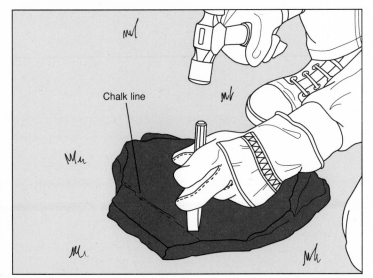

Chalk line

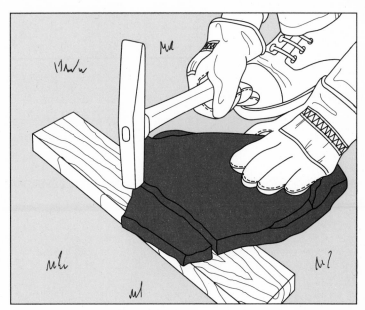

1 **Scoring a cutting line.** If the stone is over 3 inches thick, split it along the grain *(page 54)*. If the stone is no more than 3 inches thick, cut it. Cutting stone properly takes practice and patience, and is easiest along the grain; have several extra stones on hand and soak the stone with water, if necessary, to make the grain visible. Mark a cutting line on each side of the stone using chalk and a straight edge. Place the stone on a soft, flat surface. Wearing work gloves and goggles, score the cutting line on each side of the stone using a cold chisel and a ball-peen hammer *(above)*; tap lightly with the hammer, chiseling to a depth of about 1/8 inch.

2 **Breaking the stone.** Support the stone against the edge of a board, as shown, with the waste side of the stone overhanging it. Wearing work gloves and goggles, use a brick hammer to tap the waste side of the stone along the scored cutting line *(above)*, breaking the stone. If the stone does not break, score a deeper cutting line *(step 1)* and repeat the procedure. If the stone does not break evenly, chip off any sharp edges using a cold chisel and a ball-peen hammer. If necessary, face the stone *(step above)*.

SPLITTING A STONE

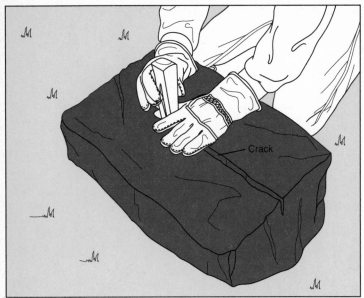

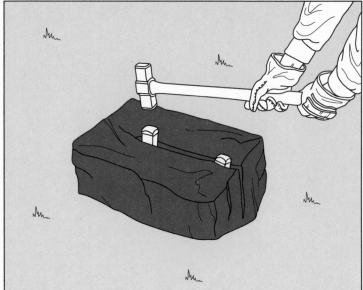

Using wedges. If the stone is no more than 3 inches thick, cut it *(page 53)*. If the stone is more than 3 inches thick, split it along the grain; have a stone more than 3 inches thick split across the grain by a professional. Scrub off dirt using a stiff fiber brush and soak the stone with water, if necessary, to make the grain visible. If there are no natural cracks along the grain, split the stone using wedges and shims *(step below)*. If there are natural cracks along the grain, wear work gloves and push a stone wedge into each end of the longest crack *(above, left)*; tap it lightly into place, if necessary, using a small sledgehammer. Wearing goggles, use a large sledgehammer to strike the top of each wedge, in turn *(above, right)*, driving them into the stone. Continue until the stone splits apart. If the stone does not split evenly, chip off any sharp edges using a cold chisel and a ball-peen hammer. If necessary, face the stone *(page 53)*.

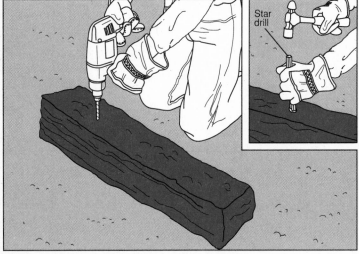

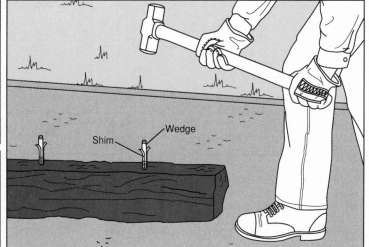

Using wedges and shims. If the stone is no more than 3 inches thick, cut it *(page 53)*. If the stone is more than 3 inches thick, split it along the grain; have a stone more than 3 inches thick split across the grain by a professional. Scrub off dirt using a stiff fiber brush and soak the stone with water, if necessary, to make the grain visible. If there are natural cracks along the grain, split the stone using wedges *(step above)*. If there are no natural cracks along the grain, drill a hole 1 to 2 inches deep about 1/3 of the way in from each end of the stone. Wearing work gloves and goggles, use a star drill and a ball-peen hammer *(inset)* or a hammer drill fitted with a 3/8-inch masonry bit *(above, left)*; stop drilling periodically to let the drill and bit cool. Blow dust out of the hole to clear it. Fit a set of stone shims into each hole, positioning the curved tips in opposite directions, as shown, at a 90-degree angle to the stone grain. Push a stone wedge between each set of shims; tap it lightly into place, if necessary, with a small sledgehammer. Use a large sledgehammer to strike the top of each wedge, in turn *(above, right)*, driving them into the stone. Continue until the stone splits apart. If the stone does not split evenly, chip off any sharp edges using a cold chisel and a ball-peen hammer. If necessary, face the stone *(page 53)*.

PLACING A STONE

Rolling a stone up a ramp. To place a heavy stone at a height above the ground, use a board as a ramp; in most instances, a 2-by-6 is sufficient. Position one end of the board at the final position for the stone and the other end of the board on the ground—or on a concrete block, if necessary, to decrease the ramp slope. Wearing work gloves, roll the stone end over end up the ramp *(above)* and into place. If you cannot budge the stone, work with a helper or use a longer board.

Dropping a stone into place. Never lower a stone completely into place; your fingers holding the stone can be crushed by its weight. Wearing work gloves, roll the stone into place, using a ramp, if necessary *(step left)*, or lift the stone *(page 52)*, slowly lower it *(above)* and drop it into place from a height of 4 to 6 inches. If necessary, raise one edge of the stone to reposition it, slowly lower the edge and drop it into place from a height of 2 to 3 inches.

REPLACING A DRY-LAID WALL STONE

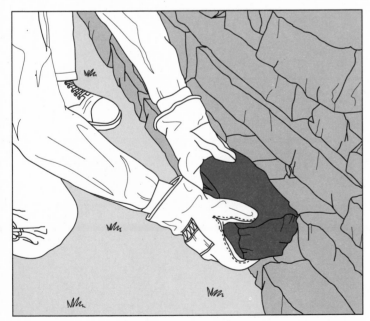

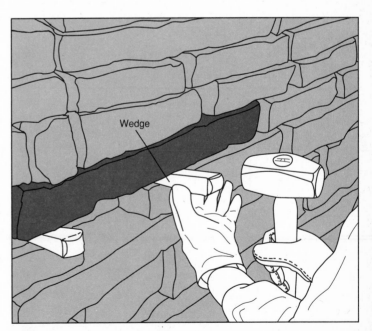

1 Chinking a stone into a wall. Over time, stones in a dry-laid wall come loose or fall out due to settling, frost heave and traffic. If the wall has settled and the stone cannot be repositioned, enlarge the opening for it by supporting the stones around the opening with wedges *(step 2)*. In many instances, a fallen stone can be repositioned by hand; wearing work gloves, push it back into place *(above)*. If necessary, tap the stone into place securely using a small sledgehammer, cushioning the blows with a block of wood.

2 Supporting a stone with wedges. Support each stone directly above the opening for the fallen stone with at least one stone wedge. Wearing work gloves and goggles, use a small sledgehammer to drive each wedge between the stone directly above the opening and a stone below it *(above)*. Drive in as many wedges as necessary to enlarge the opening and reposition the fallen stone. Then, chink the stone into the opening *(step 1)* and pull out the wedges.

REFITTING A DRY-LAID CAP STONE

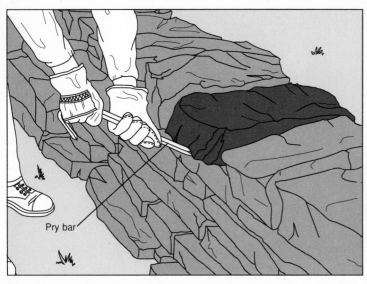

Pry bar

Reseating a cap stone. Once a year, check the cap stones of a dry-laid wall; they are especially vulnerable to shifting caused by settling, frost heave and traffic. Replace any loose or fallen stones below the cap stones *(page 55)*; rebuild a sagging or buckling wall section *(page 57)*. Wearing work gloves, use a pry bar to reposition a cap stone that is loose or out of place *(above, left)*; wiggle the cap stone to ensure it is seated securely. If a cap stone cannot be reseated securely, wedge one or more small stones under it. If necessary, raise the cap stone using the proper lifting procedure *(page 52)*; to reposition the stone, drop it into place from a height of 4 to 6 inches *(above, right)*.

REFITTING A MORTARED CAP STONE

Mortar hook

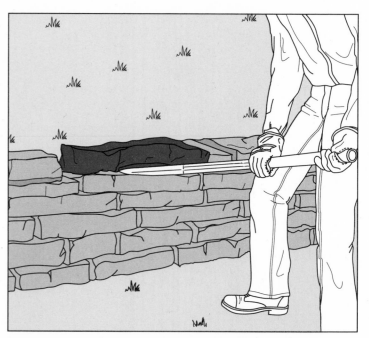

1 **Chiseling out the old mortar.** Once a year, check the cap stones of a mortared wall. Point any damaged mortar joints and replace any damaged stones below the cap stones *(page 59)*; rebuild a sagging or buckling wall section *(page 61)*. Wearing work gloves and goggles, use a cold chisel and a ball-peen hammer to cut back the mortar joints around a loose or damaged cap stone *(above)*; damaged mortar crumbles easily. Drag a mortar hook along the interior of the cut-back joints *(inset)* to scrape off mortar that is hard to reach.

2 **Prying up the cap stone.** If the cap stone is secure and not damaged, tuck-point the joints *(page 59)*. If the cap stone is loose or damaged, unseat it. Wearing work gloves, fit a long pry bar into the joint under the cap stone *(above)* and work it up and down to free the cap stone. If the cap stone is not damaged, support it *(step 3)*. If the cap stone is damaged, replace it *(page 47)*; chisel mortar off the edges of adjoining stones *(step 1)* and, if necessary, split *(page 54)* or face *(page 53)* the new cap stone before placing it *(page 55)*.

REFITTING A MORTARED CAP STONE (continued)

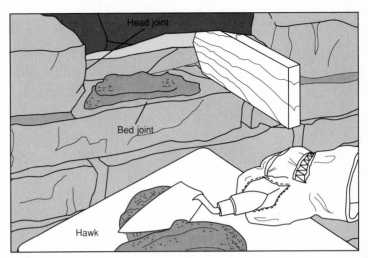

3 **Supporting the cap stone.** Use a board sawed into a point at one end *(page 120)* to prop up the cap stone; in most instances, a 1-by-4 positioned on its edge, as shown, is sufficient. Wearing work gloves, use a pry bar to raise the cap stone high enough to wedge the board under it *(above)*. If you are refitting a new cap stone, mortar it *(step 4)*. If you are refitting the same cap stone, wear goggles and chip old mortar off it and the edges of adjoining stones using a cold chisel and a ball-peen hammer. Clean off loose particles with a stiff fiber brush.

4 **Remortaring the cap stone.** Soak the cap stone and the adjoining stones with clean water. Wearing work gloves, mix a batch of mortar *(page 48)* and use a pointing trowel to spread a 3/4-inch layer on the bed joint *(above)* and each head joint. Sit small stones in the bed joint to support the cap stone as the mortar sets. Using a pry bar as a lever, pull out the board supporting the cap stone, lowering it slowly into place. Pack mortar into the joints and scrape off excess with the trowel. Wipe mortar off the face of the stones with a damp piece of burlap or rough cloth and strike the joints using a jointer *(page 119)*. Keep the mortar damp until it cures for 3 days.

REBUILDING A DRY-LAID WALL SECTION

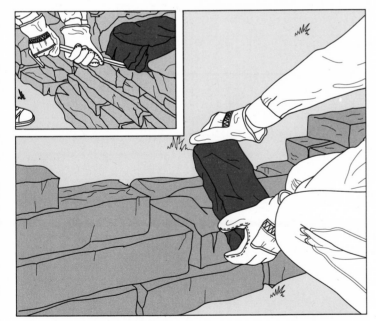

1 **Removing a damaged wall section.** Wearing work gloves, remove a V-shaped wall section, starting at the top with stones at least 2 feet beyond each side of the damaged wall section. Use a pry bar to loosen the cap stones *(inset)* and the stones in the courses below it, if necessary; number the stones for later reference with chalk. Work your way down the wall, removing progressively fewer stones from each course *(above)* and using the proper lifting procedure *(page 52)*. Continue until the damaged wall section is removed; if you stop before the base, go to step 3.

2 **Rebuilding the base.** A dry-laid wall requires a solid base of undisturbed soil or a well compacted 4- to 6-inch layer of gravel under it. If the base is sunken or heaved, make a tamper *(page 121)* and use it, alternately lifting and pounding it against the base. To build up the base, use a spade to spread a 2- to 4-inch layer of gravel on it and tamp again *(above)*. If you are rebuilding a retaining wall, slope the base slightly toward the soil being retained, away from the exposed side of the wall section.

REBUILDING A DRY-LAID WALL SECTION (continued)

3 **Relaying the stone courses.** Wearing work gloves, relay each stone, one course at a time, reversing the order in which they were removed; use the numbers chalked onto the stones as reference. Use the proper lifting procedure *(page 52)* to place each stone *(page 55)*, overlapping the joints between the stones in the course below it; if necessary, fit one or more small stones under it as shims to seat it securely *(above)*. If you are rebuilding a retaining wall, slope each course slightly toward the soil being retained. If you are rebuilding a freestanding wall, taper each course slightly inward from the course below it. Continue until all stones but the cap stones are relaid.

4 **Recapping the wall section.** Wearing work gloves, lay the cap stones, straddling them across the tiers of stones. Following the same procedure used to lay the other courses *(step 3)*, place each cap stone; with one edge in position *(above)*, drop the opposite edge into place from a height of 2 to 3 inches. Fit one or more small stones under a cap stone as shims, if necessary, to seat it securely. Continue until all the cap stones are relaid.

REBUILDING A DRY-LAID WALL CORNER

Interlocking stones at a corner. Wearing work gloves, remove a V-shaped wall section from both sides of the corner *(page 57, step 1)*; if necessary, rebuild the base *(page 57, step 2)*. Wearing work gloves, re-lay each stone, one course at a time, reversing the order in which they were removed; use the numbers chalked onto the stones as reference. Use the proper lifting procedure *(page 52)* to place each stone *(page 55)*, overlapping the joints between the stones in the course below it

(above, left); if necessary, fit one or more small stones under it as shims to seat it securely. At the corner, overlap the joints between the stones as shown *(above, right)*, alternating sides each course so the stones interlock. If you are rebuilding a retaining wall, slope each course slightly toward the soil being retained. If you are rebuilding a freestanding wall, taper each course slightly inward from the course below it. Continue relaying each course of stones and recap the wall section *(step 4, above)*.

POINTING DAMAGED MORTAR JOINTS

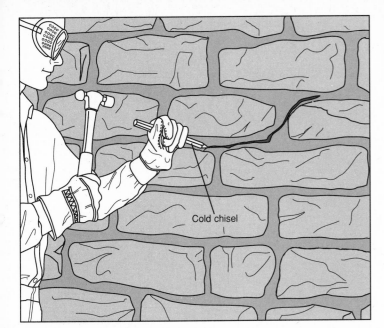

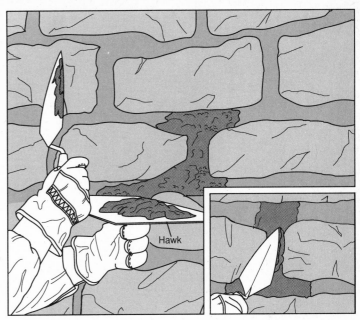

1 **Chiseling out the old mortar.** Wearing work gloves and goggles, use a cold chisel and a ball-peen hammer to cut back the damaged joints until solid mortar is reached *(above)*; work carefully to avoid damaging any stones. Drag a mortar hook along the interior of the cut-back joints *(below, right)* to scrape off mortar that is hard to reach. Clean out loose particles using a stiff fiber brush. Soak the cut-back joints and adjoining stones with clean water to prevent the leaching of moisture from fresh mortar.

2 **Tuck-pointing the joints.** Wearing work gloves, mix a batch of mortar *(page 48)* on a mason's hawk. Use a pointing trowel to tuck-point, or work mortar into the joints. Or, to force mortar into a vertical joint, flick it off the trowel with a sharp snap of your wrist *(above)*. Pack as much mortar as possible into the joints and scrape off excess with the edge of the trowel blade. Wipe mortar off the face of the stones with a damp piece of burlap or rough cloth. Strike the joints using a jointer *(page 119)* or the bottom surface of the trowel *(inset)*. Keep the mortar damp until it cures for 3 days by misting periodically with the fine spray of a garden hose.

REPLACING A MORTARED WALL STONE

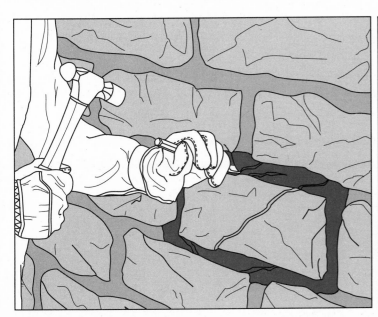

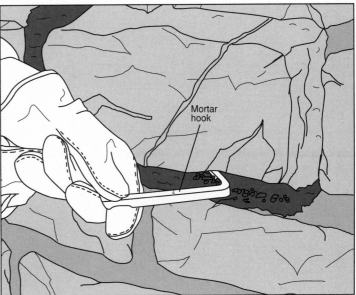

1 **Chiseling out the old mortar.** Wear work gloves and goggles, use a cold chisel and a ball-peen hammer to cut away the joints around the damaged stone *(above, left)*. Drag a mortar hook along the interior of the cut-back joints *(above, right)* to scrape off mortar that is hard to reach. Repeat the procedure, removing as much of the mortar around the damaged stone as possible; work carefully to avoid damaging any adjoining stone. Continue until the damaged stone is loosened.

REPLACING A MORTARED WALL STONE (continued)

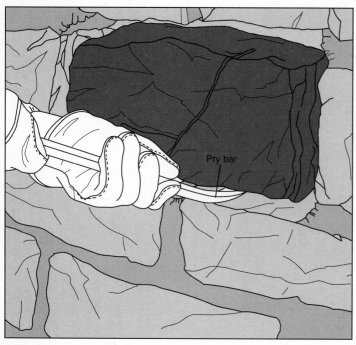

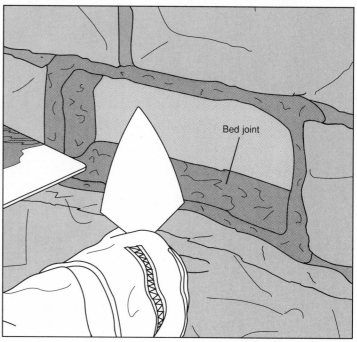

2 **Prying out the stone.** Wearing work gloves and goggles, fit a pry bar into the cleaned-out joint below the damaged stone *(above)* and work it back and forth to free the damaged stone. Pull out the pry bar and repeat the procedure on each side of the damaged stone until it can be taken out of the wall; if the stone is broken, remove it in pieces. Take out the damaged stone using the proper lifting procedure *(page 52)*. Find a replacement stone *(page 47)*; have it prepared for you, or split *(page 54)* or face *(page 53)* it yourself.

3 **Mortaring the wall cavity.** Wearing work gloves and goggles, use a cold chisel and a ball-peen hammer to chip any remaining mortar off the sides of the cavity. Clean out loose particles with a stiff fiber brush. Soak the cavity and the replacement stone with clean water to prevent the leaching of moisture from fresh mortar. Mix a batch of mortar *(page 48)* on a mason's hawk and use a pointing trowel to spread a 3/4-inch layer on the bed joint *(above)*, sides and top of the cavity. Sit small stones in the bed joint to support the replacement stone in position as the mortar sets.

4 **Placing the new stone.** Wearing work gloves, butter the top of the replacement stone with a layer of mortar and place it carefully into the cavity *(left)*, using the proper lifting procedure *(page 52)*. Push the stone straight into position in the cavity, aligning its face with the face of adjoining stones; use a pry bar, if necessary, to place the stone properly. Pack mortar into the joints around the replacement stone using a pointing trowel and scrape off excess with the edge of the trowel blade. Wipe mortar off the face of the stones with a damp piece of burlap or rough cloth. Strike the joints using a jointer *(page 119)* or the bottom surface of the trowel. Keep the mortar damp until it cures for 3 days by misting periodically with the fine spray of a garden hose or by tapping plastic over the surface of the repair using duct tape.

REBUILDING A MORTARED WALL SECTION

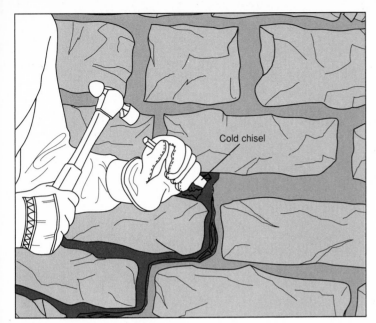

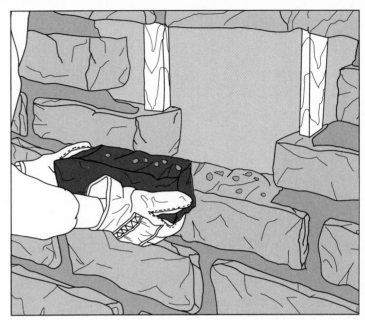

1 Chiseling out the old mortar. To repair a damaged wall section, remove a V-shaped pattern of stones, starting with stones at the top of the damaged section and at least 2 feet beyond each side of it; remove the stones one at a time, one course at a time. Wearing work gloves and goggles, use a cold chisel and a ball-peen hammer to cut away the joints around the stone (above). Drag a mortar hook along the interior of the cut-back joints to scrape off mortar that is hard to reach. Remove as much of the mortar around the stone as possible. Loosen the stone using a pry bar, if necessary, and take it out using the proper lifting procedure (page 52).

2 Removing the stones. Take out the first course as you did the first stone (step 1), numbering the stones for later reference with chalk. Brace unsupported stones at the top of the cavity with boards; in most instances, 2-by-4s are sufficient. Wedge each board, as shown, between the unsupported stone and a stone in a course below it. Work your way down the wall, removing progressively fewer stones from each course (above). Continue until all the stones of the damaged wall section are removed. Working your way back up the wall one stone and one course at a time, remortar the cavity (page 60, step 3) and place each stone (page 60, step 4); use the numbers as reference.

MAINTAINING A RETAINING WALL

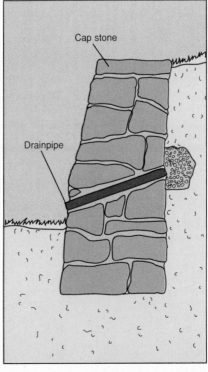

Cap stone

Drainpipe

Keeping a retaining wall in good repair. A dry-laid retaining wall and a mortared retaining wall require a solid base and adequate drainage; both should slope slightly toward the soil they are retaining. There is no drainage maintenance for a dry-laid retaining wall since the joints around the stones are open; and a mortared retaining wall is built on a maintenance-free base of concrete. Nonetheless, a retaining wall should be inspected each spring.

If the retaining wall is dry-laid, replace any loose or fallen stone (page 55), wearing work gloves to chink it into the wall (far left) or, if it is a cap stone, reseat it (page 56). If a dry-laid retaining wall is sagging or buckling, rebuild the damaged section (page 57) or corner (page 58).

If the retaining wall is mortared, refit any loose or damaged cap stone (page 56), point any damaged joint (page 59) and replace any damaged stone (page 59). If a mortared retaining wall is sagging or buckling, rebuild the damaged section (steps above); if the base is damaged, consult a professional. Clean each drainpipe, located as shown (near left), as you would for a brick retaining wall (page 31).

REPLACING STONE VENEER

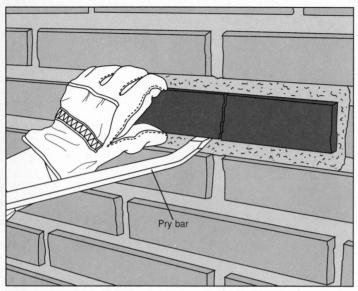

1 **Chipping out the damaged stone veneer.** Wearing work gloves and goggles, use a cold chisel and a ball-peen hammer to cut away the mortar joints around the loose or damaged stone. If necessary, drag a mortar hook along the interior of the cut-back joints to scrape off mortar that is hard to reach. Fit a pry bar into the cleaned-out joint below the damaged stone *(above)* and work it back and forth to free the damaged stone. If you expose a metal tie holding the stone in position, chip the mortar off it and leave it in place.

2 **Cleaning the wall cavity.** Wearing work gloves and goggles, use the blade of a cold chisel to carefully scrape mortar off the back and sides of the wall cavity *(above)*; if necessary, chip off stubborn mortar by tapping the chisel lightly with a ball-peen hammer. Clean out loose particles with a stiff fiber brush. If the backing material behind the stone is damaged, consult a professional. Otherwise, buy replacement stone veneer and seal it, if necessary *(step 3)*.

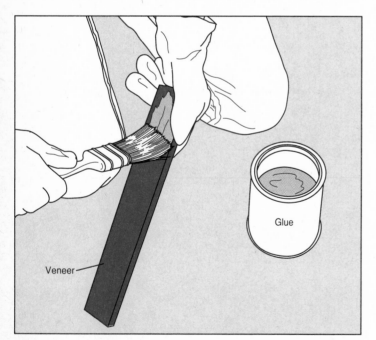

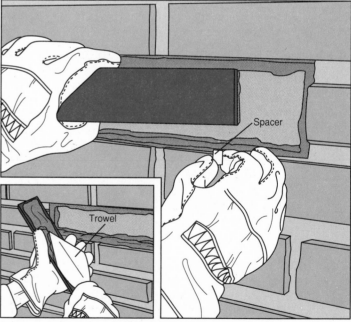

3 **Sealing the replacement stone.** Buy replacement stone veneer *(page 47)*, mason's glue and spacers at a building supply center or a stone dealer. Prepare and mortar the stone following the label instructions; for example, some precast types require sealing with mason's glue to prevent the leaching of moisture from fresh mortar. If the stone requires sealing with glue, wear rubber gloves and use a paintbrush to apply an even coat on the back of the stone *(above)*; allow the glue to set according to the label instructions. If the stone does not require sealing with glue, soak it with clean water.

4 **Mortaring the new stone.** Wearing work gloves, mix a batch of mortar *(page 48)* and add a little mason's glue to it—about 1 tablespoon or according to the label instructions. Wet the cavity with clean water. Use a pointing trowel to spread a 1-inch layer of mortar on the bed joint and sides of the cavity; also, butter the back of the stone *(inset)*. Sit spacers into the bed joint to support the stone as the mortar sets and push the stone straight into the cavity, in position on them *(above)*; align the face of the stone with the face of adjoining stones. Pack mortar into the joints around the stone using the trowel and scrape off excess with the edge of the trowel blade. Wipe mortar off the face of the stones using a damp piece of burlap or rough cloth.

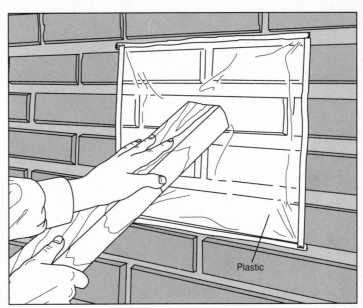

5 **Striking the joints.** Support the stone in place using a 2-by-4 or other brace. Allow the mortar to set for 30 minutes or until it is stiff enough to hold a thumbprint. Wearing work gloves, use a jointer with a shape that matches the original joints *(page 119)* to strike the joints, or press them to form a watertight seal. Wet the jointer with clean water and drag it smoothly along the joints *(above)*; for the neatest appearance, strike the vertical joints first, then the horizontal joints.

6 **Curing the mortar.** Wipe mortar forced out by the jointer off the face of the stones using a damp piece of burlap or rough cloth. Until the mortar cures for 3 days, place plastic over the repaired surface, holding it with duct tape, as shown, or mist periodically with the fine spray of a garden hose. Support the new stone in place by resting a board or other brace against it *(above)*; in most instances, a 2-by-4, as shown, is sufficient.

REPAIRING A MORTARED STEP STONE

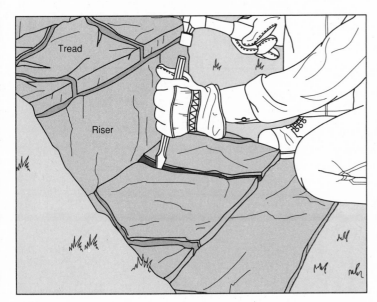

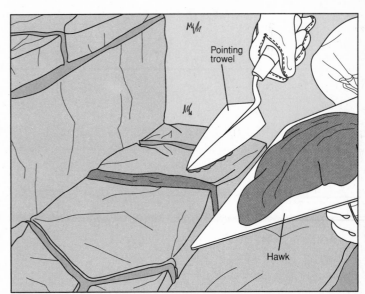

1 **Chiseling out the old mortar.** If a riser stone is damaged, replace it as you would a mortared wall stone *(page 59)*. If a tread stone is damaged, replace it as you would a mortar-bed paving stone *(page 65)*. Wearing work gloves and goggles, use a cold chisel and a ball-peen hammer to chip out damaged mortar around a step stone *(above)*. Drag a mortar hook along the interior of the cut-back joints to scrape off mortar that is hard to reach. Repeat the procedure until you reach solid mortar. Clean out loose particles using a stiff fiber brush. Soak the cut-back joints and adjoining stones with clean water to prevent the leaching of moisture from fresh mortar.

2 **Pointing the joints.** Wearing work gloves, mix a batch of mortar *(page 48)* on a mason's hawk. Use a pointing trowel to tuck-point, or work mortar into the joints. Pack as much mortar as possible into the joints, pressing it in with the trowel *(above)*. Scrape off excess mortar with the edge of the trowel blade. Wipe mortar off the face of the stones with a damp piece of burlap or rough cloth. Strike the joints using a jointer *(page 119)* or the bottom surface of the trowel. Keep the mortar damp until it cures for 3 days by misting periodically with the fine spray of a garden hose.

REPAIRING A DRY-LAID STEP

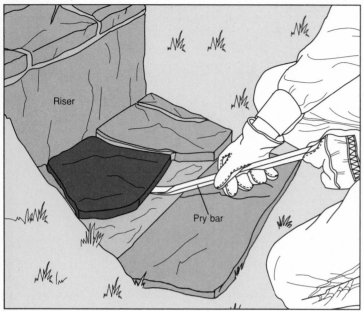

Repositioning a tread stone. Dry-laid stones of country-style steps can be positioned in a number of ways; typically, they are set against undisturbed soil or compacted sand or gravel, each tread butted against or under the riser above it and seated on any riser below it. If a tread stone is sunken or heaved, reposition it; if it is damaged, replace it. To remove the tread stone, wear work gloves and use a pry bar to raise it *(above, left)*; if it is butted under the riser above it, first remove the riser *(step below)*. Set the tread stone aside using the proper lifting procedure *(page 52)*. If necessary, find a replacement stone *(page 47)*; have it prepared for you, or cut or face it yourself *(page 53)*. To build up the base, use a spade to add sand or gravel and tamp using the end of a 4-by-4 *(above, right)*. To place the tread stone, position one edge against the riser above it, slowly lower the opposite edge into position on any riser below it and drop it from a height of 2 to 3 inches; if you removed the riser above the tread, reposition it *(step below)*. Sweep sand into the joints around the tread stone using a stiff broom.

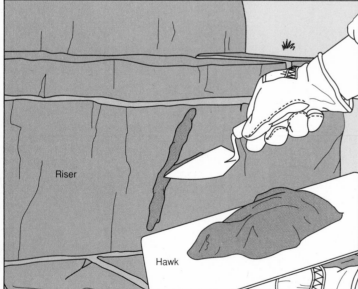

Patching or repositioning a riser stone. A dry-laid riser stone is usually set against undisturbed soil, its bottom edge butted behind or on the tread below it and its top edge butted under the tread above it. A cracked riser stone can be patched if it is still properly positioned. Sweep particles out of the crack using a stiff fiber brush and soak the crack with clean water. Wearing work gloves, mix a batch of mortar *(page 48)* on a mason's hawk. Use a pointing trowel to pack the crack with mortar *(above, left)* and scrape off excess. Wipe mortar off the face of the stone using a damp piece of burlap or rough cloth. Keep the mortar damp until it cures for 3 days by misting periodically with the fine spray of a garden hose. To reposition or replace a riser stone, wear work gloves and use a pry bar to work it out from between the treads above and below it *(above)*; if it is butted behind the tread below it, first remove the tread above it *(step above)*, as shown. Set the riser stone aside using the proper lifting procedure *(page 52)*. If the riser stone is damaged, find a replacement stone *(page 47)*; have it prepared for you, or cut or face it yourself *(page 53)*. To place the riser stone, slowly lower one edge against the tread below it and drop it into position from a height of 2 to 3 inches; angle it slightly toward the soil behind it. Then, reposition the tread above it *(step above)* or work the riser stone into position between the treads above and below it.

RELAYING A SAND-BED PAVING STONE

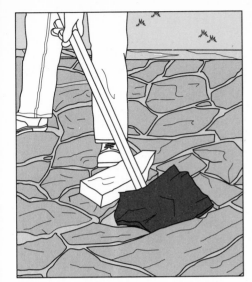

1 **Prying out the stone.** If all or most of the stones are sunken or heaved, remake the sand bed *(page 66)*. To remove a sunken or heaved stone, wear work gloves and use a long pry bar. Using another stone or a concrete block as a fulcrum, fit the end of the pry bar under the stone and raise it *(above)*; set the stone aside using the proper lifting procedure *(page 52)*.

2 **Preparing the sand bed.** Use a tape measure to measure the thickness of the stone you removed; raise or lower the sand bed to a depth equal to the measurement. Add or remove sand using a spade and tamp the bed to compact it with the end of a 4-by-4 *(above)* or your feet. Smooth the sand bed using a gloved hand.

3 **Reseating the stone.** Wearing work gloves, use the proper lifting procedure *(page 52)* to position one edge of the stone. Slowly lower the opposite edge of the stone *(above)* and drop it into place from a height of 2 to 3 inches. Sweep sand into the joints using a stiff broom, dampen them using the fine spray of a garden hose; refill them, if necessary, after the sand dries and settles.

REPLACING A MORTAR-BED PAVING STONE

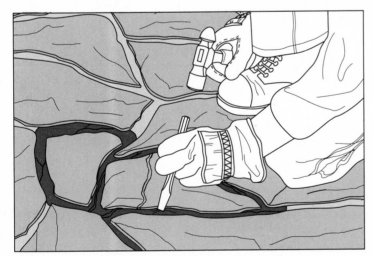

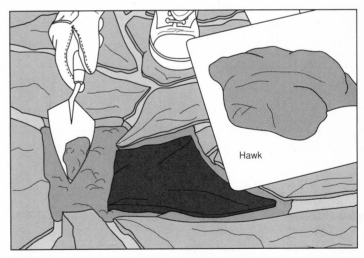

1 **Chiseling out the old mortar.** If the mortar around a stone is damaged, chisel out and point the joints as you would to repair a mortared step stone *(page 63)*. Wearing work gloves and goggles, use a cold chisel and a ball-peen hammer to chip out all the mortar around a damaged stone *(above)*. Drag a mortar hook along the interior of the cut-back joints to scrape off mortar that is hard to reach. Repeat the procedure until the damaged stone can be removed using the proper lifting procedure *(page 52)*; use a pry bar to loosen the stone, if necessary. Chip any remaining mortar off the sides and bottom of the cavity. Clean out loose particles with a stiff fiber brush. Find a replacement stone *(page 47)*; have it prepared for you, or cut or face it yourself *(page 53)*. Soak the cavity with clean water to prevent the leaching of moisture from fresh mortar.

2 **Mortaring the replacement stone.** Wearing work gloves, mix a batch of mortar *(page 48)* on a mason's hawk and use a pointing trowel to spread a 3/4-inch layer on the bottom and sides of the cavity *(above)*. Using the proper lifting procedure *(page 52)*, place the stone; position one edge, slowly lower the opposite edge and drop it into place from a height of 2 to 3 inches. Pack as much mortar as possible into the joints, pressing it in with the trowel, and scrape off excess. Wipe mortar off the face of the stones with a damp piece of burlap or rough cloth. Strike the joints using a jointer *(page 119)* or the bottom surface of the trowel. Keep the mortar damp until it cures for 3 days by misting periodically with the fine spray of a garden hose.

REMAKING A SAND BED

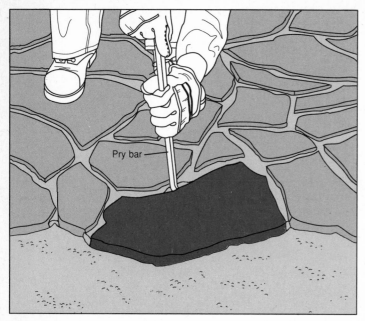

1 Prying out the stones. Starting at one corner of the paving, wear work gloves and use a pry bar to remove each stone. Fit the end of the pry bar under the stone and raise it *(above)*, using another stone or a concrete block as a fulcrum under the pry bar, if necessary. Set the stone aside using the proper lifting procedure *(page 52)*. Repeat the procedure to remove the other stones, one course at a time, numbering the bottom of them with chalk for later reference.

2 Preparing the sand bed. For proper drainage, stone paving should be set on a well-compacted bed of 3 to 4 inches of gravel covered with at least 1 inch of sand. To build up the bed, if necessary, buy fine sand at a building supply center. Use a spade to add the sand to the bed *(above)*, spreading it evenly.

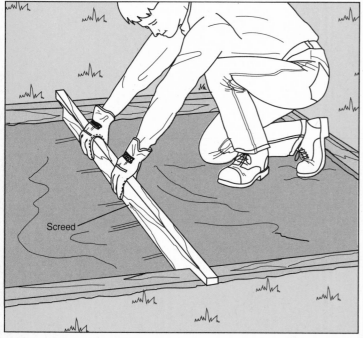

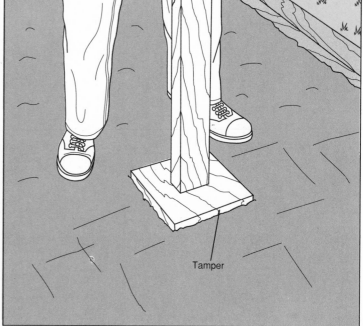

3 Striking off and tamping the sand bed. Use a straight 2-by-4 to make a leveling tool or screed about 6 inches longer than the width of the sand bed; if there is edging, as shown, cut a notch *(page 121)* at each end of the screed 3 inches long and equal in width to the thickness of the stones to fit on the edging. Starting at one end of the bed, drag the screed across the sand to level the bed *(above, left)*, filling in your footprints as you go. To compact the bed, use a tamper *(page 121)*, alternately lifting it and pounding it against the base *(above, right)*. Strike off again using the screed, adding more sand *(step 2)*, if necessary, and tamp again.

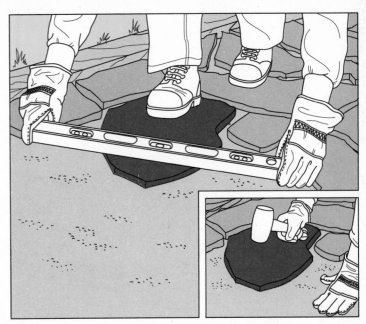

4 **Relaying the stones.** Starting at one corner of the paving, wear work gloves to relay each stone, one course at a time. Use the proper lifting procedure *(page 52)* to position one edge of the stone. Supporting the stone with one hand, use the other hand to gently work the sand *(above)*, matching it as much as possible to the bottom contour of the stone. Slowly lower the raised edge of the stone and drop it into place from a height of 2 to 3 inches. Seat the stone *(step 5)* and relay the other stones the same way, using the numbers chalked onto them for reference. Repeat the procedure until all the stones are relaid.

5 **Seating the stones.** After relaying each stone, wear work gloves and wiggle it to embed it in the sand, seating it securely. If the stone can be rocked, raise one edge of it back up and relay it again *(step 4)*. When the stone is seated securely, check its position with a carpenter's level *(above)*; rest the level across the stone, as shown, in two directions at a 90-degree angle to each other. If necessary, tap the stone using a rubber mallet *(inset)* to seat it even with adjoining stones. Relay the other stones and repeat the procedure to seat them. Continue until all the stones are relaid and seated.

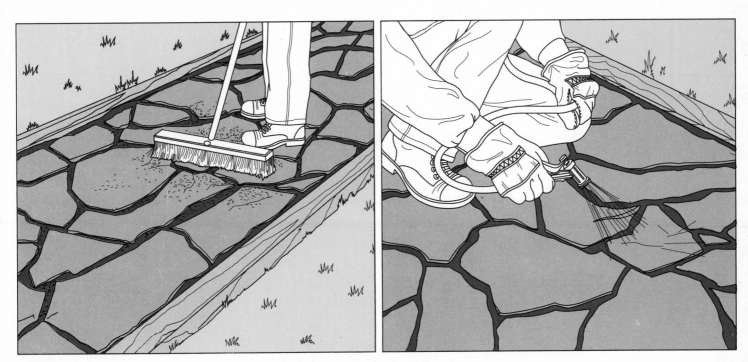

6 **Filling the joints.** Wearing work gloves, use a spade to spread a fine layer of sand on the stones. Work the sand into the joints around the stones using a stiff broom *(above, left)* and sweep off excess. Water the surface using the fine spray of a garden hose to settle the sand in the joints *(above, right)*. After the sand has dried, check that the joints are level with the stones. If necessary, add more sand and water the surface again.

POINTING CHIMNEY JOINTS

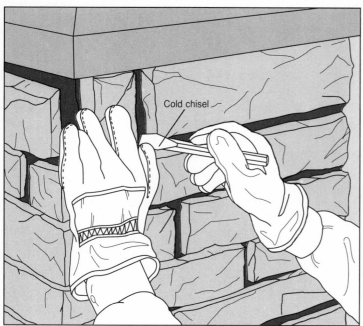

Cold chisel

1 **Inspecting chimney joints and locating leaks. Caution:** Prepare to work safely on the roof *(page 114)*. Wearing work gloves, check the condition of the chimney mortar joints by running the blade of a cold chisel along them *(above, left)*; the mortar should remain intact. If the mortar crumbles easily, chisel out the damaged joints *(step 2)*. Next, alert your neighbors that you are checking your chimney. In the room with the fireplace, open the windows and close the doors or seal off the doorways with plastic and masking tape. Have a helper build a small,

smokey fire in the fireplace when you are on the roof. Block off the top of the chimney using a section of plywood weighted down with a brick. Check for signs of leaking smoke and mark the spots with chalk *(above, right)*; have your helper do the same indoors. Remove the brick and the plywood, leaving the chimney blocked for no more than 2 to 3 minutes at one time. Leaking smoke is a sign of a possible problem with the flue liner; have it inspected and repaired by a professional.

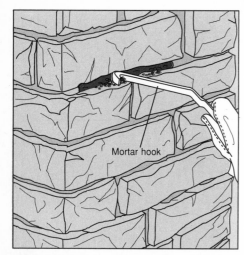

Mortar hook

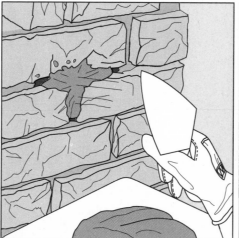

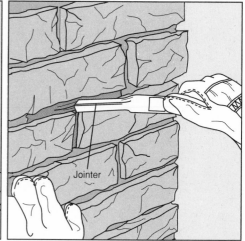

Jointer

2 **Cutting back damaged mortar joints.** Wearing work gloves and goggles, use a cold chisel and a ball-peen hammer to cut back the damaged joints at least 2 inches or until solid mortar is reached; work carefully to avoid damaging any stones. Drag a mortar hook along the cut-back joints *(above)* to scrape off mortar that is hard to reach. Clean out loose particles using a stiff fiber brush. Soak the cut-back joints and adjoining stones with water to prevent the leaching of moisture from fresh mortar.

3 **Tuck-pointing and striking the joints.** Wearing work gloves, mix a batch of mortar *(page 48)* on a mason's hawk. Hold the hawk just below the damaged area to catch any mortar that is accidentally dropped. Use a pointing trowel to tuck-point, or work mortar into the joints. Or, to force mortar into a vertical joint, flick it off the trowel with a sharp snap of your wrist *(above, left)*. Pack as much mortar as possible into the joints with the trowel and scrape off excess with the edge of the blade. Wipe mortar off the face of the stones with a damp piece of burlap or rough cloth. Allow the mortar to set for 30 minutes or until it is stiff enough to hold a thumbprint. Using a jointer with a shape that matches the original joints *(page 119)*, strike the joints, or press them to form a watertight seal. Wet the jointer with clean water and drag it smoothly along the joints *(above, right)*; for the neatest appearance, strike the vertical joints first, then the horizontal joints. Keep the mortar damp until it cures for 3 days by taping plastic over the surface of the repair using duct tape.

REPLACING A CHIMNEY CAP

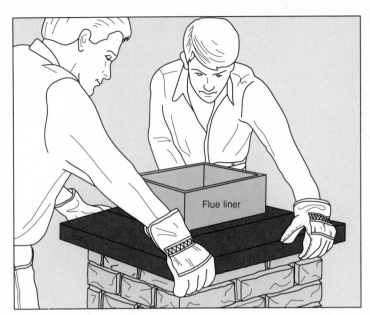

1 **Chiseling off the old cap. Caution:** Prepare to work safely on the roof *(page 114)*. Replace the chimney cap if it is badly damaged or a repaired crack recurs; take the cap measurements before removing it. To remove the old cap, break it into pieces small enough to take off by hand using a cold chisel and a small sledge-hammer *(above)* or a ball-peen hammer; wear work gloves and goggles. Buy a precast cap at a building supply center or have a cap custom made and install it *(step 2)*; or, make a concrete cap yourself *(steps below)*. Make sure the chimney cap overhangs the chimney top by at least 3 inches.

2 **Installing a chimney cap.** Wearing work gloves, mix a batch of mortar *(page 48)*; use a stiff mix to prevent the mortar from oozing out when the cap is positioned. Using a mason's trowel, spread a 1-inch layer of mortar on the top course of chimney bricks and furrow the bed *(page 118)*. Working with a helper, carefully lower the cap over the flue liner and into position on the chimney top *(above)*. Fill the joint between the cap and the flue liner with mortar, sloping it slightly away from the liner. Use the edge of the trowel blade to scrape off any excess mortar, then strike the joints using a jointer *(page 119)* or a moistened gloved finger. Tape plastic over the cap using duct tape and leave it until the mortar cures for 3 days; do not use the fireplace until the plastic is removed.

MAKING A CHIMNEY CAP

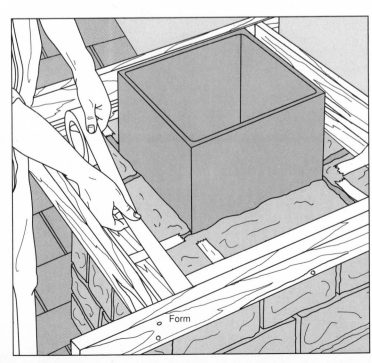

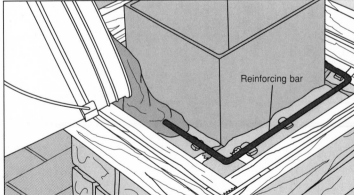

1 **Preparing the form and placing concrete.** Build a chimney cap form *(page 121)*. With one or more helpers, hoist the form onto the roof and carefully position it on the chimney top; check its position using a carpenter's level and adjust it, if necessary. Use masking tape to cover the bolts for the metal straps *(left)*, preventing concrete from adhering to them, and position the reinforcing bars. Wearing work gloves, mix a batch of concrete *(page 86)* and pass it up to the roof one bucketful at a time. Place concrete into the form and against the flue liner *(above)*, distributing it evenly until the form is filled up to within 1 inch of the top.

MAKING A CHIMNEY CAP (continued)

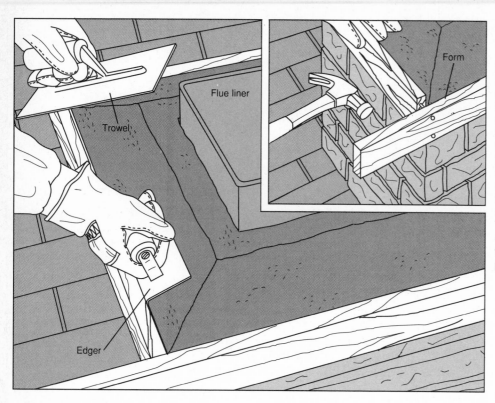

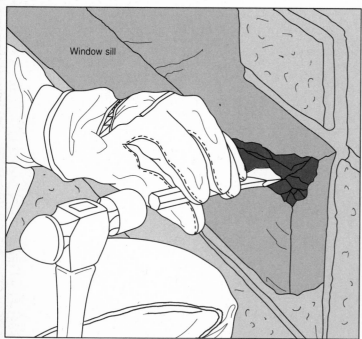

2 **Finishing the cap.** Add concrete to fill the form and use a wooden float to shape the cap for drainage, sloping it away from the flue liner; the cap should be 1/2 inch higher at its inside edge against the flue liner than at its outside edge. Avoid using metal tools for shaping; they draw moisture to the top of the concrete, weakening it. After the cap is shaped, smooth the surface using a rectangular trowel and curve the outside edge with an edger *(left)*; work with two hands, as shown. Cover the cap with plastic and tape the edges with duct tape. Allow the concrete to cure for 3 days before removing the plastic and the form. **Caution:** Keep people away from the house when removing the form. To take apart the form, hammer on the inside edge of the extended sides *(inset)*. Remove the bolts from the bottom of the form and use pliers to pry the metal straps out of the cap.

REBUILDING A DECORATIVE STONE EDGE

1 **Preparing the surface.** A decorative stone edge broken 1 to 3 inches from the surface can be rebuilt for aesthetic reasons. The repair, however, does not provide structural support and is appropriate only on a stone that is not load-bearing—such as a window sill or an ornamental corner. Position a pan or have a helper hold it below the damaged edge to catch stone dust for later use. Wearing work gloves and goggles, use a cold chisel and a ball-peen hammer to chip off the edge until solid stone is reached *(above, left)*. To help the bonding of a mortar patch, chisel a 1/4-inch groove every 1 to 2 inches into the edge. Or, use a power drill fitted with a masonry bit to drill 1/4-inch holes 1/2 inch deep as keys every 2 to 3 inches into the edge *(above, right)*; wrap masking tape around the bit, as shown, to know when to stop drilling.

REBUILDING A DECORATIVE STONE EDGE (continued)

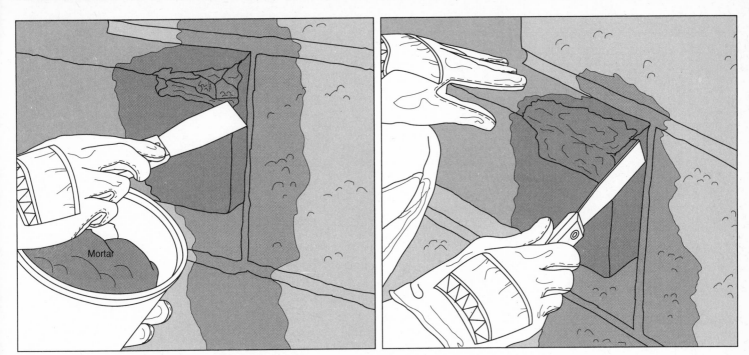

2 **Patching with mortar.** Clean off loose particles using a stiff fiber brush. Dampen the edge with clean water to prevent the leaching of moisture from fresh mortar. Wearing work gloves, mix a batch of mortar *(page 48)* in a small plastic container; color the mortar to match the undamaged stone, if necessary *(page 119)*. Use a putty knife to apply a thin, even layer of mortar on the edge *(above, left)* and allow the mortar to set for 5 to 10 minutes. Scratch grooves in the mortar with the blade of the putty knife and apply more mortar, building up and forming the edge *(above, right)*.

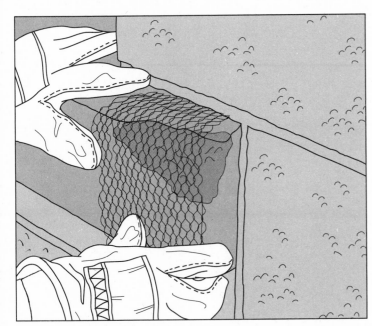

3 **Shaping the patch.** To match the original shape of the edge, wear work gloves and use tin snips to cut a piece of stiff wire mesh to apply as a mold. Press the wire mesh against an undamaged edge of the stone, forming it into a mold of the same shape as the stone. Position the molded wire mesh on the mortar *(above)*, pressing lightly into it to shape it. Remove the wire mesh and smooth the mortar by making light passes with a putty knife.

4 **Smoothing and coating the patch.** Wet the putty knife with clean water and smooth the mortar again, if necessary, to match the undamaged stone. Gather the stone dust you collected in step 1; wearing goggles, use a ball-peen hammer to crush any small chunks into fine powder. Before the mortar stiffens, sprinkle the stone dust onto it *(above)*. Keep the mortar damp until it cures for 3 days by taping plastic over the surface of the repair using duct tape.

CONCRETE

Concrete is a mixture of portland cement (named after a popular building stone of the nineteenth century), gravel, sand and water; it can be formed into practically any shape, resists decay and is economical. Around the home, concrete is a common feature, used for walkways, driveways, patios, post footings and foundation walls. Typical locations of concrete are shown at right. Stucco, a covering for exterior walls, also has a base of portland cement; mixed with sand, hydrated lime and water, it is applied on a wire mesh material called lath, or over bricks, stones or concrete. Concrete that is properly mixed, placed (the correct term for poured), finished and cured is durable and almost maintenance-free; stucco, likewise, enjoys the same characteristics. Consult the Troubleshooting Guide on page 74 for guidance in diagnosing problems. For specific information on cleaning and removing stains, refer to the chart on page 75; in addition to the cleaning agents listed there, many special products are now available on the market. Clean stucco surfaces as shown on page 102. Many small concrete repairs can be performed quickly and easily using concrete patching compound *(page 79)*. The biggest challenge in repairing stucco is usually matching the surrounding texture *(page 105)*.

Although rigorous work, replacing a concrete walkway, driveway, patio or post footing can be done by the homeowner; consult a professional about a major repair to a foundation wall, or a basement or garage floor. Break up damaged concrete paving as shown on page 81. Although you may encounter wire mesh or other reinforcing material, its use for residential purposes today is controversial; adding an inch to the thickness of the new concrete is as effective and more economical. Refer to pages 82 to 84 for information on installing a form and consult page 85 for guidance in determining the volume of concrete you require. If you live in a climate of freeze and thaw conditions, use concrete that is air-entrained—an air-entraining agent added to portland cement to cushion the effects of water expansion and contraction. Place concrete as shown on page 88 and finish it using the techniques on pages 88 to 90; keep in mind that too much finishing, or overworking, of the concrete weakens it. Concrete requires about 5 days at a temperature above 50 degrees fahrenheit to fully cure—a hardening process resulting from a chemical reaction between the portland cement and water. Cure concrete using one of the methods on page 90.

Once a year, inspect all concrete structures and stucco surfaces around your home. Undertake repairs as soon as problems are detected to prevent further damage. Most of the tools, materials and supplies required for repairs are readily available at a building supply center. Refer to the Tools & Techniques chapter *(page 106)* for the proper use and cleaning of tools; be sure to clean tools before concrete hardens on them. Work carefully with portland cement; it is caustic when wet. Concrete weighs about 135 to 145 pounds per cubic foot; use proper lifting techniques *(page 111)* when handling it.

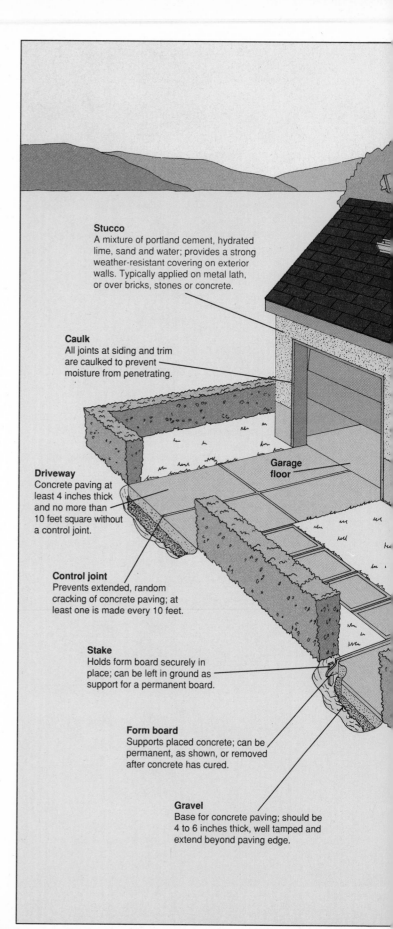

Stucco
A mixture of portland cement, hydrated lime, sand and water; provides a strong weather-resistant covering on exterior walls. Typically applied on metal lath, or over bricks, stones or concrete.

Caulk
All joints at siding and trim are caulked to prevent moisture from penetrating.

Driveway
Concrete paving at least 4 inches thick and no more than 10 feet square without a control joint.

Garage floor

Control joint
Prevents extended, random cracking of concrete paving; at least one is made every 10 feet.

Stake
Holds form board securely in place; can be left in ground as support for a permanent board.

Form board
Supports placed concrete; can be permanent, as shown, or removed after concrete has cured.

Gravel
Base for concrete paving; should be 4 to 6 inches thick, well tamped and extend beyond paving edge.

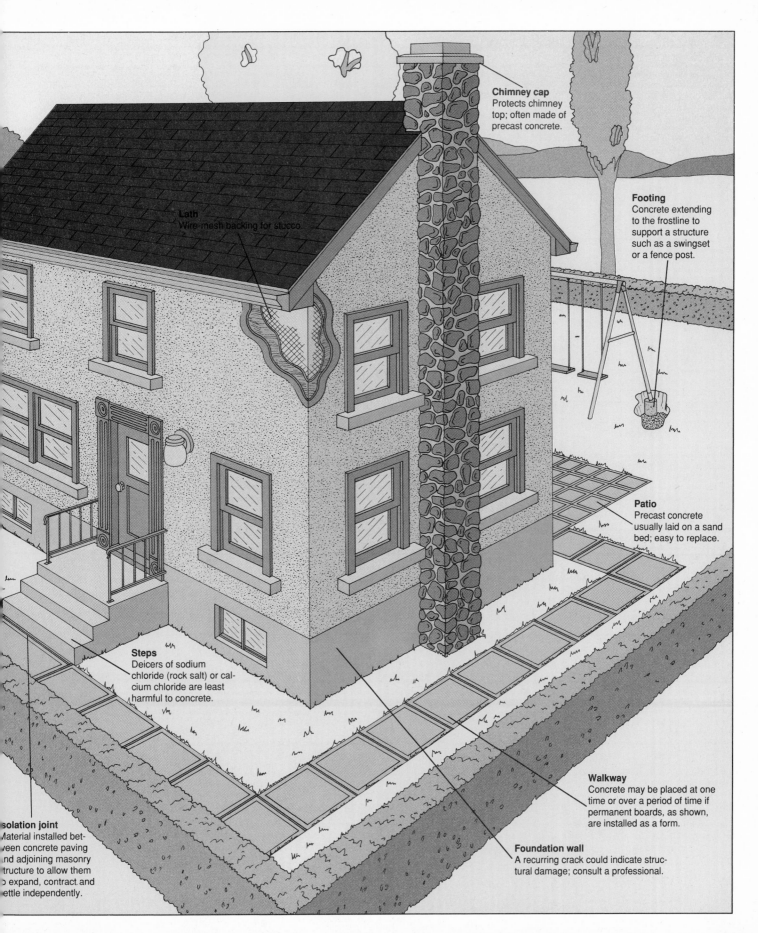

Chimney cap
Protects chimney top; often made of precast concrete.

Lath
Wire-mesh backing for stucco.

Footing
Concrete extending to the frostline to support a structure such as a swingset or a fence post.

Patio
Precast concrete usually laid on a sand bed; easy to replace.

Steps
Deicers of sodium chloride (rock salt) or calcium chloride are least harmful to concrete.

Walkway
Concrete may be placed at one time or over a period of time if permanent boards, as shown, are installed as a form.

Isolation joint
Material installed between concrete paving and adjoining masonry structure to allow them to expand, contract and settle independently.

Foundation wall
A recurring crack could indicate structural damage; consult a professional.

TROUBLESHOOTING GUIDE

SYMPTOM	POSSIBLE CAUSE	PROCEDURE
CONCRETE		
Surface dirty or stained	Weather, wear and pollution	Clean surfaces *(p. 75)* □●
Surface efflorescence (white, powdery deposits of dissolved salts)	High humidity or poor air circulation	Clean surfaces *(p. 75)* □●; indoors, seal or paint concrete *(p. 77)* □●, install dehumidifier or increase ventilation
Wall or floor damp	High humidity or poor air circulation	Seal or paint concrete *(p. 77)* □◗, install dehumidifier or increase ventilation
	Moisture penetrating door or window trim	Recaulk exterior trim *(p. 78)* ◗◗
	Moisture penetrating wall or floor crack	Fill wall crack *(p. 80)* ◗◗ or repair floor crack with concrete patching compound *(p. 79)* ◗◗; if crack recurs, consult a professional
	Insufficient drainage or leak in roof or plumbing	Inspect gutters, downspouts and soil grading *(p. 110)* □○; if necessary, consult a professional
Water damage around door or window	Caulk at joint between concrete and trim loose or damaged	Recaulk exterior trim *(p. 78)* ◗◗
Wall or floor cracked	Structure settlement	Fill wall crack *(p. 80)* ◗◗ or repair floor crack with concrete patching compound *(p. 79)* ◗◗; if crack recurs, consult a professional
Wall leaning or buckling	Structure settlement or damaged foundation	Consult a professional
Paving or step icy	Precipitation and freezing temperatures	Deice paving or step *(p. 76)* □○
Weeds between paving	Windblown seeds and pods rooting in dirt accumulated in control joints	Pull out weeds and cut back roots *(p. 77)* □○
Paving or step dusting (surface powder)	Weather and traffic	Seal or paint concrete *(p. 77)* □●; resurface paving *(p. 81)* ◗◗ or repair paving surface *(p. 94)* ◗●; repair step surface *(p. 93)* ◗●
Paving or step rough, crazing (minor surface cracks) or scaling (minor surface peeling)	Weather and traffic; deicing salts	Resurface paving *(p. 81)* ◗◗ or repair paving surface *(p. 94)* ◗●; repair step surface *(p. 93)* ◗●; limit use of deicing salts *(p. 76)* □○
Paving or step popouts (shallow surface holes)	Expansion of gravel near concrete surface due to freezing	Repair popouts with concrete patching compound *(p. 79)* ◗◗; repair paving surface *(p. 94)* ◗● or, if damage extensive, replace paving *(page 95)* ■●; repair step surface *(p. 93)* ◗●
Paving or step surface chipped or cracked	Weather and traffic; deicing salts	Repair paving surface *(p. 94)* ◗● or repair step surface *(p. 93)* ◗●; limit use of deicing salts *(p. 76)* □○
Step corner broken off	Blow by heavy object	Repair step corner with concrete glue *(p. 80)* □○
Step edge chipped, cracked or broken	Weather and traffic	Repair step edge *(p. 80)* ◗●
Paving corner or edge chipped, cracked or broken	Weather and traffic; blow by heavy object; spreading root networks	Cut back roots *(p. 77)* □○; repair paving edge *(p. 92)* ◗●
Paving cracked, sunken or heaved	Weather and traffic; erosion	Replace paving *(page 95)* ■●
Post footing cracked, sunken or heaved	Weather; erosion	Repair *(p. 100)* □◗ or replace *(p. 100)* ◗● post footing
STUCCO		
Surface dirty or stained	Weather, wear and pollution	Clean or repaint stucco *(p. 102)* □●
Water damage around door or window	Caulk at joint between stucco and trim loose or damaged	Recaulk exterior trim *(p. 78)* ◗◗
Surface cracked	Structure settlement	Repair stucco crack *(p. 102)* □◗; if crack recurs, consult a professional
Surface hole	Blow by heavy object	Repair stucco hole *(p. 103)* □●; if hole larger than 2 feet square, consult a professional
Wall leaning or buckling	Structure settlement or damaged foundation	Consult a professional

DEGREE OF DIFFICULTY: □ Easy ◗ Moderate ■ Complex
ESTIMATED TIME: ○ Less than 1 hour ◗ 1 to 3 hours ● Over 3 hours

MAINTAINING CONCRETE

Stains on concrete surfaces, especially if they are outdoors, are virtually unavoidable. Weather, wear and pollution eventually result in the discoloring of most walls, patios, walkways and driveways. Garage and basement floors, as well as driveways, are vulnerable to oil, grease and paint stains. And any concrete surface subjected to moisture can be prey to unsightly efflorescence—white, powdery deposits of dissolved salts. For guidance in removing stains, refer to the chart below; in addition to the common cleaning agents listed, many special products are now available on the market.

Always begin by trying out the mildest cleaning agent possible; do not underestimate the effectiveness of household detergent and water (step below). If you must resort to more powerful acids, solvents and cleaners, be sure to read the label instructions carefully and follow all safety precautions. **Caution:** When mixing acid solutions, add the acid to the water; never add the water to the acid. Before applying a cleaning agent on a stain, test it on a small, inconspicuous surface to determine if it has any damaging side-effects. When you have finished cleaning, safely dispose of all leftover products (page 116).

PROBLEM	CLEANING AGENT	PROCEDURE (Test first on inconspicuous surface)
Efflorescence (white, powdery deposits)	Water	Scrub with stiff fiber brush and rinse
	Trisodium phosphate (TSP)***, household detergent and water	Wearing rubber gloves and goggles, add 1 cup of TSP and 1 cup of detergent to 1 gallon of water; apply solution (page 76)
Paint	Commercial paint remover*	Wearing rubber gloves and goggles, apply paint remover according to label instructions; use putty knife, scraper or wire brush to remove it
Rust	Oxalic acid crystals*	Wearing rubber gloves and goggles, mix 1 pound of oxalic acid to 1 gallon of water in a plastic or glass container. **Caution:** Add acid to water. Presoak surface with water, use stiff fiber brush to scrub surface with acid solution and rinse surface
Oil	Trisodium phosphate (TSP)*, thickener (talcum powder*** or fuller's earth***) and water	Wearing rubber gloves and goggles, add 1 pound of TSP to 1 gallon of water and mix in thickener until pasty; apply poultice (page 20)
Grease	Oil-dissolving solvent* and thickener (talcum powder*** or fuller's earth***)	Scrape off excess grease with putty knife. Wearing rubber gloves and goggles, mix solvent and thickener until pasty; apply poultice (page 20)
Tar	Kerosene and thickener (talcum powder*** or fuller's earth***)	Scrape off excess tar with putty knife; wearing work gloves, apply dry ice to make globs brittle. Wearing rubber gloves and goggles, mix kerosene and thickener until pasty; apply poultice (page 20)
Dirt, grime, smoke or general discoloration	Household scouring powder	Wearing rubber gloves and goggles, apply powder (page 76)
	Trisodium phosphate (TSP)***, household detergent and water	Wearing rubber gloves and goggles, add 1/2 cup of TSP and 1/2 cup of detergent to 1 gallon of water; apply solution (page 76)

*Available at a building supply center   *** Available at a drug store

Scrubbing with detergent and water. Sweep off the surface using a stiff broom and presoak the concrete using clean water from a garden hose. Mix a solution of household detergent and water in a bucket; use 1/2 to 1 cup of detergent per gallon of water. Apply the solution on the surface, scrubbing with a stiff fiber brush; or, on a large paving surface, use a push-broom to avoid bending (left). Rinse off the surface thoroughly and allow it to dry. If the surface is still dirty or it is stained, try cleaning with household scouring powder or trisodium phosphate (TSP) solution (page 76), or refer to the chart above for guidance in choosing an alternative cleaning agent.

MAINTAINING CONCRETE (continued)

Cleaning with scouring powder or trisodium phosphate (TSP) solution. For stubborn dirt and grime, and for common stains, use scouring powder or a mixture of 1/2 cup of TSP and 1/2 cup of household detergent in one gallon of clean water *(chart, page 75)*; wear rubber gloves and goggles. Wet the surface thoroughly and apply the powder or solution, scrubbing vigorously with a stiff fiber brush *(above, left)*. Rinse off the surface thoroughly using a garden hose *(above, right)* or several bucketfuls of clean water. Repeat the procedure, if necessary.

PREVENTING CONCRETE DAMAGE

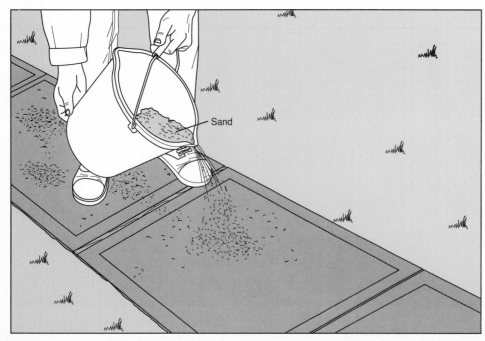

Sand

Deicing concrete. In cold, wet weather, concrete paving is vulnerable to icing, potentially making walkways, steps and driveways dangerously slippery. In these conditions, sand or fine gravel is the best abrasive for the concrete; neither is likely to damage the surface. Spread a fine layer of the sand *(left)* or gravel using a bucket, sprinkling it ahead of you, as shown, while you stand on a surface you have already covered. For safety reasons, however, a commercial deicer is sometimes required to melt ice and prevent it from building up on the surface. Under these circumstances, choose a deicer carefully. A deicer of sodium chloride (rock salt), calcium chloride or urea is less harmful to a concrete surface than a deicer of ammonium nitrate or ammonium sulphate; these latter deicers are caustic and can be more damaging—and are best avoided. Keep in mind that concrete is most susceptible to damage in the first 3 months after it is placed; during this time, the use of a commercial deicer is likely to be especially harmful to the surface.

PREVENTING CONCRETE DAMAGE (continued)

Pulling out weeds. Prevent damage to concrete paving by keeping the edges and the control joints between sections clean and free of seedlings. Wearing work gloves, pull up any seedlings by hand *(above)*, taking out as much of their roots as possible. To prevent seedlings from growing back, buy a herbicide such as glyphosate at a garden center and apply it according to label instructions. **Caution:** Spray herbicide only on a calm day, never when it is windy. Scrape dirt out of control joints using the edge of a putty knife and use a stiff broom to sweep away loosened particles.

Cutting back roots. Large, spreading root systems of trees, shrubs and plants can seriously damage concrete, causing it to buckle and crack. At least once each growing season, cut back the root systems along the edges of concrete paving. Wearing work gloves, use a spade to slice straight into the soil at the edge of the concrete *(above)*; use your full weight to push down on the blade of the spade, as shown, in order to reach a depth of at least 6 to 8 inches. Pull out the spade and repeat the procedure along the edges of the concrete, overlapping each slice of the blade slightly.

SEALING AND PAINTING CONCRETE

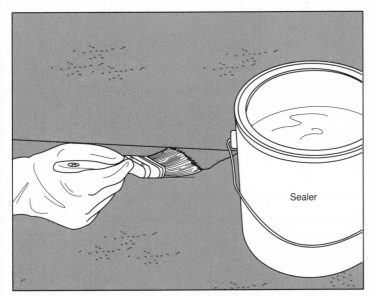

Applying a sealer. Apply a sealer only on concrete that is unpainted; if the concrete is painted, repaint it *(step right)*. For many surfaces, an acrylic or silicone sealer is recommended; consult your local building supply center, however, since applying a sealer can be controversial. Remove any dirt and stains from the concrete *(page 75)*, rinsing it thoroughly, and allow it to dry. Wearing rubber gloves, use a paintbrush to test the sealer for discoloration on a small, inconspicuous surface *(above)* and allow it to dry for at least 48 hours; or, plan to paint over the sealer. Apply the sealer following the label instructions, using a paintbrush and a roller as you would to paint.

Applying paint. Buy cementitious paint at a building supply center. Remove any dirt and stains from the concrete *(page 75)*, rinsing it thoroughly; while the surface is still damp, wear rubber gloves and apply the paint following the label instructions. On a large surface, use a medium- or long-nap roller fitted with an extension *(above)*, working the paint into the surface. Apply at least one thick coat; on new concrete, two coats may be required. Keep the finish coat damp for at least 48 hours by misting it periodically with the fine spray of a garden hose.

RECAULKING EXTERIOR TRIM

1 **Removing old caulk.** Over time, the caulk around exterior door and window trim dries out, letting in moisture. To remove damaged caulk, run the blade of a utility knife under it *(above)* along both sides of the joint and pry it out with the corner of a paint scraper or a putty knife. Using a stiff fiber brush, scrub the joint and clean the outer edge of the trim with a solution of mild detergent and water. Rinse the joint and dry it thoroughly with a clean cloth; if the finish of wood trim is damaged, touch it up with finish or preservative.

2 **Applying new caulk.** Buy a tube of exterior silicone or acrylic caulk at a building supply center. Load the tube into a caulking gun. Following the label instructions, use a utility knife to cut the tip of the tube at a 45-degree angle, providing an opening for a 1/4-inch bead. Use a long nail or an awl to break the tube seal. Holding the gun at a 45-degree angle, squeeze the gun trigger to lay a continuous bead of caulk along the joint *(above)*. Wearing a rubber glove, run a wet finger along the caulk to press it into the joint, smoothing and shaping it.

CHIPPING OFF DAMAGED CONCRETE

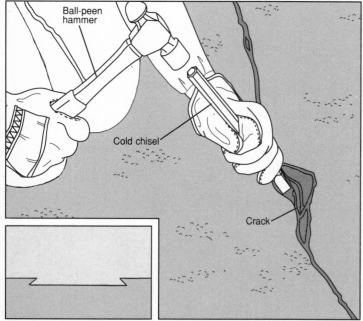

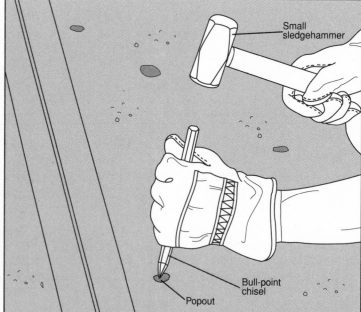

Using chisels and hammers. To break up a large area of concrete, use a large sledgehammer or a demolition hammer *(page 81)*. To remove a small area of concrete, use a cold chisel or a bull-point chisel and a ball-peen hammer or a small sledgehammer. If repairing a crack, for example, the cutting action of a cold chisel and a ball-peen hammer is easiest to control. Wearing work gloves and goggles, fit the blade of the cold chisel into the crack and strike the top of it with the ball-peen hammer *(above, left)*; work along the crack, widening and deepening it slightly, and undercut the edges *(inset)*. If repairing a popout, for example, the cutting action of a bull-point chisel and a sledgehammer is most forceful. Wearing work gloves and goggles, fit the blade of the bull-point chisel into the popout and strike the top of it with the sledgehammer *(above, right)*, enlarging and deepening the hole about 1/4 inch; break up any gravel visible at the bottom of the hole.

REPAIRING WITH CONCRETE PATCHING COMPOUND

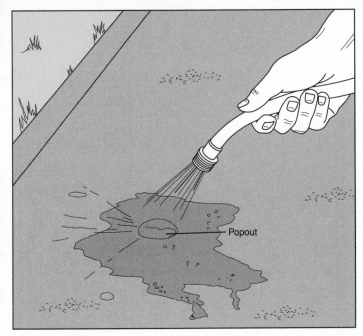

1 **Preparing the surface.** Buy concrete patching compound at a building supply center; a type with a base of latex, vinyl or epoxy will bond to old concrete. Also buy a bonding agent if the patching compound does not contain one. Chip off the damaged concrete *(page 78)* and use a stiff fiber brush to clean off loose particles. Wet the damaged area with clean water using a garden hose *(above)*; allow any puddles formed to dry. If the patching compound contains a bonding agent, apply it *(step 3)*.

2 **Applying a bonding agent.** Wearing rubber gloves, pour a small amount of the bonding agent into a plastic or glass container. Following the label instructions, apply an even coat of the bonding agent on the damaged concrete using a paintbrush *(above)*. Wait for the concrete surface to become tacky—usually about 15 minutes; then, apply patching compound *(step 3)*.

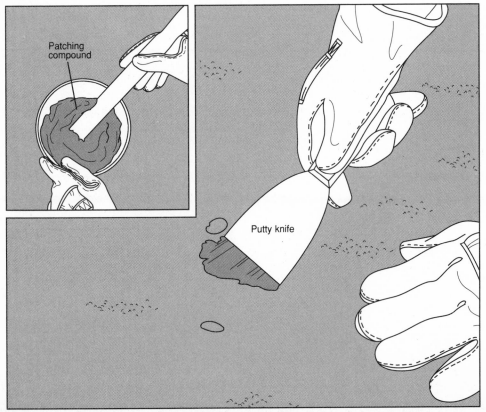

3 **Applying patching compound.** Wearing work gloves, prepare the patching compound following the label instructions, mixing a small amount in a plastic or glass container with a clean stick *(inset)*. For a small repair, use a putty knife to apply the patching compound; pack the damaged area as tightly as possible, scrape off excess and smooth the surface *(left)*. For a large repair, use a pointing trowel or a mason's trowel to apply the patching compound; if necessary, smooth the surface with a wooden float or a metal rectangular trowel. Allow the patching compound to cure according to the label instructions; until it cures, use a plant sprayer to mist it with water whenever it begins to lighten around the patch edges.

FILLING A CRACK IN A CONCRETE WALL

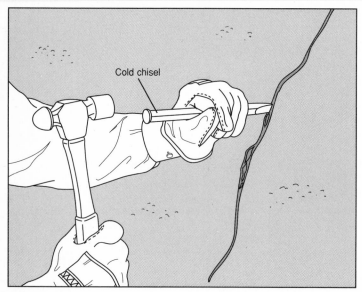

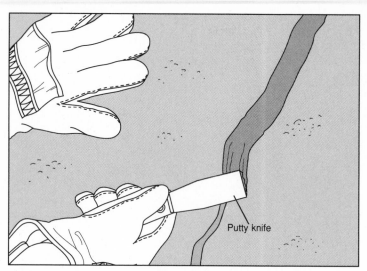

1 **Preparing the crack.** Wearing work gloves and goggles, use a cold chisel and a ball-peen hammer to enlarge the crack slightly and undercut the edges *(above)*. Clean out loose particles using a stiff fiber brush and flush the crack with clean water. To repair a dry crack, use concrete patching compound; to repair a leaking crack, use quick-set hydraulic cement. Buy patching compound or hydraulic cement at a building supply center and prepare it following the label instructions.

2 **Patching the crack.** For a dry crack, wear work gloves and use a putty knife or a pointing trowel to pack it with patching compound *(above)*, scrape off excess and smooth the surface. For a leaking crack, wear rubber gloves and use your hands to work the hydraulic cement into a plug with the consistency of putty. Starting at the top of the crack and working downward, press the plug into the crack with your fingers and hold it until it sets—about 3 minutes. Scrape off excess and smooth the surface with a pointing trowel. Allow the patch to cure according to the label instructions.

REPAIRING A CONCRETE STEP

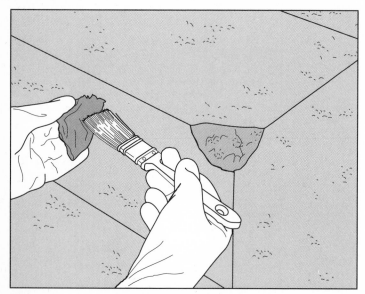

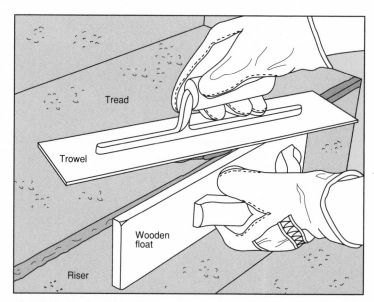

Repairing a step corner. If the step corner has broken off in pieces, repair the step edges *(step right)*. If the step corner has broken off in one piece, brush off any loose particles with a stiff fiber brush. Buy concrete glue at a building supply center and prepare it following the label instructions. Wearing rubber gloves, use a paintbrush to apply an even coat of the glue on the bottom surface of the piece *(above)* and the top surface of the step corner. Press the piece into position on the step corner; hold it or prop it in place until the glue sets. Allow the glue to cure for 24 hours before walking on the step corner.

Repairing a step edge. Prepare the surface of the step tread and riser *(page 79)*. Wearing work gloves, use a putty knife to apply patching compound on the damaged surfaces, working it into the undercut edges. To square the step edge, use the bottom of a wooden float as a form against the riser and use a metal rectangular trowel to smooth the tread *(above)*. Allow the patching compound to set for at least 48 hours before walking on the step edge. Until the patching compound cures, use a plant sprayer to mist it with water whenever it begins to lighten around the patch edges.

RESURFACING CONCRETE PAVING

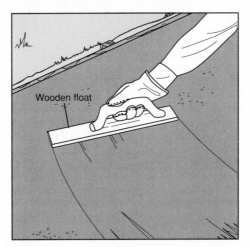

1 **Cleaning off the surface.** To repair minor crazing or scaling of concrete, sweep off loose particles with a stiff broom *(above)* and clean the surface *(page 75)*. Buy concrete patching compound at a building supply center and prepare it following the label instructions; to help it bond with the undamaged concrete, apply it while the surface is still damp.

2 **Applying patching compound.** Wearing work gloves, use a wooden float to apply a thin coat of patching compound. Smooth the surface using a broad arcing motion *(above)*, overlapping passes; keep the leading edge of the float lifted slightly. For a smooth final-finish, repeat with a metal rectangular trowel; or, final-finish using a broom *(step 3)*. Otherwise, allow the compound to cure according to the label instructions.

3 **Final-finishing the surface.** For a rough final-finish with good skid resistance, use a stiff broom; for a coarser final-finish, first dampen the broom bristles with clean water. Applying even pressure, pull the broom gently across the surface in one direction without overlapping passes *(above)*. Allow the compound to cure according to the label instructions.

BREAKING UP DAMAGED CONCRETE

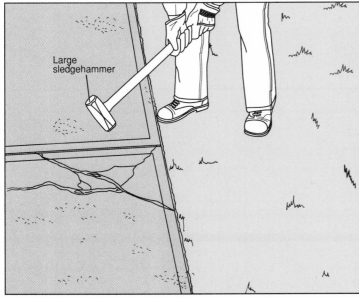

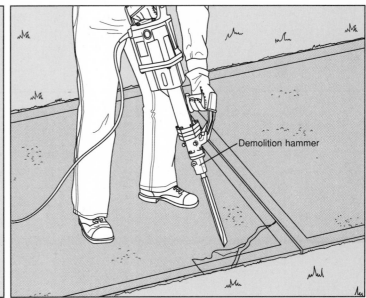

Using a sledgehammer or a demolition hammer. To remove a small area of concrete, use a cold chisel or a bull-point chisel and a ball-peen hammer or a small sledgehammer *(page 78)*. To break up a large area of concrete, use a large sledgehammer or, for easier and faster results, a demolition hammer. To work with a sledgehammer, wear work gloves, goggles and steel-toed work boots. Start at an edge and progress toward the center of the concrete, standing off the concrete and back from the edge you are breaking up, as shown. Raise the sledgehammer, gripping the handle firmly with both hands, and allow its weight to pull it down *(above, left)*. Repeat the procedure, breaking up the concrete into chunks small enough to remove by hand.

A demolition hammer can be readily obtained at a tool rental agency. **Caution:** Ask for and follow all operating instructions for the demolition hammer. To work with a demolition hammer, wear work gloves, goggles, ear protection and steel-toed work boots. Start at an edge and progress toward the center of the concrete, standing on the concrete and back from the edge you are breaking up, as shown. Support the demolition hammer firmly with both hands and pull the trigger *(above, right)*. Release the trigger, lift up the demolition hammer to reposition it, and repeat the procedure, breaking up the concrete into chunks small enough to remove by hand.

SETTING UP A CONCRETE FORM

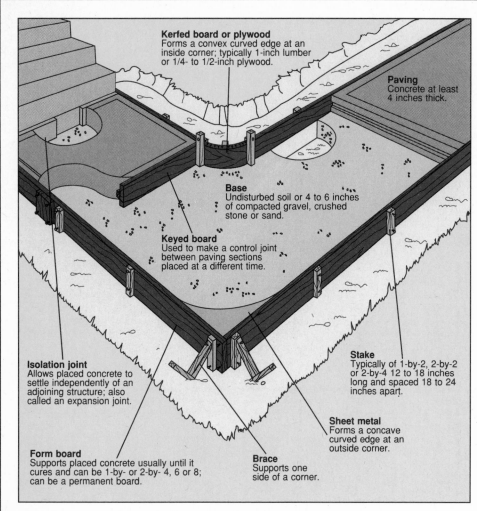

Kerfed board or plywood
Forms a convex curved edge at an inside corner; typically 1-inch lumber or 1/4- to 1/2-inch plywood.

Paving
Concrete at least 4 inches thick.

Base
Undisturbed soil or 4 to 6 inches of compacted gravel, crushed stone or sand.

Keyed board
Used to make a control joint between paving sections placed at a different time.

Isolation joint
Allows placed concrete to settle independently of an adjoining structure; also called an expansion joint.

Form board
Supports placed concrete usually until it cures and can be 1-by- or 2-by- 4, 6 or 8; can be a permanent board.

Brace
Supports one side of a corner.

Stake
Typically of 1-by-2, 2-by-2 or 2-by-4 12 to 18 inches long and spaced 18 to 24 inches apart.

Sheet metal
Forms a concave curved edge at an outside corner.

Preparing to place concrete. A form is used to support placed concrete. Check at left to determine what you require for a form, and below and pages 83 to 84 for how to build it; for easiest disassembly, use duplex nails and apply form oil or old motor oil on the inside surfaces.

For each straight side, 1-by-4 boards and 1-by-2 stakes in most instances are sufficient. For a curved side, use similar lumber or plywood, or sheet metal *(page 84)*. Keep in mind that the nominal size of a board is not its actual size; a 2-by-4, for example, is only 1 1/2 inches by 3 1/2 inches. If you use 2-by-4s for sides, therefore, the base will need to be 1/2 inch below them to place concrete 4 inches thick—the minimum required. Backfill soil into the trench along the outside edges of the boards to keep placed concrete from escaping.

Placed concrete should be no more than 10 feet square without at least one control joint to limit cracking; although the strongest section is as long as it is wide, a length up to 1 1/2 times the width is acceptable. Make control joints by using a jointer *(page 89)*, a keyed board *(page 96)* or a permanent board. Make sure permanent boards are decay-resistant redwood, cedar or cypress, or pressure-treated; position them 1/2 inch below the surface to allow for settling of the placed concrete. Install isolation-joint material along each masonry structure adjoining the concrete to be placed *(page 97)*.

The base must be undisturbed soil or a compacted 4- to 6-inch layer of gravel, crushed stone or sand; to compact it, make a tamper *(page 121)*. Although wire mesh can be installed to reinforce the concrete, it is not required; for equivalent strength, place new concrete an inch thicker than the old. See page 85 to determine the volume of concrete required.

INSTALLING A STRAIGHT FORM SIDE

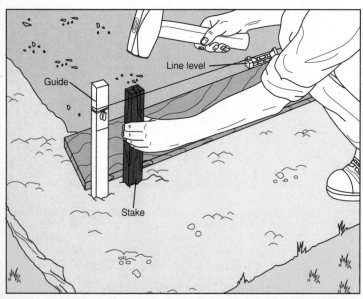

Guide

Line level

Stake

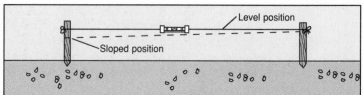

Level position

Sloped position

1 Positioning a form. Position the sides of a form using a line level, string and 1-by-2 stakes as guides. Drive a guide for each corner of the form into the ground with a small sledgehammer; if necessary, position the guides using string cut into lengths equal to the form sides. Working on one side of the form at a time, run a string tautly between the guides and tie it at the desired height of the concrete, leveling it with the line level. If drainage is important, as with a walkway, for example, lower one end of the string 1/8 inch for each foot the string is in length *(above)*, 1/2 inch if it is 4 feet long, 1 inch if it is 8 feet long. Cut the boards, if necessary, and make 12- to 18-inch long stakes for the form *(page 120)*. Then, place a board on the base against the guides and use a small sledgehammer to drive stakes into the ground every 18 to 24 inches along it *(left)*; align each stake with the string and the board, as shown, and drive it flush with or below the string.

INSTALLING A STRAIGHT FORM SIDE (continued)

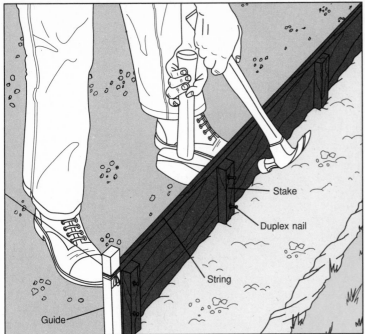

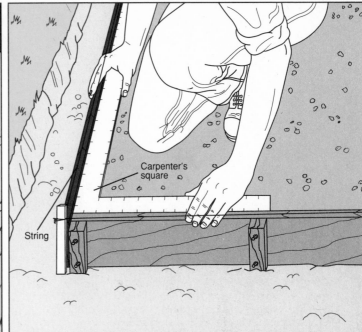

2 **Installing a form board and checking corners.** Position the board on the stakes, level with the string; if necessary, use a spade to dig up the soil under the board to place it properly. Drive at least two nails through each stake into the board *(above, left)*; use a small sledgehammer to support the board against the stake while you hammer, as shown. Then, position a second board adjacent to the first board and level with the string, butting their ends, and drive in a nail to hold them together. Check that the corner is square with a carpenter's

square *(above, right)* and reposition the second board, if necessary. When the second board is in position, drive stakes into the ground along it and install it on the stakes as you did with the first board. Drive at least one more nail into the corner to hold the boards together. Repeat the procedure to install boards for each side of the form. If you install two or more boards along any side of the form, nail a section of plywood 2 to 4 inches wide over each joint on the outside surface of the boards to keep the concrete to be placed from escaping.

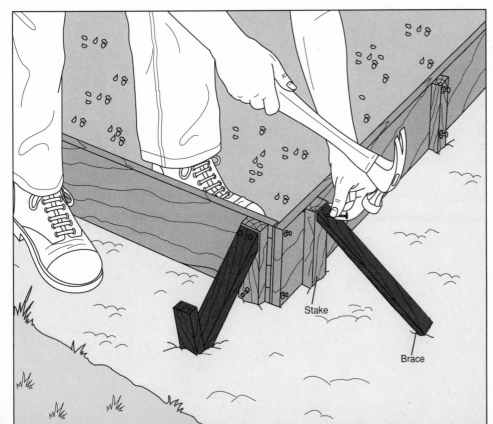

3 **Bracing a form corner.** After each straight side of the form is in place, install any curved sides required *(page 84)* and a brace on both sides of each corner. Use a saw *(page 120)* to cut braces from lumber of the same dimensions as the stakes and equal in length to them; bevel one end of each brace at a 45-degree angle. To install a brace, dig the flat end into the ground and nail the beveled end to the stake nearest the corner *(left)*; drive in at least two nails. Then, use a small sledgehammer to drive a stake into the ground at the flat end of the brace, wedging it securely in place.

Wearing work gloves, use a paintbrush to apply a coat of form oil or old motor oil on the inside surface of each form board. Prepare the base, using a spade to dig up soil or add gravel, crushed stone or sand; to compact the base, make a tamper *(page 121)* and use it, alternately lifting it and pounding it against the base. Fill in any low spots under the sides of the form to keep the concrete to be placed from escaping; if necessary, use the spade to backfill a layer of soil into the trench along the sides of the form and tamp the soil with your feet. Refer to page 85 to determine the volume of concrete required and the amount of each ingredient needed to make it.

MAKING A CURVE WITH METAL

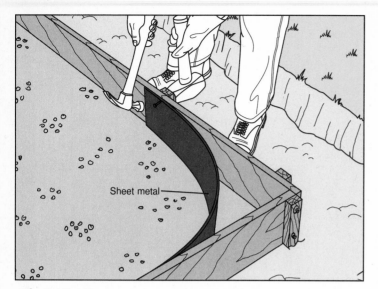

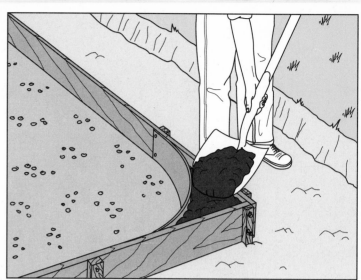

1 Setting the curve. For a convex, inside corner, use wood *(steps below)*; for a concave, outside corner, use wood or sheet metal. With metal, position and install straight boards *(page 82)* and use string to shape a curve; allowing for 6 inches of overlap along each board, cut the string to the curve length. Wearing work gloves, use tin snips to cut the metal equal to the string length. Bending the metal gently to form the curve, drive at least two nails through each end of it *(above)*.

2 Supporting the curve. Use a spade to backfill soil into the space between the metal and the boards at the corner *(above)*; work carefully to avoid misshaping or damaging the metal, or dislodging it from the boards. Distribute the soil evenly, pushing it gently against the metal and the boards. Tamp the soil with your feet. Refer to page 85 to determine the volume of concrete required and the amount of each ingredient needed to make it.

MAKING A CURVE WITH WOOD

1 Positioning the curve. To make a concave, outside corner, use sheet metal *(steps above)* or wood; to make a convex inside corner, use wood. Position and install boards for each straight form side *(page 82)*. Use string to mark off the position and shape of a gentle curve between the boards at each end of the straight form sides; cut the string to the length of the curve. Use a saw to cut a 1-inch thick board of the same width as the other boards to the length of the string, and make enough 12- to 18-inch long stakes to install one every 12 inches along it *(page 120)*; instead of a board, you may use plywood. Drive the stakes into the ground on alternate sides of the curve with a small sledgehammer *(above)*, using the string as a guide.

2 Installing the curved board. To help shape the board, saw kerfs across it every 1/4 to 1 inch along one side *(page 120)* and soak it in water. Working with a helper, if necessary, gently bend the board inward on the kerfed side and fit it between the stakes *(above)*, butting it with the straight form sides. Reposition stakes, if necessary, to fit the curved board into place. Align the top of the curved board with the top of the straight form sides and drive at least two nails through each stake on the kerfed side into the curved board. Pull out the stakes along the curved board opposite the kerfed side; use a small sledgehammer to loosen them, if necessary. Nail a section of plywood over any gap in the outside surface of the boards to keep concrete from escaping. Refer to page 85 to determine the volume of concrete required and the amount of each ingredient needed to make it.

MIXING CONCRETE

Concrete is made of portland cement, gravel, sand and water. In climates with extreme freeze and thaw conditions, use concrete that is air-entrained—containing portland cement with an air-entraining agent in it to cushion the consequences of water expansion and contraction. Air-entrained concrete must be mixed in a portable concrete mixer *(page 86)* or be ordered ready-mixed *(page 87)*. Concrete that is not air-entrained is suitable for most small repairs and can be mixed in a wheelbarrow *(page 86)*, on plywood or in a mortar box.

Working with concrete is time-consuming and rigorous. Plan to place no more than 18 cubic feet at one time—the volume equivalent of an area measuring 6 feet long by 6 feet wide, with a thickness of 6 inches. Determine the volume of concrete required *(center, left)*, using the chart *(center, right)* for guidance, if necessary. If you choose to mix the concrete yourself, use the charts at the bottom of the page to calculate the amount of each ingredient you require.

Determining the volume of concrete required. Use a tape measure to determine the area of the concrete to be placed; measure the length and width *(above, left)* in feet. With the thickness of the concrete to be placed in inches, compare the measurements to those listed in the chart *(above, top right)*. If your measurements are not listed, multiply the length, width and thickness measurements, and divide by 12; the result is the volume of concrete required in cubic feet. Use the volume to decide on the concrete materials most appropriate *(above, bottom right)*.

CONCRETE VOLUME: CUBIC FOOTAGE

AREA		THICKNESS	
(feet)	4 inches	5 inches	6 inches
3 by 3	3	3 3/4	4 1/2
4 by 4	5 1/2	6 3/4	8
4 by 5	6 3/4	8 1/2	10
4 by 6	8	10	12
5 by 5	8 1/2	10 1/2	12 1/2
5 by 6	10	12 1/2	15
6 by 6	12	15	18

Ready-mixed concrete. For more than 27 cubic feet (1 cubic yard) of concrete, order ready-mixed concrete *(page 87)*.

Premixed concrete. Usually available in 45- and 90-pound bags, premixed concrete contains portland cement, gravel and sand; a 90-pound bag makes 2/3 cubic foot of concrete. Following the label instructions, add water and mix in a wheelbarrow or portable mixer *(page 86)*.

Dry ingredients. Refer to the charts below to determine the amounts of gravel, portland cement, sand and water needed. Weigh the ingredients on a bathroom scale in separate containers, "zeroing" the scale with the empty container first. After weighing each ingredient once, mark the material level inside the container to measure subsequent batches.

AIR-ENTRAINED CONCRETE: INGREDIENTS FOR 1 CUBIC FOOT

GRAVEL SIZE (inches)	GRAVEL WEIGHT (pounds)	CEMENT* WEIGHT (pounds)	SAND** WEIGHT (pounds)	WATER WEIGHT (pounds)
3/8	29	53	46	10
1/2	27	46	55	10
3/4	25	42	65	10
1	24	39	70	9
1 1/2	23	38	75	9

NON-AIR-ENTRAINED CONCRETE: INGREDIENTS FOR 1 CUBIC FOOT

GRAVEL SIZE (inches)	GRAVEL WEIGHT (pounds)	CEMENT WEIGHT (pounds)	SAND** WEIGHT (pounds)	WATER WEIGHT (pounds)
3/8	29	59	46	11
1/2	27	53	55	11
3/4	25	47	65	10
1	24	45	70	10
1 1/2	23	43	75	9

*With an air-entraining agent in it. If this type of portland cement is not available at a building supply center, find a concrete-delivery company that will sell you an air entraining agent.

**Based on wet sand, its usual condition. Test sand condition by squeezing a handful; adjust the quantities in the mix, if necessary. *Wet sand* forms a ball, without moistening the palm; use the quantities given. *Damp sand* falls apart (will not form a ball); decrease the sand by 1 pound and increase the water by 1 pound. *Very wet sand* (exposed to rain) forms a ball and moistens the palm; increase the sand by 1 pound and decrease the water by 1 pound.

MIXING CONCRETE IN A WHEELBARROW

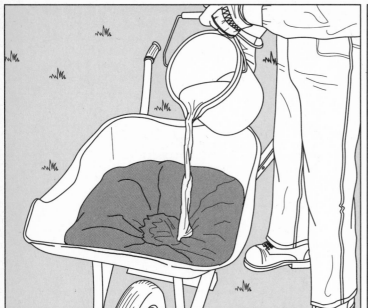

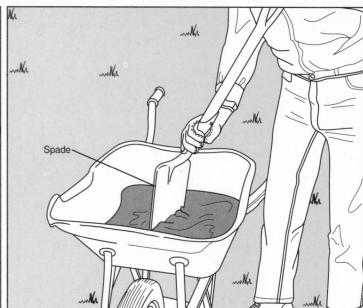

Adding the concrete ingredients. To mix a batch of air-entrained concrete, use a portable concrete mixer *(step 1, below)*. To mix a small batch of concrete, use a wheelbarrow. Determine the volume of concrete required and the amount of each ingredient needed *(page 85)*. Wearing work gloves, use a spade to fill the wheelbarrow no more than 3/4 full with the dry ingredients, mix them together thoroughly and form a crater in the center of them. Add the required amount of clean water using a bucket *(above, left)*, pouring and mixing in only a little at one time.

Mix in the water thoroughly with the spade *(above, right)*, using it to lift and turn over the ingredients. When the concrete is uniform in appearance, test its consistency and adjust it, if necessary *(page 87)*. When the concrete is of the proper consistency, roll the wheelbarrow to the work site and place the concrete *(page 88)*. Repeat the procedure to mix and place more concrete, if necessary. When you finish mixing and placing concrete, use a garden hose to wash off the wheelbarrow; if necessary, loosen hardened particles by scrubbing with a wire brush.

MIXING CONCRETE IN A PORTABLE MIXER

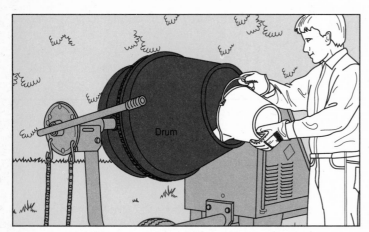

1 Adding the concrete ingredients. To mix a small batch of concrete, use a wheelbarrow *(step above)*. To mix a batch of air-entrained concrete, use a portable concrete mixer, available at a tool rental agency. Determine the volume of concrete required and the amount of each ingredient needed to make it *(page 85)*. Wearing work gloves, follow the operating instructions for the mixer and add the ingredients into the drum; avoid filling it much more than half full. Use a spade to shovel in the dry ingredients; use a bucket to pour in the required amount of clean water *(above)*. Turn on the mixer and allow the drum to spin for 3 to 5 minutes; then, test the concrete consistency and adjust it, if necessary *(page 87)*. When the concrete is of the proper consistency, place it *(page 88)*. Repeat the procedure to mix and place more concrete, if necessary.

2 Cleaning the mixer. When you finish mixing and placing concrete, clean out the drum. Turn on the mixer, use a garden hose to spray inside the drum with clean water *(above)* and use a spade to add several scoops of gravel or crushed stone. Allow the drum to spin for 2 to 3 minutes and dump out the water and gravel or crushed stone. Spray more water into the drum to rinse it and dump out the water. If necessary, turn off the mixer and loosen hardened particles by scrubbing with a wire brush, then repeat the procedure. Turn off the mixer after cleaning the inside of the drum and allow it to dry.

TESTING CONCRETE CONSISTENCY

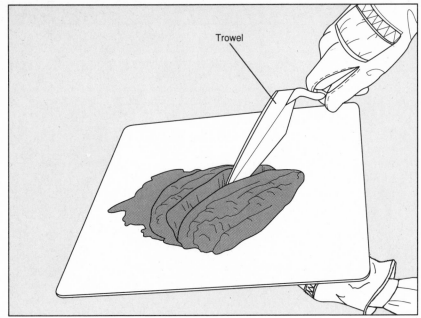

Trowel

Slicing mixed concrete. For a strong, durable repair, proper consistency of the mixed concrete is essential. Concrete should not be so dry that it crumbles nor contain so much water that it is soupy. After mixing a batch of concrete using one of the methods described on page 86, wear work gloves and use a spade to place a small, rectangular mound of it on a scrap piece of plywood or a mason's hawk. To test the concrete consistency, slice it in half along its length with the blade of a mason's trowel *(left)*. The concrete should separate firmly, as shown, without crumbling or collapsing. If the concrete is soupy, mix in more sand and gravel, adding no more than half a spadeful at one time. If the concrete crumbles, mix in more water, using a bucket to add only a little at one time. When the concrete is of the proper consistency, place it *(page 88)*.

WORKING WITH CONCRETE PROFESSIONALS

Chute

Ordering ready-mixed concrete. To place more than 27 cubic feet, or 1 cubic yard, of concrete, order ready-mixed concrete from a concrete-delivery company. Determine the volume of concrete required *(page 85)* and consult a professional of the company on the correct amount to order; be sure to specify the use of the concrete and make your order in cubic yards. The cost of the ready-mixed concrete depends on the amount ordered and includes a charge for the distance the delivery truck travels and a standard delivery time, usually 30 to 45 minutes; typically, there is an additional hourly charge for jobs that require more time. To keep the cost to a minimum, prepare in advance for the concrete delivery. Make sure that a concrete form is properly made and installed, and that the base for the concrete is properly prepared *(page 82)*. Provide access to the work site for the delivery truck so that the concrete can be placed directly from its chute *(above)*; have helpers on hand to place the concrete *(page 88)*, transporting it in wheelbarrows or buckets from the delivery truck to the work site, if necessary, and to finish the concrete *(page 88)*.

PLACING CONCRETE

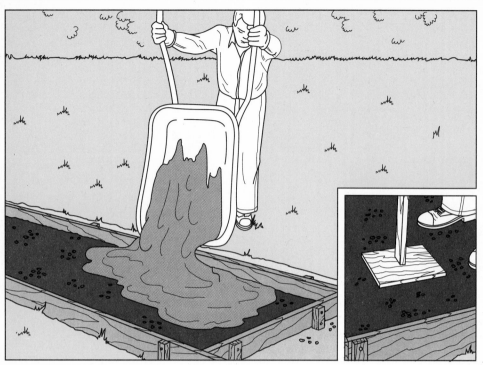

Placing mixed concrete. Concrete requires a solid base of undisturbed soil, or a compacted, 4- to 6-inch layer of gravel, crushed stone or sand. Before mixing and placing the concrete, install a form, if necessary, and make sure the base is properly prepared *(page 82)*. To compact the base, construct a tamper *(page 121)* and use it *(inset)*, alternately lifting it and pounding it against the base. To prevent the leaching of moisture from fresh concrete, use the fine spray of a garden hose to dampen the base and any adjacent old concrete.

Whenever possible, place fresh concrete directly from where it is mixed—the wheelbarrow, the portable mixer or the delivery truck. If necessary, transport the concrete from where it is mixed to the work site with a wheelbarrow *(page 112)* or a bucket and place it evenly on the bed *(left)*. Use a spade or a shovel to distribute the placed concrete, pushing it into corners and against the sides of a form; avoid overworking the concrete, however, since this can cause the gravel in it to sink to the bottom, weakening the top. Place as much concrete as necessary to completely fill any form, then finish the surface *(steps below)*.

FINISHING CONCRETE

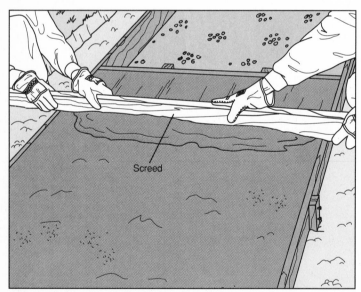

1 **Striking off using a screed.** To level, or strike off, the surface, use a screed; for the screed, use a straight 2-by-4 about 18 to 24 inches longer than the width of the surface. If necessary, strike off with a helper holding one end of the screed. Wearing work gloves, position the screed across the width of the surface, resting on the top of a form, with its leading edge at a slight angle to the surface. Pull the screed slowly across the surface *(above)*, working it back and forth to prevent concrete from adhering to it; to fill in any low spots, keep a small amount of concrete ahead of the screed, adding it with a trowel, if necessary. Scrape excess concrete off the screed using the trowel and rinse the screed with clean water. To rid the concrete of air pockets, pull the screed slowly across the length of the surface, gently working it up and down in the concrete. Strike off again using the screed.

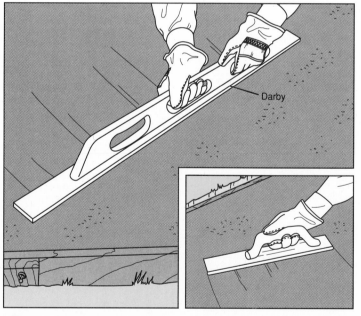

Darby

2 **Floating the surface.** Float the surface immediately after striking off to smooth the concrete and embed the gravel in it below the surface. On a large surface, use a darby. Wearing work gloves, use both hands to sweep the darby lightly across the surface in a broad arcing motion *(above)*, overlapping passes; keep the leading edge of the darby lifted slightly, as shown, to avoid digging into the concrete and use even pressure. If necessary, position scrap pieces of plywood on the concrete to use as kneeboards in order to reach the entire surface. On a small surface, use a wooden float; work with one hand and follow the same procedure *(inset)*. Edge the concrete as soon as it is stiff enough to hold a thumbprint *(step 3)*.

FINISHING CONCRETE (continued)

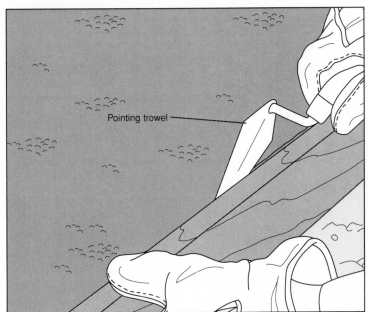

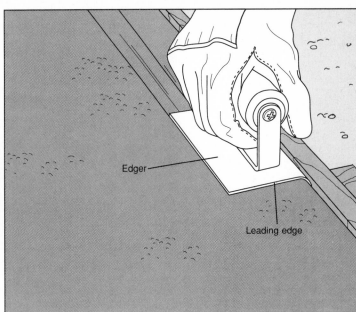

3 Edging the concrete. Edging the perimeter of a concrete surface provides smooth, durable, rounded edges that resist chipping. Allow any water on the surface to evaporate before edging. Then, wearing work gloves, cut along the inside edge of the form with the blade of a pointing trowel *(above, left)*, creating a narrow opening between the form and the concrete for an edger. Place the edger flat on the surface, with the curve of its blade against the form *(above, right)*. Slide the edger back and forth across the surface, keeping the leading edge of its blade lifted slightly to avoid digging into the concrete. If the surface is more than 10 feet square, make control joints *(step 4)*. If the surface is less than 10 feet square, float it for final-finishing *(step 5)*.

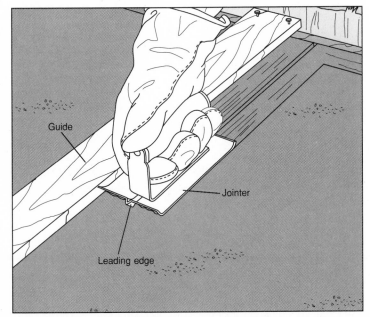

4 Making control joints. Control joints prevent random, extended cracking in concrete paving. Make a control joint at least every 10 feet across the surface; for appearance, place control joints at equal intervals: across the width every 3 or 4 feet along a walkway that is 3 feet wide and 12 feet long, for example. To make a control joint, use a jointer with a cutting edge equal to about 1/4 of the concrete thickness. Position and gently nail a straight 1-by-6 or 2-by-6 across the form to use as a guide; keep in mind that the center of the control joint is formed by the center of the jointer. Wearing work gloves, position the jointer against the guide and push it into the concrete; with its leading edge lifted slightly, slide it lightly across the surface *(above)*. Make another pass in the opposite direction.

5 Floating for final-finishing. Use a wooden float to prepare for final-finishing, or for a rough final-finish on a surface exposed to the weather and subjected to heavy foot traffic—a walkway, for example, that can become slippery. Begin floating after the moisture sheen disappears, but before the concrete stiffens completely. Wearing work gloves, sweep the float lightly across the surface in a broad arcing motion *(above)*, overlapping passes; keep the leading edge lifted slightly to avoid digging into the concrete and use even pressure. If necessary, position scrap pieces of plywood on the concrete to use as kneeboards, as shown, in order to reach the entire surface. Touch up the edging *(step 3)* and the control joints *(step 4)*, if necessary; then, final-finish *(step 6)* or cure the concrete *(page 90)*.

FINISHING CONCRETE (continued)

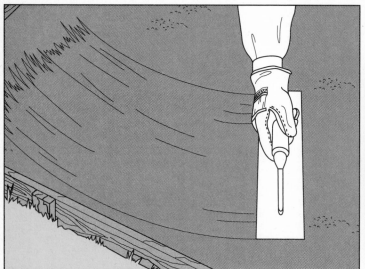

6 **Final-finishing with a trowel or a broom.** Use a metal rectangular trowel for a smooth final-finish that is easy to clean—on a garage floor, for example. Wearing work gloves, sweep the trowel lightly across the surface in a broad arcing motion *(above, left)*, overlapping passes; keep the leading edge lifted slightly to avoid digging into the concrete and use even pressure. If necessary, position scrap pieces of plywood on the concrete to use as kneeboards in order to reach the

entire surface. For a rough final-finish with good skid-resistance, use a stiff broom; for a coarser final-finish, first dampen the broom bristles with clean water. Applying even pressure, pull or push the broom gently across the surface in one direction without overlapping passes *(above, right)*. After troweling or brooming, touch up the edging *(step 3)* and the control joints *(step 4)*, if necessary; then, cure the concrete *(steps below)*.

CURING CONCRETE

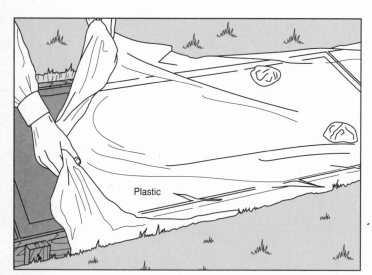

Plastic

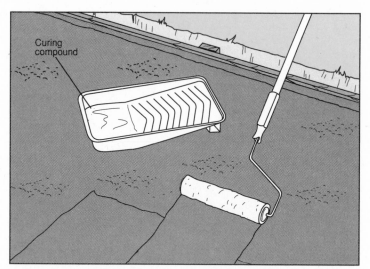

Curing compound

Curing with plastic. Constant sprinkling of the concrete with water for 5 days is typically the recommended curing method, but it is often impractical. For a concrete surface that can withstand the weight of traffic within this period of time, apply curing compound *(step right)*. Although a variety of other curing methods can be used, curing with plastic both seals the concrete and protects its surface. Buy plastic in sheets or on a roll at a building supply center. Lay the plastic flat on the concrete, completely covering the surface *(above)*, and anchor it with large stones. Overlap the plastic by 2 inches at any seam and tape the sections with duct tape. Then, pull the plastic taut and use a staple gun to staple it onto each side of the form, sealing the surface. Be sure the plastic lies flat; wrinkles in it can cause discoloration of the concrete. Keep the plastic in place for 5 days, patching any tears that occur in it; then, remove the plastic and disassemble the form *(page 91)*.

Applying curing compound. To seal the concrete and protect its surface while it cures, use plastic *(step left)*. For a concrete surface that can withstand the weight of traffic before the concrete cures, apply curing compound. Buy concrete curing compound at a building supply center and follow the label instructions to apply it. Wearing rubber gloves, pour a small amount of the curing compound into a roller pan at one time and spread it evenly on the surface using a paint roller fitted with an extension *(above)*; be sure to work the curing compound into any control joint. To ensure adequate coverage, apply two coats of the curing compound: the first in one direction, the second at a 90-degree angle to the first. Before subjecting the concrete to foot traffic, allow at least 24 hours; to heavier traffic, allow at least 48 hours. After the concrete cures for 5 days, disassemble the form *(page 91)*.

REMOVING A CONCRETE FORM

Disassembling a form. After the concrete cures for 5 days, disassemble the form; leave in place any permanent board installed and any isolation joint. Pull out the nails with a hammer *(left)*, using the claws to grip the shank just below the head, as shown. To loosen the nails in a stake, if necessary, pull the stake away from the board by wedging a pry bar or driving a wooden shim between them. After the nails are removed, rock each stake back and forth to loosen it and pull it out of the ground; if necessary, hammer on the sides of it at ground level. Pull the form boards away from the concrete using a pry bar, working carefully to avoid chipping the edges of the concrete. When the form is disassembled, use a spade to fill in the trench with soil, grading it slightly away from the edges of the concrete. Tamp the soil with your feet, put back any sod removed and tamp again.

ETCHING CONCRETE WITH MURIATIC ACID

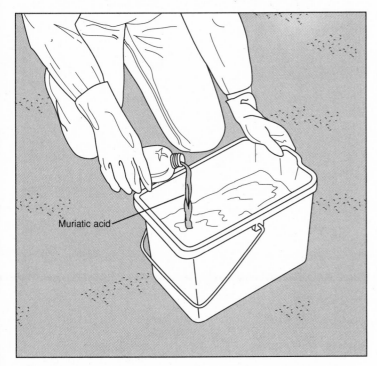

Muriatic acid

1 Mixing the solution. To prepare old concrete and help it bond with new concrete, etch it with a solution of muriatic acid. Buy muriatic acid at a building supply center. Wearing rubber gloves and goggles, follow the label instructions to mix a solution of 1 part acid and between 3 to 5 parts water in a plastic bucket or container *(above)*; avoiding filling the bucket or container up to the top. **Caution:** Always add the acid to the water, as shown; never add the water to the acid. If you are etching a large area or a number of small areas at one time, mix the weaker solution to slow the reaction with the concrete.

2 Applying the solution. Use clean water to soak the concrete evenly, without creating puddles. Wearing rubber gloves and goggles, apply the solution while the concrete is wet. To etch one large area, slowly pour the solution a little at a time *(above)*, working carefully to avoid splashing; to etch a small area, apply the solution using a paintbrush. Work the solution into the concrete by scrubbing with a stiff fiber brush. Etching occurs for as long as the solution bubbles. To stop the etching and neutralize the solution, sprinkle a layer of sodium bicarbonate (baking soda) on the concrete, wait about 15 minutes, then flush the concrete thoroughly with clean water.

REPAIRING A PAVING EDGE

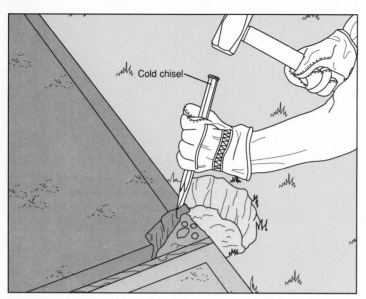

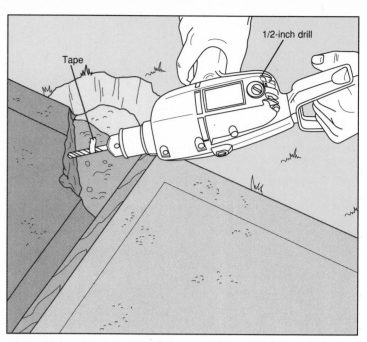

1 **Removing the damage.** Use a spade to cut and remove any sod and dig up the soil around the damaged concrete. Wearing work gloves and goggles, chip off the damaged concrete into chunks small enough to remove by hand *(page 78)*. To help the bonding of new concrete, break up the damaged concrete until you reach the base and use a cold chisel and a ball-peen hammer to square or undercut the edges of the undamaged concrete *(above)*. If you find any embedded wire mesh or a reinforcing bar, chip the concrete off it and leave it in place; if any wire mesh cannot be repositioned flat on the base, cut it off with wire cutters or cutting pliers. If the base has sunk, rebuild it *(page 97)*. Clean loose particles off the edges of the undamaged concrete using a stiff fiber brush and etch with muriatic acid *(page 91)*.

2 **Drilling holes for lag bolts or reinforcing bars.** To help anchor new concrete, install 6-inch lag bolts with expansion shields or reinforcing bars half way into the undamaged concrete, positioning them at least 2 inches below the surface and 2 to 4 inches apart. Buy lag bolts with expansion shields or reinforcing bars at a building supply center. Drill holes equal in diameter to the expansion shields or reinforcing bars using a 1/2-inch drill fitted with a masonry bit *(above)* or a hammer drill; use tape to know when to stop drilling: after 6 inches for an expansion shield, after 3 inches for a reinforcing bar.

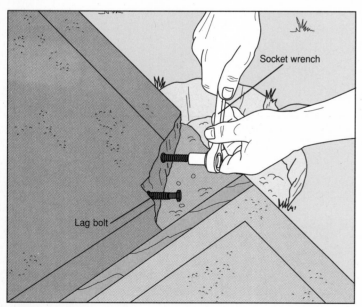

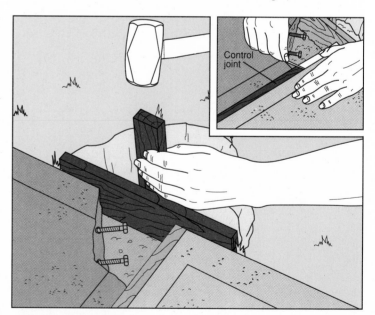

3 **Installing lag bolts or reinforcing bars.** To install each lag bolt and expansion shield, fit the expansion shield into the hole and tap it flush with the top of the hole using a ball-peen hammer. Then, use a socket wrench to drive the lag bolt half way into the expansion shield *(above)*. To install each reinforcing bar, slide it into the hole by hand; if necessary, tap it into place lightly with a ball-peen hammer.

4 **Installing a form.** To support new concrete along more than one side, install a form *(page 82)*; along one side, use a 1-by-4 or 1-by-6 at least 4 to 6 inches longer than it. Cut 1-by-2 stakes *(page 120)* 12 to 18 inches long; make enough to drive one into the ground every 18 to 24 inches along the board. Center the board along the damaged side, as shown, and drive each stake into the ground using a sledgehammer *(above)*. Drive at least two nails through each stake into the board. Tape the top of any adjacent permanent board installed as a control joint to protect it from concrete stains *(inset)*.

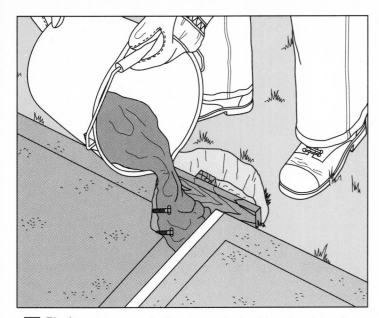

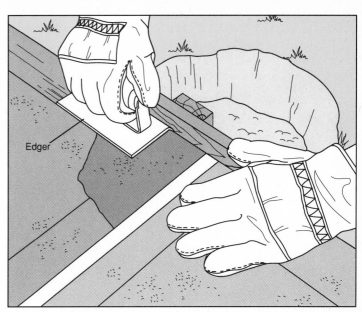

5 **Placing new concrete.** To prevent the leaching of moisture from fresh concrete, soak the old concrete with clean water. Apply a bonding agent on the old concrete *(page 79)* or use fresh concrete with a bonding agent in it *(page 85)*. Wearing work gloves, mix a batch of concrete in a wheelbarrow or a portable mixer *(page 86)* and place it *(page 88)* using a bucket *(above)*. Place concrete until it is flush with the undamaged concrete.

6 **Finishing the concrete.** Float the surface after placing the concrete *(page 88)* and allow any water on the surface to evaporate. As soon as the concrete is stiff enough to hold a thumbprint, edge the perimeter using an edger *(page 89)*, sliding it along the surface against the board *(above)*; also edge any adjacent control joint. Float the surface for final-finishing *(page 89)* and, if necessary, final-finish the surface *(page 90)*. Cure the concrete *(page 90)* and disassemble the form *(page 91)*.

REPAIRING A STEP SURFACE

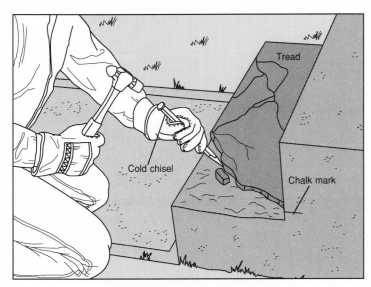

1 **Chipping off the surface.** If the concrete surface of a step tread is damaged, replace it. For later reference, first mark the top of the tread on each side of the step with chalk, as shown. Wearing work gloves and goggles, chip at least a 1-inch layer of concrete off the entire tread surface *(page 78)* using a cold chisel and a ball-peen hammer *(above)*. Then, to help the bonding of new concrete, chip a groove about 1 inch wide and 1 inch deep every 8 to 10 inches along the surface; start and stop each groove about 1 inch from the edge of the tread. Work carefully to avoid damaging any adjacent riser surfaces. Clean off loose particles with a stiff fiber brush.

2 **Etching the surface.** To protect undamaged concrete and other surfaces from etching, use scrap pieces of wood, plastic or other material; tape plastic over the risers adjacent to the damaged tread with duct tape, as shown, for example. Wearing rubber gloves and goggles, etch the damaged concrete surface *(page 91)*, applying the solution evenly using a paintbrush *(above)*. Flush the etched concrete with clean water and uncover the protected surfaces.

REPAIRING A STEP SURFACE (continued)

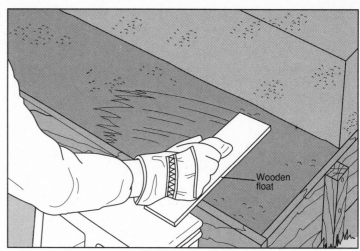

Wooden
float

3 **Installing a form.** Use three boards 1 inch thick to make a form along the length and sides of the tread. To support the form, cut stakes *(page 120)* 12 to 18 inches long for the sides and use a concrete block for the length. Position the boards and drive nails into each corner with a hammer. Drive the stakes into the ground alongside the form with a sledgehammer. Align the top of the form with the chalk marks and use the hammer to drive at least two nails through each stake into the form. Place the concrete block flush against the length of the form *(above)*. To prevent the leaching of moisture from fresh concrete, soak the old concrete with clean water.

4 **Placing and finishing new concrete.** Apply a bonding agent on the old concrete *(page 79)* or use fresh concrete with a bonding agent in it *(page 85)*. Wearing work gloves, mix a batch of concrete *(page 86)* and place it *(page 88)*. When the placed concrete is flush with the top of the form, use a wooden float to smooth the surface. Sweep the float across the surface in a broad arcing motion *(above)*, overlapping passes; keep the leading edge lifted slightly to avoid digging into the concrete and use even pressure. Allow any water on the surface to evaporate. Edge the perimeter, if necessary *(page 89)*. Then, float the surface for final-finishing *(page 89)*. Cure the concrete *(page 90)* and disassemble the form *(page 91)*.

REPAIRING A PAVING SURFACE

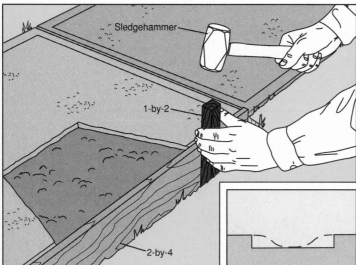

Sledgehammer

1-by-2

2-by-4

1 **Preparing the surface.** Wearing work gloves and goggles, chip off the damaged concrete *(page 78)* into chunks small enough to remove by hand. To help the bonding of new concrete, break up the damaged concrete to a depth of at least 1 inch and square or undercut the edges of the undamaged concrete *(inset)*. Clean off loose particles using a stiff fiber brush. Etch the damaged concrete with muriatic acid *(page 91)* . If the damaged concrete extends to an outside edge, support is required for new concrete: along more than one outside edge, install a form *(page 82)*; along only one outside edge, use a board 1 or 2 inches thick and at least 4 to 6 inches longer than the edge for a form. Cut stakes *(page 120)* 12 to 18 inches long; make enough to drive one

into the ground at least every 18 to 24 inches along the form. Use a spade to cut and remove any sod next to the edge and dig a trench for the form. Center the form along the damaged edge, as shown, its width and thickness flush with the undamaged concrete. Drive each stake into the ground using a sledgehammer *(above, left)* until the top is flush with the form. Use a hammer to drive at least two nails through each stake into the form. Tape the top of any adjacent permanent board installed as a control joint to protect it from concrete stains. To prevent the leaching of moisture from fresh concrete, soak the old concrete with clean water. Apply a bonding agent on the old concrete *(page 79)* using a paintbrush *(above, right)* or use fresh concrete with a bonding agent in it *(page 85)*.

REPAIRING A PAVING SURFACE (continued)

2 **Placing and finishing new concrete.** Wearing work gloves, mix a batch of concrete *(page 86)* and place it *(page 88)* using a shovel *(above, left)*. Place concrete until it is flush with the top of the form and the undamaged concrete. If the placed concrete surface is large, strike it off using a screed *(page 88)*, moving it slowly across the surface *(above, right)* and working it back and forth to prevent concrete from adhering to it. Float the surface after striking off or if the placed concrete surface is small *(page 88)*. Allow any water on the surface to evaporate. Edge the perimeter, if necessary *(page 89)*, and any adjacent control joint. Float the surface for final-finishing *(page 89)* and, if necessary, final-finish the surface *(page 90)*. Cure the concrete *(page 90)* and disassemble any form installed *(page 91)*.

REPLACING PAVING

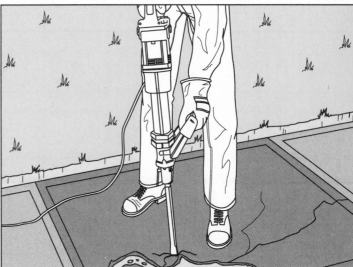

1 **Removing the paving.** If the paving is divided into sections by control joints, you may replace only the damaged sections, one at a time or all together. If the paving is not divided into sections by control joints, replace all the paving. Wearing work gloves, use a spade to cut and remove any sod within 4 to 6 inches along the edges of the damaged paving *(above, left)* and dig a trench to the depth of the base. Wearing goggles, break up the damaged concrete into chunks small enough to remove by hand *(page 81)* using a demolition hammer *(above, right)*. Work from the perimeter of the paving toward the center, as shown, breaking up the concrete until you reach the base. To remove chunks of concrete adhering to any wire mesh on the base, use wire cutters or cutting pliers to cut the mesh. Chip off concrete along the control joint of any undamaged paving you wish to leave in place *(page 78)*, squaring or undercutting the edges; then, clean off loose particles with a stiff fiber brush and etch with muriatic acid *(page 91)*.

REPLACING PAVING (continued)

2 **Estimating lumber for a form.** To estimate the amount and sizes of lumber required for a form *(page 82)*, use a tape measure to measure the width *(above)*, length, and depth below ground level of the base. As a rule of thumb, a paving section should be no less than 4 inches thick and no more than 10 feet square without a control joint *(page 72)*; although the strongest paving section is as long as it is wide, a length up to 1 1/2 times the width is acceptable. Plan on making control joints using a jointer *(page 89)*, a keyed board *(step 4)*, or a permanent board *(page 82)*. If necessary, plan also for isolation joints *(step 7)* and curved sides *(page 84)*. Buy materials for a form at a building supply center.

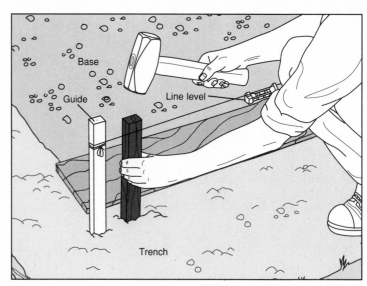

3 **Installing a form board.** Position the form sides *(page 82)* and make stakes *(page 120)*. For a straight side, place a board on the base against its guides and drive stakes into the ground every 18 to 24 inches along it using a small sledgehammer *(above)*; align each stake with the string and the board, as shown, and drive it flush with or below the string. Position the board on the stakes, level with the string, and drive at least two nails through each stake into it *(page 83)*. Install each straight side the same way, checking corners with a carpenter's square *(page 83)*; if necessary, install a permanent board 1/2 inch below the top of the other boards or make a keyed board *(step 4)*. Then, install any curved sides required *(page 84)*.

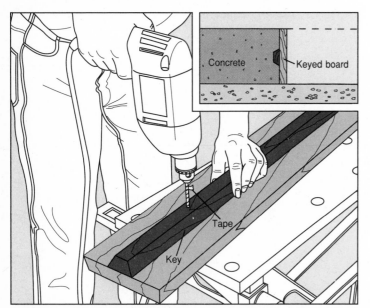

4 **Making a keyed board.** If the concrete is to be placed at one time, oil the boards *(step 5)*. If the concrete is not to be placed at one time, use a keyed board to make a control joint between the paving sections. A keyed board allows two adjoining paving sections to interlock, helping to keep them level; concrete placed against a keyed board *(inset)* forms a groove which shapes a tongue in concrete subsequently placed. To make a keyed board, use a 1-by-2 or 2-by-2 equal in length to the board as a key; bevel two opposite sides of it at a 20- to 30-degree angle with a saber saw *(page 120)*. Position the key along the center of the board, bore pilot holes every 12 to 18 inches along it using a drill *(above)*, and screw it onto the board.

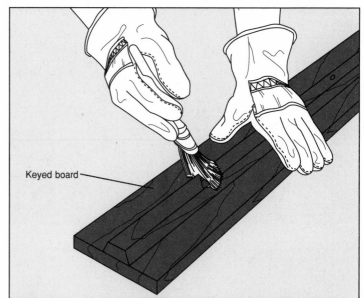

5 **Oiling the form boards.** To keep the concrete from adhering to the boards, buy form oil at a building supply center or use old motor oil. Wearing work gloves, apply a thin, even coat of oil on the inside surface of each board with a paintbrush; if you are using a keyed board, make sure that the key, in particular, is adequately coated *(above)*. If you installed two or more boards along any form side, nail a section of plywood 2 to 4 inches wide over each joint on the outside surface to keep concrete from escaping. Brace the corners of the form *(page 83)*, install the keyed board *(step 6)* if you are using one, and make any isolation joint required *(step 7)*. If you are not using a keyed board and no isolation joint is required, prepare the paving base *(step 8)*.

6 **Installing a keyed board.** After installing the boards for the other form sides *(step 3)*, install the keyed board; position it with the key facing into the concrete to be placed and no farther than 10 feet away from its opposite form side. Wedge the keyed board between its adjacent form sides, tapping it into place with a hammer. Check the position of the keyed board using a carpenter's level and a carpenter's square *(page 83)*; reposition it, if necessary. When the keyed board is correctly positioned, drive at least two nails through each adjacent form side into the end of it *(above)*. Then, drive stakes into the ground every 18 to 24 inches along the keyed board using a small sledgehammer and drive at least two nails through each stake into the keyed board.

7 **Making an isolation joint.** To allow a paving section to expand, contract and settle independently, make an isolation joint between it and each adjoining masonry structure--a step, a curb, a wall or a foundation, for example. If no isolation joint is required, prepare the paving base *(step 8)*. For an isolation joint, buy 1/2-inch thick isolation-joint material at a building supply center; cut it to size using a utility knife and a straight edge. Position the joint material along the structure adjoining the concrete to be placed, with the top of it 1/2 inch below the top of the form sides. Then, drive masonry nails through the joint material every 18 to 24 inches along it into the adjoining structure *(above)*.

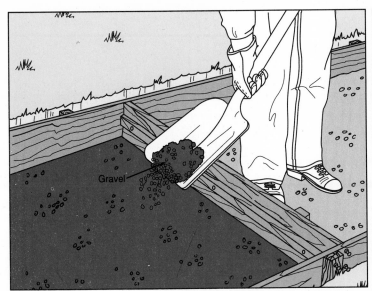

8 **Preparing the paving base.** A paving section must be at least 4 inches thick and requires a solid base of undisturbed soil, or a compacted 4- to 6-inch layer of gravel, crushed stone or sand. Use a spade to dig the base to a uniform depth, if necessary. To build up the base, buy gravel, crushed stone or sand at a building supply center and distribute it using a shovel *(above, left)*. Level the base, if necessary, with a rake. Fill in any low spots under the form sides to keep the concrete to be placed from escaping; if necessary, use a spade to backfill a layer of soil into the trench around the form sides and tamp the soil with your feet. To compact the base, construct a tamper *(page 121)* and use it *(above, right)*, alternately lifting it and pounding it against the base.

REPLACING PAVING (continued)

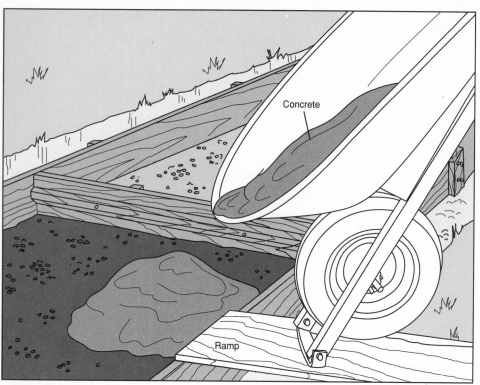

9 **Placing new concrete.** Determine the volume of concrete required *(page 85)*. If the volume to be placed at one time is less than 27 cubic feet, mix the concrete yourself using a wheelbarrow or a portable mixer *(page 86)*; if the volume to be placed at one time is more than 27 cubic feet, order ready-mixed concrete *(page 87)*. To prevent the leaching of moisture from the fresh concrete, use the fine spray of a garden hose to dampen the base, without creating puddles. If you are using a permanent board to make a control joint, protect the top of it from concrete stains with masking tape.

Whenever possible, place fresh concrete directly from where it is mixed--the wheelbarrow, the portable mixer or the delivery truck. If necessary, transport the concrete from where it is mixed to the work site with a wheelbarrow *(page 112)* or a bucket and place it evenly on the base *(left)*. Use a spade or a shovel to distribute the placed concrete, pushing it into corners and against the form sides; avoid overworking the concrete, however, since this can cause the gravel in it to sink to the bottom, weakening the top. Place as much concrete as necessary to completely fill the form.

10 **Striking off using a screed.** To level, or strike off, the surface, use a screed; for the screed, use a straight 2-by-4 about 18 to 24 inches longer than the width of the surface. If necessary, strike off with a helper holding one end of the screed. Wearing work gloves, position the screed across the width of the surface, resting on the top of the form, with its leading edge at a slight angle to the surface. Pull the screed slowly across the surface *(above)*, working it back and forth to prevent concrete from adhering to it; to fill in any low spots, keep a small amount of concrete ahead of the screed. To rid the concrete of air pockets, pull the screed slowly across the length of the surface, gently working it up and down in the concrete. Strike off again using the screed.

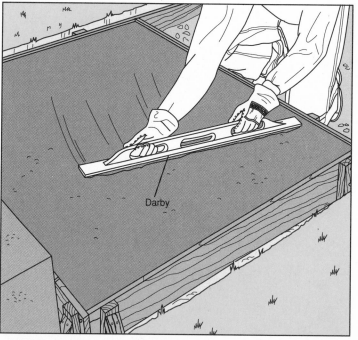

11 **Floating the surface.** Float the surface with a darby immediately after striking off to smooth the concrete and embed the gravel in it below the surface. Wearing work gloves, use both hands to sweep the darby lightly across the surface in a broad arcing motion *(above)*, overlapping passes; keep the leading edge of the darby lifted slightly to avoid digging into the concrete and use even pressure. If necessary, position scrap pieces of plywood on the concrete to use as kneeboards in order to reach the entire surface. Edge the concrete as soon as it is stiff enough to hold a thumbprint *(step 12)*.

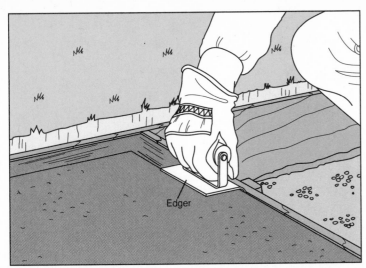

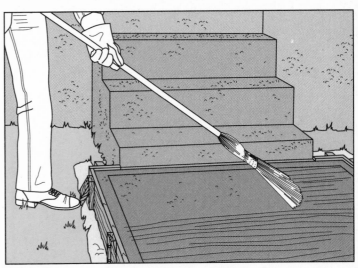

12 **Edging the concrete.** Edge the perimeter of the concrete along the form sides and isolation joints for smooth, durable, rounded edges that resist chipping. Allow any water on the surface to evaporate before edging. Then, wearing work gloves, use the blade of a pointing trowel to cut along the inside edge of each form and isolation joint, creating a narrow opening for an edger. Place the edger flat on the surface, with the curve of its blade against the form *(above)* or isolation joint, and slide it back and forth across the surface; keep the leading edge lifted slightly to avoid digging into the concrete. If you are not using a keyed board or permanent boards and the placed concrete is over 10 feet square, make control joints with a jointer *(page 96)*.

13 **Final-finishing the surface.** Float the surface using a wooden float to prepare for final-finishing, or for a rough final-finish. Begin floating after the moisture sheen disappears, but before the concrete stiffens completely. Wearing work gloves, use one hand to sweep the float lightly across the surface, following the technique used with a darby *(step 11)*. For a smoother final-finish, follow up with a metal rectangular trowel, again using the same technique; for a rougher final-finish, follow up with a broom, pulling it gently across the surface without overlapping passes *(above)*. After final-finishing, touch up the edging *(step 12)* and any control joints made with a jointer *(page 89)*, if necessary.

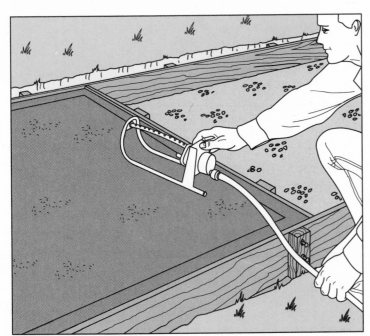

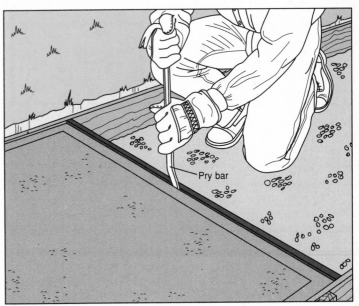

14 **Curing the concrete.** To cure the placed concrete, constant sprinkling of it with water for 5 days is the recommended method. Set up a garden sprinkler *(above)*, for example, if the concrete is outdoors. Often, however, this method is impractical or the concrete requires protection while it cures; in these instances, cure with plastic or apply curing compound *(page 90)*. If you are using a keyed board to place concrete for more than one paving section, you may remove it after 24 hours *(step 15)*. Otherwise, allow the concrete to fully cure and then disassemble the form *(page 91)*.

15 **Removing a keyed board.** Remove the keyed board to place concrete for the subsequent paving section. Use a hammer to pull the nails out of the ends of the keyed board and the stakes along it. If necessary, loosen the nails in a stake by pulling the stake away from the keyed board; wedge a pry bar or drive a wooden shim between them. After the nails are removed, rock each stake back and forth to loosen it and pull it out of the ground. Pull the keyed board away from the concrete using a pry bar *(above)*, working carefully to avoid chipping the edges of the concrete or damaging the keyed board. Repeat steps 7 to 14 for the subsequent paving section; if necessary, first reinstall the keyed board *(step 6)* to make a control joint along it or install a board without a key *(step 3)* along an outside edge.

REPAIRING A POST FOOTING

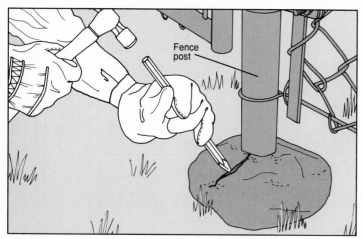

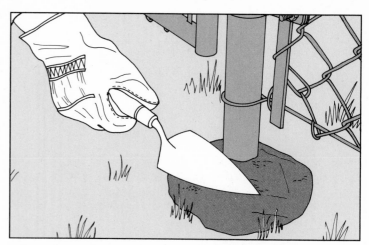

1 Removing the damage. Wearing work gloves and goggles, chip off the damaged concrete *(page 78)* using a bull-point chisel and a ball-peen hammer *(above)*. If the concrete is damaged below the surface, use a spade to cut and remove any sod and dig up the soil around the footing; dig to the depth required to chip off the damaged concrete. If the entire footing is damaged, replace it *(steps below)*. If a portion of the footing is damaged, clean loose particles off the un-damaged concrete using a stiff fiber brush and etch with muriatic acid *(page 91)*. For a small repair on the surface, apply concrete patching compound *(page 79)*.

2 Placing new concrete. For a large repair, use concrete *(page 85)*; if it does not have a bonding agent in it, first apply a bonding agent on the undamaged concrete *(page 79)*. Wearing work gloves, use a spade to mix the concrete in a wheelbarrow *(page 86)* and place it until the top of the footing is at least 1 inch above the ground. Shape the top of the footing with a mason's trowel, sloping it away from the post *(above)*. Cure the concrete *(page 90)*, then caulk around the base of the post. Use a spade to fill in around the footing with soil, grading it slightly away from the concrete. Tamp the soil with your feet, put back any sod removed and tamp again.

REPLACING A POST FOOTING

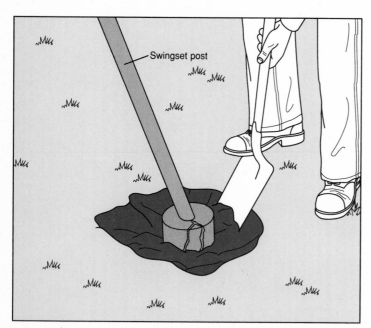

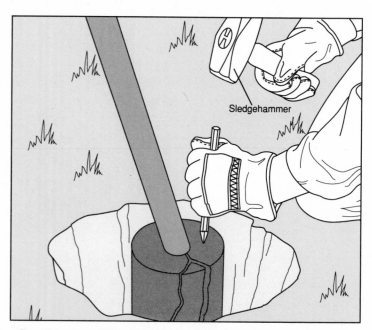

1 Digging up the footing. To replace a footing, use a spade to cut and remove any sod and dig up the soil around the footing *(above)*; dig to the depth required to reach the bottom of the footing. If the footing is for a post that is not independent and not easily isolated, such as with a swingset, as shown, chip off concrete to remove the footing *(step 2)*. If the footing is for a post that is independent or easily isolated, such as with a fence, disassemble any structure connected to it and, working with at least one helper, try pulling the post and footing out of the ground; if necessary, wedge 2-by-4s under the footing to use as levers.

2 Chipping off the concrete. Wearing work gloves and goggles, chip off the concrete *(page 78)* into chunks small enough to remove by hand using a bull-point chisel and a small sledge-hammer *(above)*. If you did not remove the post and footing, as shown, enlarge the hole using a spade to reach the entire footing, if necessary. If you removed the post and footing, position the footing on its side, supporting it with stones to keep it from moving, if necessary. Continue chipping off concrete until the entire footing is removed; work carefully to avoid damaging the post.

REPLACING A POST FOOTING (continued)

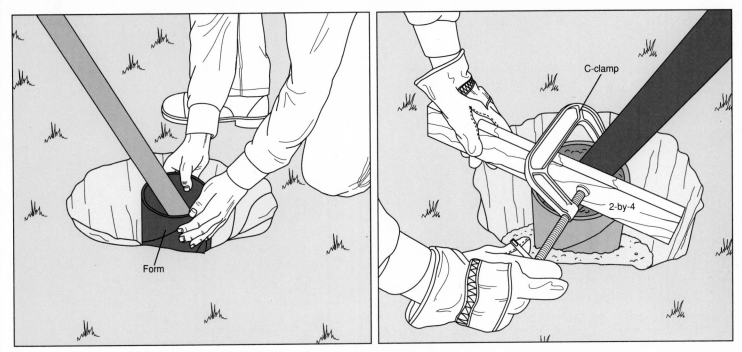

Form

C-clamp

2-by-4

3 **Installing a form and placing new concrete.** To keep a new footing from shifting in the ground, use a spade to enlarge the hole to a depth of 6 inches beyond the frostline and tamp the bottom of the hole with the end of a 2-by-4. Fill the hole with a 6-inch layer of gravel and tamp again. If desired, buy a cylindrical form 2 to 3 times the diameter or thickness of the post at a building supply center; a form is not necessary, however, and may be awkward to use if you did not remove the post. To install the form, cut it to length using a saw *(page 120)* and position it in the hole with the post in it *(above, left)*; position it high enough to place concrete up to at least 1 inch above ground level. If you did not remove the post, you may have to widen the hole or cut the form along its length and tie it closed in place using wire and pliers. After positioning the form, use the spade to backfill around it with soil, tamping after each 6-inch layer is applied; backfill and tamp until about 6 to 8 inches below ground level. Wearing work gloves, mix a batch of concrete in a wheelbarrow *(page 86)* and place it using the spade until the top of the footing is at least 1 inch above ground level. Check the position of the post and adjust it, if necessary. Shape the top of the footing with a mason's trowel, sloping it away from the post. Support the post in position until the concrete sets, bracing it, for example, with 2-by-4s and stakes or with a 2-by-4 and a C-clamp *(above, right)*.

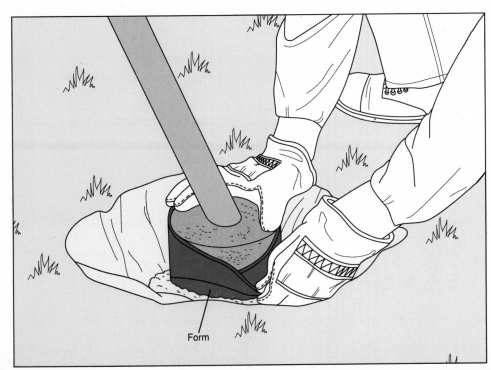

Form

4 **Curing the concrete and removing the form.** After the concrete sets for 48 hours, remove any braces used to support the post in position. If you used a form, peel back the top of it *(left)*, if desired, and cut it off using a utility knife. Keep the concrete damp until it cures for 5 days; cover it with wet sand or spray it periodically using a garden hose to prevent it from drying out. When the concrete cures, caulk around the base of the post. Use a spade to fill in around the footing with soil, grading it slightly away from the concrete. Tamp the soil with your feet, put back any sod removed and tamp again.

CLEANING AND REFINISHING STUCCO

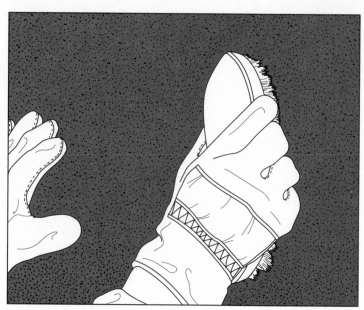

Washing off dirt and stains. Clean dirt off the surface with a garden hose. To avoid stains from the rundown of dirty water, presoak the surface first, working slowly from the bottom to the top of it using only a fine spray. Then, use a strong spray to dislodge dirt particles from the surface *(above)*, working slowly from the top to the bottom of it. To remove stains, refer to the chart on page 75 for guidance in choosing an appropriate cleaning agent and procedure. After applying any cleaning agent, rinse off the surface thoroughly using clean water. If stains cannot be removed or the stucco is discolored, repaint the surface *(step right)*.

Repainting the surface. Wash dirt and stains off the surface *(step left)*. To refinish the surface, buy cementitious paint at a building supply center and follow the label instructions to apply it; a primer may be required. Wearing rubber gloves and goggles, apply the paint while the surface is still damp, scrubbing it in with a stiff fiber brush *(above)*, or working it in with a stucco paintbrush or a long-nap roller. Apply at least one thick coat of the paint; on new stucco, two coats may be required. Keep the finish coat damp for at least 48 hours by misting it periodically with the fine spray of a garden hose.

REPAIRING A STUCCO CRACK

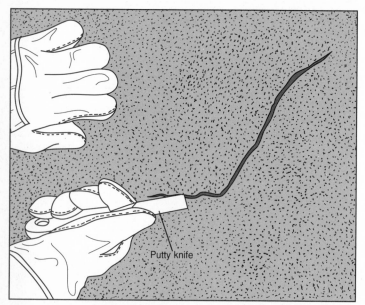

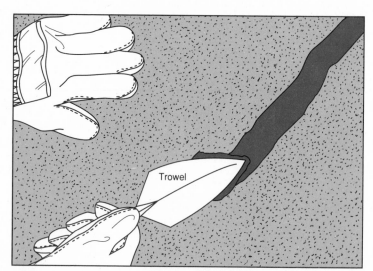

Trowel

1 **Preparing the crack.** Wearing work gloves and goggles, use a small putty knife to clean loose particles out of the crack, deepening it slightly and undercutting the edges. If the crack is wide, carefully chip off the damaged stucco and undercut the edges with a cold chisel and a ball-peen hammer *(page 78)*. Sweep dust out of the crack using a stiff fiber brush and soak the damaged area thoroughly with clean water.

Putty knife

2 **Applying stucco compound.** Buy premixed or ready-mixed stucco compound at a building supply center and follow the label instructions to apply it. Prepare premixed stucco compound in a bucket or on a scrap piece of plywood, adding water gradually and mixing with a stick until the compound is the consistency of a thick paste. Wearing work gloves, use a pointing trowel to work compound into the crack, packing it as tightly as possible *(above)*. Scrape off excess with the flat edge of the trowel blade and use the bottom surface of the trowel to smooth the compound in the crack. Match the texture of the undamaged stucco *(page 104)* and repaint the surface *(step above, right)*.

REPAIRING A STUCCO HOLE

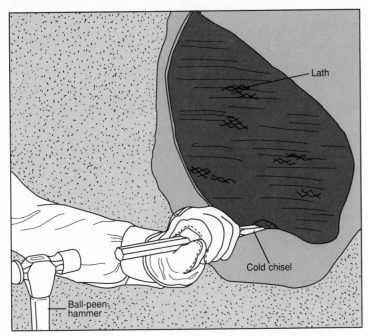

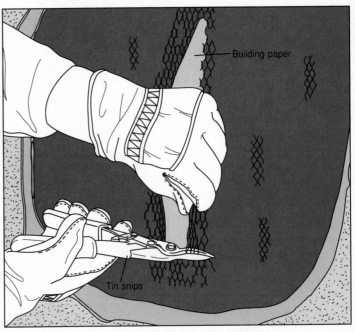

1 **Removing the damaged stucco.** If the hole is larger than 2 feet square, the entire surface may have to be replaced; consult a professional. Otherwise, wearing work gloves and goggles, use a cold chisel and a ball-peen hammer *(above)* to carefully chip off the damaged stucco, exposing the metal lath behind it, and undercut the edges *(page 78)*. Clean off loose particles with a stiff fiber brush.

2 **Removing the damaged lath.** Inspect the lath for rust and breaks in its webs. If the lath is not damaged, make a scarifier and prepare stucco compound *(step 4)*. If the lath is damaged, replace it. Wearing work gloves and goggles, use tin snips to cut off and remove the damaged lath section *(above)*. Work carefully, holding the lath with one hand while you cut it, as shown, to avoid tearing any building paper behind it.

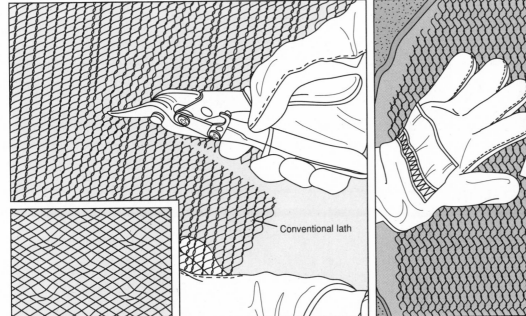

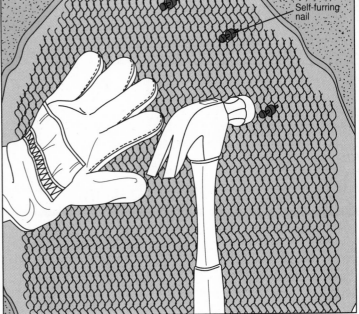

3 **Installing new lath.** Buy galvanized lath and fasteners at a building supply center; use conventional lath and self-furring nails, or self-furring lath and conventional nails. Self-furring lath *(inset)* has dimples which position it correctly, 1/4 inch away from the surface behind it; self-furring nails *(page 124)* perform the same function for conventional lath. Wearing work gloves and goggles, use tin snips to cut a replacement section of conventional *(above, left)* or self-furring lath 2 to 4 inches larger than the damaged section. Position the lath and drive in nails every 4 to 6 inches along the edges *(above, right)*.

REPAIRING A STUCCO HOLE (continued)

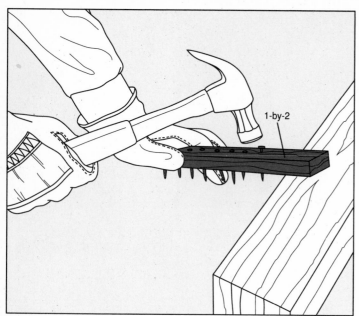

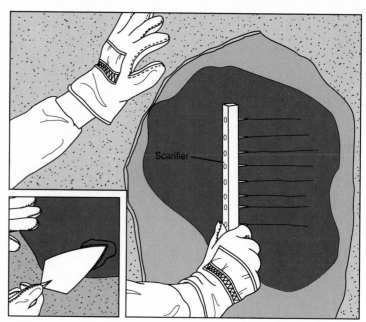

4 **Making a scarifier and preparing stucco compound.** Use a scarifier to help the bonding between coats of stucco compound. To make a scarifier, saw off *(page 120)* a 10- to 12-inch length of 1-by-2 and drive 3-inch nails into the center of it every 1 inch along it *(above)*. Start each nail with the 1-by-2 section under it positioned on a solid, flat surface; then, drive the nail through, as shown, with the 1-by-2 section under it overhanging the edge of the surface. Buy premixed or ready-mixed stucco compound at a building supply center. Prepare premixed stucco compound in a bucket or on a scrap piece of plywood, adding water gradually and mixing with a stick until the compound is the consistency of a thick paste. Soak the damaged area with clean water.

5 **Applying stucco compound.** Wearing work gloves, use a mason's trowel to apply the stucco compound, following the label instructions. Work compound into the hole, packing it against the lath as tightly as possible *(inset)*. Fill the hole to within 1/4 inch of the undamaged surface. Scrape off excess compound with the flat edge of the trowel blade and use the bottom surface of the trowel to smooth the compound in the hole. Drag the scarifier lightly across the surface, scratching lines into the compound *(above)*. Allow the compound to set for 48 hours, misting it periodically with the fine spray of a garden hose. Use the mason's trowel to apply a finish coat of compound flush with the undamaged surface; then, match the texture of the undamaged stucco *(step 6)*.

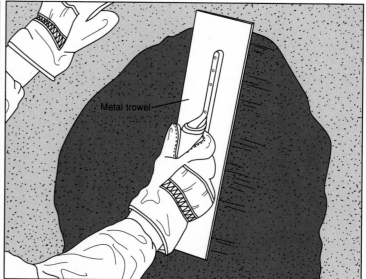

6 **Matching the stucco texture.** Matching a stucco texture requires practice and patience; begin as soon as the finish coat of compound starts to set. Refer to page 105 for guidance in identifying the texture of the undamaged stucco and adopting a procedure to match it. Experiment, if necessary; sometimes a combination of procedures may be required. Wear work gloves to protect your hands. For a coarse, uniform texture, use a wooden float. Working from the center of the repair to the edges, sweep the float across the surface in a broad arcing

motion *(above, left)* or in a tight circular motion, overlapping passes. For a smooth, even texture, use a metal rectangular trowel; slide it slowly across the surface *(above, right)*, applying even, moderate pressure, and keep the leading edge lifted slightly to avoid digging into the compound. After matching the stucco texture, allow the compound to cure, misting it periodically with the fine spray of a garden hose. When the compound cures, repaint the surface *(page 102)*.

CREATING STUCCO TEXTURES

Swirl finish. When the finish coat begins to set, wear work gloves and use a paintbrush to lightly stroke the surface with the bristle tips *(above)*; work with the width of the paintbrush, as shown. Dampen a clean rag with water and wipe off compound that builds up on the bristles. Allow the compound to cure, misting it periodically with the fine spray of a garden hose. Repaint the surface *(page 102)*.

Stipple finish. When the finish coat begins to set, wear work gloves and gently press the bristle tips of a stiff fiber brush into the surface *(above)* without sweeping or overlapping passes. Dampen a clean rag with water and wipe off compound that builds up on the bristles. Allow the compound to cure, misting it periodically with the fine spray of a garden hose. Repaint the surface *(page 102)*.

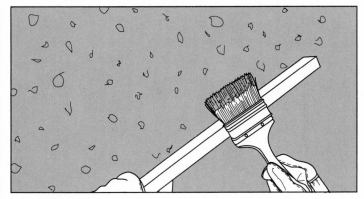

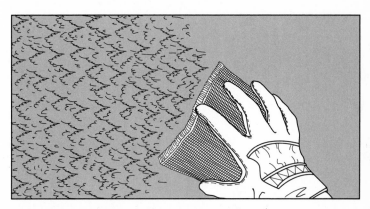

Dash or spatter finish. When the finish coat begins to set, wear work gloves and prepare a thin batch of premixed or ready-mixed stucco compound, adding extra water to dilute it. Load a paintbrush with compound and spatter it onto the surface by striking a short piece of 1-by-2 *(above)*. Allow the compound to cure, misting it periodically with the fine spray of a garden hose. Repaint the surface *(page 102)*.

Rough finish. When the finish coat begins to set, wear work gloves and press a small piece of thick-pile carpeting into the surface *(above)* without wiping or overlapping passes. Clean off compound that builds up on the pile in water and squeeze out the excess. Allow the compound to cure, misting it periodically with the fine spray of a garden hose. Repaint the surface *(page 102)*.

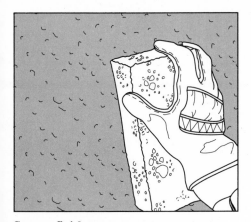

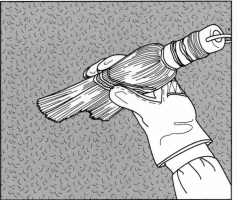

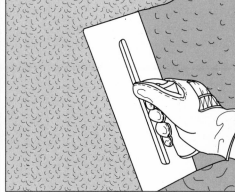

Sponge finish. When the finish coat begins to set, wear work gloves and press a damp sponge into the surface *(above)* without wiping or overlapping passes. Let the compound cure, misting it periodically with the fine spray of a garden hose. Repaint the surface *(page 102)*.

Travertine (marble-like) finish. Before the finish coat begins to set, wear work gloves and gently jab the bristles of a whisk broom into the surface *(above, left)* without sweeping or over-lapping passes; wipe excess compound off the bristles. When the compound begins to set, use a metal rectangular trowel to sweep lightly across it in a broad, arcing motion *(above, right)*, smoothing the edges slightly without filling the craters. Allow the compound to cure, misting it periodically with the fine spray of a garden hose. Repaint the surface *(page 102)*.

TOOLS & TECHNIQUES

This section introduces tools and techniques that are basic to repairing brick, stone and concrete structures, such as moving heavy masonry units *(page 111)*, using a wheelbarrow *(page 112)* and working safely on the roof; refer to page 112 for the proper use of a ladder, page 114 for the proper use of scaffolding. The section on working with mortar *(page 117)* includes basic mortaring techniques. Charts on mixing mortar *(page 117)* and on masonry fasteners *(page 124)* are designed for easy reference. You can handle most repairs with the basic kit of tools and supplies shown below and on pages 108 and 109. Special tools, such as a demolition hammer, an extension ladder and scaffolding can be obtained at a tool rental agency. For the best results, always use the right tool for the job — and be sure to use the tool correctly.

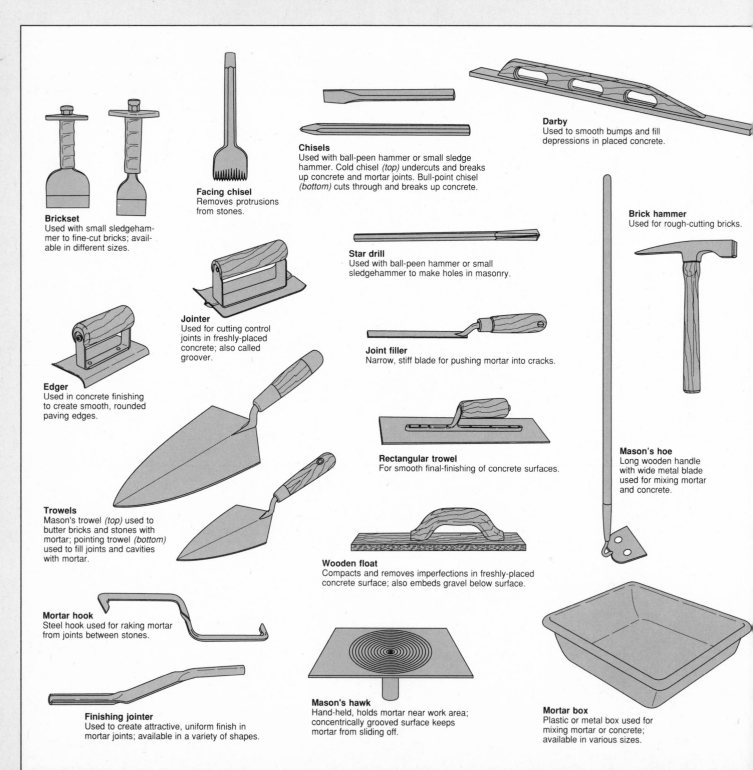

Brickset
Used with small sledgehammer to fine-cut bricks; available in different sizes.

Facing chisel
Removes protrusions from stones.

Chisels
Used with ball-peen hammer or small sledge hammer. Cold chisel *(top)* undercuts and breaks up concrete and mortar joints. Bull-point chisel *(bottom)* cuts through and breaks up concrete.

Darby
Used to smooth bumps and fill depressions in placed concrete.

Jointer
Used for cutting control joints in freshly-placed concrete; also called groover.

Star drill
Used with ball-peen hammer or small sledgehammer to make holes in masonry.

Brick hammer
Used for rough-cutting bricks.

Edger
Used in concrete finishing to create smooth, rounded paving edges.

Joint filler
Narrow, stiff blade for pushing mortar into cracks.

Trowels
Mason's trowel *(top)* used to butter bricks and stones with mortar; pointing trowel *(bottom)* used to fill joints and cavities with mortar.

Rectangular trowel
For smooth final-finishing of concrete surfaces.

Mason's hoe
Long wooden handle with wide metal blade used for mixing mortar and concrete.

Wooden float
Compacts and removes imperfections in freshly-placed concrete surface; also embeds gravel below surface.

Mortar hook
Steel hook used for raking mortar from joints between stones.

Finishing jointer
Used to create attractive, uniform finish in mortar joints; available in a variety of shapes.

Mason's hawk
Hand-held, holds mortar near work area; concentrically grooved surface keeps mortar from sliding off.

Mortar box
Plastic or metal box used for mixing mortar or concrete; available in various sizes.

When shopping for new tools, purchase the highest-quality ones you can afford. Take the time to care for and store your tools properly. When working with mortar, concrete or stucco, clean tools immediately after use; keep metal tools from rusting by applying a thin coat of oil, and remove any rust with steel wool *(page 110)*. Store tools on a shelf safely away from children, in a locked metal or plastic tool box, or hang them up on hooks. When a saw blade becomes dull, buy a replacement or have it sharpened by a professional. While you are working, avoid laying tools on the ground unprotected; spread out a drop cloth or a tarp for them. Clean and lubricate power tools according to the manufacturer's instructions.

A thorough house inspection each spring can help you pinpoint many masonry problems early — and their causes.

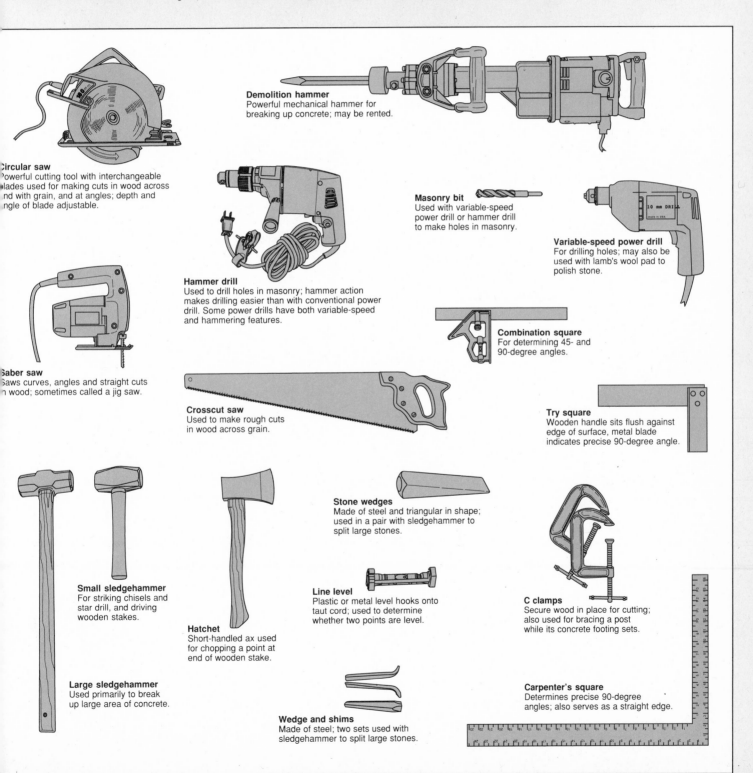

Demolition hammer
Powerful mechanical hammer for breaking up concrete; may be rented.

Circular saw
Powerful cutting tool with interchangeable blades used for making cuts in wood across and with grain, and at angles; depth and angle of blade adjustable.

Masonry bit
Used with variable-speed power drill or hammer drill to make holes in masonry.

Variable-speed power drill
For drilling holes; may also be used with lamb's wool pad to polish stone.

Hammer drill
Used to drill holes in masonry; hammer action makes drilling easier than with conventional power drill. Some power drills have both variable-speed and hammering features.

Combination square
For determining 45- and 90-degree angles.

Saber saw
Saws curves, angles and straight cuts in wood; sometimes called a jig saw.

Crosscut saw
Used to make rough cuts in wood across grain.

Try square
Wooden handle sits flush against edge of surface, metal blade indicates precise 90-degree angle.

Stone wedges
Made of steel and triangular in shape; used in a pair with sledgehammer to split large stones.

Small sledgehammer
For striking chisels and star drill, and driving wooden stakes.

Line level
Plastic or metal level hooks onto taut cord; used to determine whether two points are level.

C clamps
Secure wood in place for cutting; also used for bracing a post while its concrete footing sets.

Hatchet
Short-handled ax used for chopping a point at end of wooden stake.

Large sledgehammer
Used primarily to break up large area of concrete.

Carpenter's square
Determines precise 90-degree angles; also serves as a straight edge.

Wedge and shims
Made of steel; two sets used with sledgehammer to split large stones.

Clean out clogged gutters and downspouts; inspect flashing and eavestroughing for breaks and repair any damage to them as soon as possible. Check the base of the house for drainage problems *(page 110)*. Covering the job site with plastic or newspapers *(page 111)* before you begin a repair can save you hours of cleanup time and help avoid damage to nearby plants. Make sure the work area is safe by keeping it clean and free of clutter. To work on the roof, use a sturdy ladder to get there; always have a helper hold the base of an extension ladder while you climb up and down *(page 112)*. Do not work on a wall from a ladder; instead, rent scaffolding *(page 114)*. Attempt chimney repairs only on a roof with a pitch no more than 4 in 12 — that is, the roof rises 4 feet vertically for every 12 feet horizontally; follow all safety procedures for working

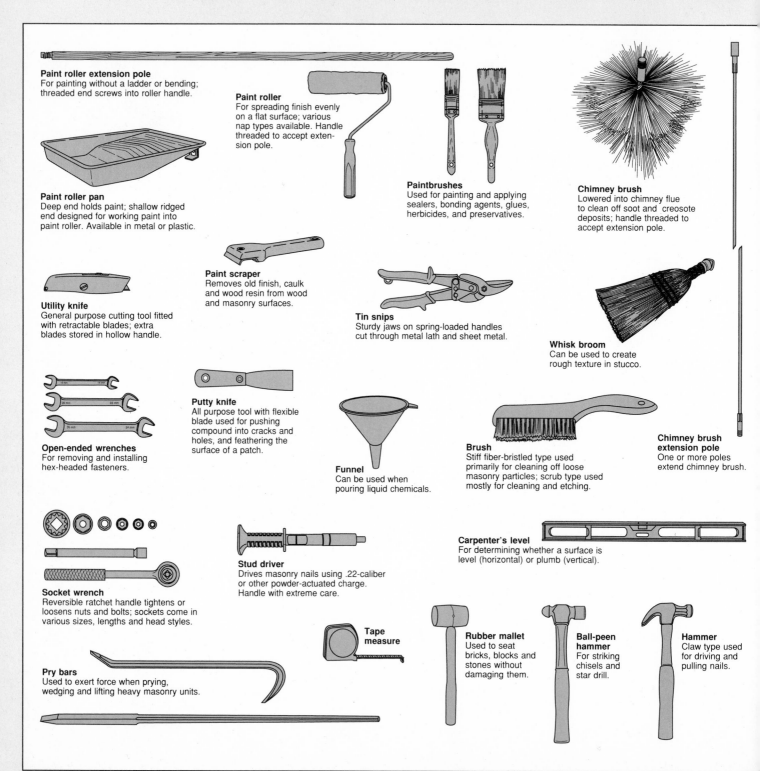

Paint roller extension pole
For painting without a ladder or bending; threaded end screws into roller handle.

Paint roller
For spreading finish evenly on a flat surface; various nap types available. Handle threaded to accept extension pole.

Paintbrushes
Used for painting and applying sealers, bonding agents, glues, herbicides, and preservatives.

Chimney brush
Lowered into chimney flue to clean off soot and creosote deposits; handle threaded to accept extension pole.

Paint roller pan
Deep end holds paint; shallow ridged end designed for working paint into paint roller. Available in metal or plastic.

Paint scraper
Removes old finish, caulk and wood resin from wood and masonry surfaces.

Utility knife
General purpose cutting tool fitted with retractable blades; extra blades stored in hollow handle.

Tin snips
Sturdy jaws on spring-loaded handles cut through metal lath and sheet metal.

Whisk broom
Can be used to create rough texture in stucco.

Open-ended wrenches
For removing and installing hex-headed fasteners.

Putty knife
All purpose tool with flexible blade used for pushing compound into cracks and holes, and feathering the surface of a patch.

Funnel
Can be used when pouring liquid chemicals.

Brush
Stiff fiber-bristled type used primarily for cleaning off loose masonry particles; scrub type used mostly for cleaning and etching.

Chimney brush extension pole
One or more poles extend chimney brush.

Socket wrench
Reversible ratchet handle tightens or loosens nuts and bolts; sockets come in various sizes, lengths and head styles.

Stud driver
Drives masonry nails using .22-caliber or other powder-actuated charge. Handle with extreme care.

Carpenter's level
For determining whether a surface is level (horizontal) or plumb (vertical).

Tape measure

Rubber mallet
Used to seat bricks, blocks and stones without damaging them.

Ball-peen hammer
For striking chisels and star drill.

Hammer
Claw type used for driving and pulling nails.

Pry bars
Used to exert force when prying, wedging and lifting heavy masonry units.

on the roof *(page 114)*. For repairs on a roof with a pitch greater than 4 in 12, consult a professional.

Also follow safety rules when working with power tools. Do not operate power tools in a damp area, and wear the recommended safety gear. Always use grounded or double-insulated power tools and plug them into a grounded outlet or a portable ground-fault circuit interrupter (GFCI). Keep an ABC-rated fire extinguisher nearby *(page 11)*, along with a well-stocked first-aid kit. Wear the proper protective clothing and gear for the job; when working with a stud driver or a demolition hammer, wear ear protection as well as work gloves and goggles. Especially when working above the ground, keep others away from the work area. If in doubt about your ability to complete a repair, do not hesitate to consult a professional.

Steel-toed work boots
Protect toes when working with heavy objects.

Ear protectors
Protect ears from noise of demolition hammer and stud driver.

Caulking gun
Accepts replaceable caulk tubes; trigger-operated ratchet slowly pushes out caulking compound.

Work gloves
Heavy gloves protect hands against splinters and abrasions, and burns when working with mortar and concrete.

Dust mask
Prevents inhalation of masonry dust, sawdust and chimney soot.

Garden hose
May be made of rubber, nylon, vinyl or plastic; available with a variety of nozzles and heads. Perforated hose used to clean stone walls should be equipped with plastic coupling.

Spade
A multi-purpose digger. Square blade useful for slicing through sod or edging around a form; pointed blade for digging into compacted soil.

Duct tape
Waterproof tape used to hold plastic against masonry.

Rubber gloves
Protect hands from burns when working with chemicals.

Safety goggles
Protect eyes from chips, dust and chemicals. Should be worn when breaking concrete and chipping mortar.

Pail
Plastic container used for mixing cleaning agents and chemicals.

Shovel
Can be used to place and spread sand, gravel or concrete.

Wheelbarrow
Handy for transporting materials and mixing concrete.

Push broom
Used on large, horizontal surfaces for cleaning and sweeping sand into joints; push broom or other stiff broom can be used for rough final-finishing of concrete.

Extension ladder
Available in various heights; used for access to roof.

PREVENTING MOISTURE DAMAGE

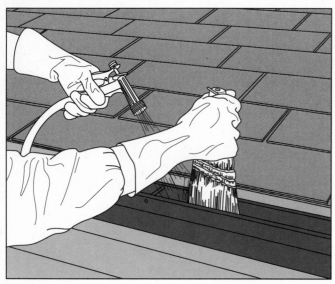

Checking for moisture problems. Spalling or flaking, mildew and efflorescence (white, powdery deposits of dissolved salts) are common problems on masonry surfaces, and may result from faulty drainage. With some simple preventive maintenance, you can often stop moisture problems at the source. Several times a year, clean fallen leaves and other debris out of house gutters *(left)* and downspouts. Inspect flashing around the chimney for corrosion and use roofing cement to seal any holes *(page 40)*; if necessary, recaulk the joints between the chimney and the siding *(page 40)*. When replacing a chimney cap, make sure the space between the flue liner and the chimney cap is properly sealed with mortar; water penetration can lead to severe damage. Keep weep holes in exterior brick walls of your house clear *(page 30)* and clean out retaining wall drainpipes *(page 31)*. If the basement leaks, inspect the ground outdoors around the foundation walls; if the soil has settled enough to prevent water from draining away from the house, add more soil, compact it, then slope it away from the house. If a moisture problem in the basement persists, consult a professional.

CLEANING TOOLS

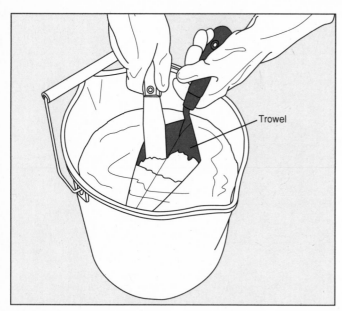

Trowel

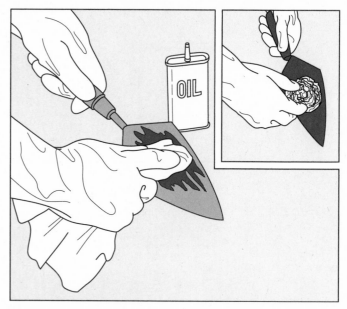

OIL

Washing off masonry tools. If your work with mortar, concrete or stucco is temporarily suspended, place hand tools in a bucket of water; otherwise, clean them right away. Wearing rubber gloves, use a bucket of clean water to rinse off the tools; if you have many tools to clean, put them in a wheelbarrow and hose them. Remove hardened particles using a stiff fiber brush or a putty knife *(above)*. Dig a hole with a spade and dump the used water; masonry particles are caustic and can ruin lawns and clog drains. Use a clean, absorbent cloth to dry off each tool. Clean a portable cement mixer as shown on page 86.

Removing rust. Clean rust off a tool as soon as you notice it. Wearing rubber gloves, dip the rusted tool in clean water, then rub off the rust with a piece of steel wool *(inset)*; rub until the metal is shiny. Use a clean, absorbent cloth to dry off the tool, then use another cloth to coat the metal of the tool with a small amount of light machine oil *(above)*; be sure not to get any oil on the tool handle.

PROTECTING AREAS NEAR THE WORK SITE

Covering plants and undamaged surfaces. Spilled cleaning solutions, mortar and concrete can damage grass and plants as well as paving, wood decks and other structures. Before beginning a cleaning job or repairs using mortar or concrete, cover plants and nearby surfaces with a large plastic drop cloth *(left)*; protect surrounding masonry from mortar or concrete spills by using duct tape to cover the surface with newspapers *(inset)*. When the job is finished, roll up the plastic drop cloth and shake any spilled materials into a garbage can. Also remove and throw out any newspapers used.

WORKING SAFELY WITH MASONRY

Handling heavy materials. Repairs to masonry walls, patios, driveways and walkways can be done safely if the materials are handled properly. Wear work gloves to protect your hands and steel-toed work boots to protect your feet; be sure to take periodic breaks. When loading a concrete block or other heavy masonry unit into a wheelbarrow, for example, minimize the use of back muscles: Always lift heavy materials with a straight back *(above)*, relying on the muscles in your legs for strength.

Rolling heavy units up a ramp. To place a heavy masonry unit such as a stone at a height above the ground, use a board as a ramp; in most instances, a 2-by-6 is sufficient. Position one end of the board at the final position for the stone and the other end of the board on the ground—or on a concrete block, if necessary, to decrease the ramp slope. Wearing work gloves, roll the stone end over end up the ramp *(above)* and into place. If you cannot budge the stone, work with a helper or use a longer board.

USING A WHEELBARROW

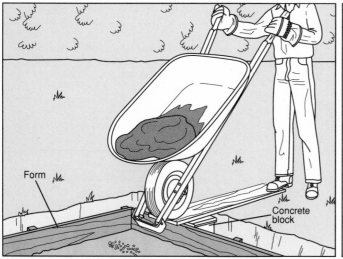

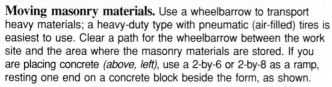

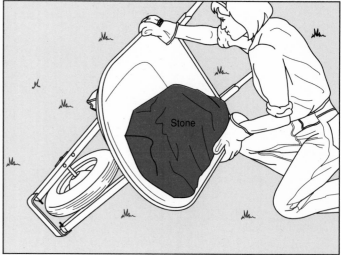

Moving masonry materials. Use a wheelbarrow to transport heavy materials; a heavy-duty type with pneumatic (air-filled) tires is easiest to use. Clear a path for the wheelbarrow between the work site and the area where the masonry materials are stored. If you are placing concrete *(above, left)*, use a 2-by-6 or 2-by-8 as a ramp, resting one end on a concrete block beside the form, as shown.

To move a heavy stone, lay the wheelbarrow on its side. Wearing work gloves, roll the stone into the wheelbarrow; be careful not to twist your back. Work with a helper, if possible. Use both hands to push the wheelbarrow upright *(above, right)*, gripping it by the sides, as shown. **Caution:** To avoid back injury, do not use the wheelbarrow handles to reposition the wheelbarrow.

USING A LADDER

Use a ladder to inspect high walls and to get to and from the roof; never, however, set up a ladder near overhead power lines. For extensive work on a wall at a height above 5 feet, use scaffolding *(page 114)*. To work on the roof, make sure the ladder extends at least 3 feet beyond the roof line. Depending on the height you want to reach, use a 12-foot straight ladder or an extension ladder; both can be obtained at a tool rental agency. Select a Type 1 industrial ladder with non-skid rubber feet.

1 Positioning a ladder. Place the ladder flat on the ground, perpendicular to the wall where it will be positioned, with its feet out from the wall by at least 1/4 of the ladder height —out 3 feet, for example, for a 12-foot ladder; if you are using an extension ladder, position it with the movable section on the bottom. Standing at the end of the ladder farthest from the wall, use both hands to lift the end of the ladder above your head. Walk under the ladder toward the opposite end of it, moving your hands from rung to rung *(left)* until you can position the ladder against the wall. If the ladder is heavy, work side-by-side with a helper using the same procedure.

USING A LADDER (continued)

Locking
mechanism

2 **Raising an extension ladder.** If you are working with
a straight ladder, secure the feet *(step 3)*. If you are working
with an extension ladder, use the hoisting rope to raise the
movable section to the proper height *(above)*; brace the ladder by
resting one foot on the bottom rung, as shown, while you pull the
hoisting rope, lifting the ladder slightly off the wall as you raise it to
avoid damaging the wall. If the ladder is heavy, have a helper stand
behind it and support it. If you are raising the ladder to reach the
roof, you may need to reposition the feet farther from the wall in order for the top to clear the roof edge. The movable section should
lock in place; check that the locking mechanism is secure. Make
sure that the two ladder sections overlap by at least 3 feet and
that the ladder is resting firmly against the wall or roof edge;
if you raised it to the roof, it should extend at least 3 feet, or
rungs, above the roof line.

3 **Securing the ladder feet.** Make sure that the ladder feet
are placed on hard, flat ground, at a distance from the wall
equal to 1/4 of the ladder height. If the ground is uneven or
soft, position a board the correct distance away from the wall and
lift the ladder to place the feet on it *(above)*; if the ladder is heavy,
work with a helper. Make a stake *(page 120)* and use a small sledgehammer to drive it into the ground near the ladder, between it and
the wall. Use a rope to secure the ladder siderails to the stake.

4 **Climbing the ladder.** Wear foot gear with a well-defined
heel for a secure grip on the rungs. When climbing up or
down the ladder, face it and use both hands to grasp the
rungs—not the siderails; have a helper steady the ladder *(above)*.
Avoid carrying tools in your hands or pockets; place tools in a
bucket and hoist it up with a rope looped over a ladder rung.
Do not overreach: Keep your belt buckle within the limits of the
siderails. If necessary, use the siderails as guide tracks to pull up
bulky materials such as a chimney cap form *(page 121)*, working
from the roof with a rope.

WORKING SAFELY ON THE ROOF

Security on the roof. Work only on a roof with a pitch no more than 4 in 12—that is, the roof rises 4 feet vertically every 12 feet horizontally; for a steeper roof, consult a professional. Never walk on a roof with slate or terracotta tiles; they can be easily damaged. Work on a roof only in good weather conditions and when there is no wind. Make sure someone is within earshot and can lend assistance if necessary. Wear soft-soled shoes and work gloves. Keep people and pets away from the work site.

Use an extension ladder *(page 112)* to gain access to the roof. For maximum security, wear a safety harness attached behind you to a rope; throw the rope over the roof ridge and tie it to a permanent structure. If the ladder is resting against eaves-troughing, place wood blocks in the gutter to keep from crushing it. For a secure toehold to the roof, rent a second ladder fitted with a pair of ladder hooks; hoist the ladder up to the roof with a rope *(left)* and hang it from the roof ridge.

WORKING WITH SCAFFOLDING

For extensive work on a wall at a height above 5 feet, rent scaffolding at a tool rental company. Estimate the height at which you will work and order the appropriate number of scaffolding units—each unit includes end frames, cross braces, lock arms, baseplate jacks and wooden planks. When ordering, ask for installation directions; some companies will deliver the scaffolding.

Use the procedure below to set up the scaffolding; work with a helper and wear work gloves. Be sure the planks extend at least 1 foot beyond the end frames and anchor each end of the scaffolding *(page 115)*. Follow the same safety guidelines for climbing scaffolding as for a ladder *(page 113)*. **Caution:** Pay attention to where you are stepping; do not rely on a safety rope to catch you.

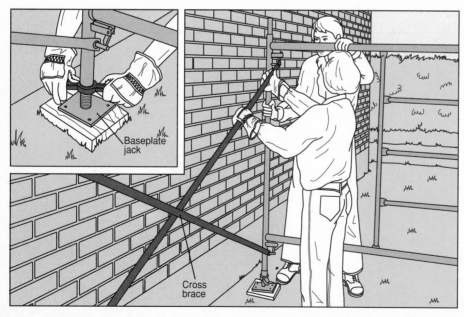

1 Installing the first level. Many types of scaffolding have holes in the baseplate jacks; for maximum stability, nail a 1-inch thick piece of wood under each one. Have a helper hold one end frame upright and raised, then slide a baseplate jack into the bottom of each end of the end frame; make sure it rests on solid, even ground. Spread the arms of a cross brace and slip them into place on one end of the end frame, attaching first the lower arm, then the upper arm *(left)*. (The cross brace arms are usually held in place by a gravity-type lock, as shown.) Install a cross brace on the other end of the end frame the same way. Use the same procedure to set up the second end frame and attach the other end of the cross brace arms. Rock the scaffolding to check its stability; if it is uneven, adjust the baseplate jacks *(inset)* until it is steady.

WORKING WITH SCAFFOLDING (continued)

2 **Installing the other levels.** Slide at least three planks into position on the end frames; the planks should extend at least 1 foot beyond each end frame. Climb up the scaffolding and stand on the planks to install the second level. Have a helper pass an end frame up to you, and fit it onto one of the end frames for the first level; align the climbing bars on it with those on the end frame below it for easy climbing. Install cross braces as you did in step 1, then repeat the procedure with another end frame at the other end of the second level *(left)*. If the scaffolding is equipped with lock arms to prevent the levels from separating, install them: Slide each one over the top assembly pin of the lower end frame and the bottom assembly pin of the upper end frame *(inset)*. With a helper, move the planks from the first level to the second level. Install other levels the same way as you did for the second level; every fourth level, change the side on which the climbing bars are positioned and leave the planks in place.

3 **Attaching a safety rope.** Every scaffold should have a safety rail or rope secured along the edge of the plank farthest from the wall to prevent anyone from falling. If the scaffolding is not equipped with a safety rail, tie a 1/2-inch rope at waist level between the end frames at the end of the plank *(above)*.

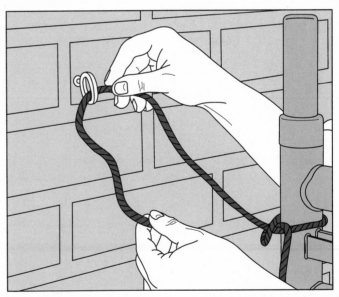

4 **Anchoring the scaffolding to the wall.** Anchor each end of the scaffolding to a window or to the wall. To use a window, tie one end of a rope to an end frame and tie the other end of the rope to a 2-by-4 positioned indoors across the window. To use the wall, use an eye bolt and anchor: drill a hole in the wall for the anchor *(page 124)*, fit it into the hole and screw in the eye bolt; then, tie a rope between the eye bolt and an end frame *(above)*.

WORKING WITH MURIATIC ACID

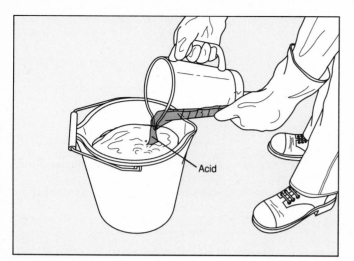

1 Diluting muriatic acid. Muriatic acid, available at a building supply center, is used for etching concrete to improve the bonding of a patch *(page 91)* and for cleaning efflorescence and old mortar off clay bricks *(page 20)*. Wearing rubber gloves and goggles, use a plastic bucket *(above)* or container to dilute the acid in water, following the label instructions for the correct proportions. **Caution:** Always add acid to water; never add water to acid. If you are using the acid for cleaning, prepare only a small amount of the solution and test it on the surface first *(step 2)*.

2 Testing the acid solution. Wearing rubber gloves and goggles, dip a stiff fiber brush into the solution and scrub it onto an inconspicuous spot on the surface. Wait one week; if the spot is not damaged by the solution, dilute more muriatic acid *(step 1)* and apply it on the entire surface using the same procedure *(above)*. After cleaning, sprinkle a layer of sodium bicarbonate (baking soda) on the surface to neutralize the solution and rinse off the surface thoroughly with clean water. Also neutralize any unused solution *(step below)*.

DISPOSING OF ACID SOLUTIONS AND CHEMICALS

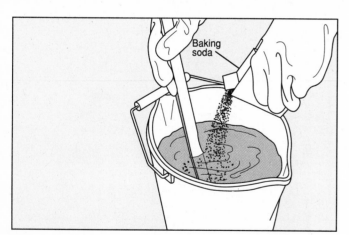

1 Neutralizing acid solutions and chemicals. Before disposing of unused acid solutions and other chemicals, neutralize them, if possible, following any instructions given on the label. For example, to neutralize a bucketful of acid solution, wear rubber gloves and goggles, and add the contents of a 1-pound box of sodium bicarbonate (baking soda); use a stick to stir the solution *(above)*. Dispose of a neutralized acid solution or chemical as you would another liquid. If you cannot neutralize an acid solution or chemical, store it *(step 2)* for safe disposal later.

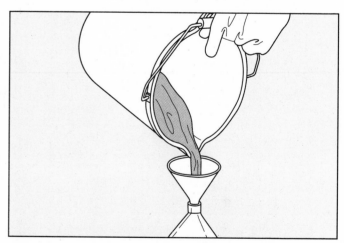

2 Storing acid solutions and chemicals. To dispose of an acid solution or chemical that you cannot neutralize, wear rubber gloves and goggles to pour it into a glass or plastic container *(above)*. Label the container with its contents and store it out of reach until you can dispose of it safely. Many communities have designated Household Hazardous Waste Clean-up Days; if your community does not, consult your fire department or local environmental agency for the proper disposal method.

WORKING WITH MORTAR

Mortar is the basic bonding material that holds bricks, blocks and stones together; it must be properly mixed in the right proportions. For most jobs, you can produce workable mortar using one of the recipes below. (Different proportions may be required, especially in colder climates; check your local building code, or consult your local builders association or masonry distributor.) Use one of two types of cement: Portland cement, a bonding agent, must be mixed with hydrated lime which gives the mixture workability; masonry cement is a portland cement and lime mixture. All recipes use finely-graded building sand and clean water (preferably with low mineral content to prevent efflorescence). For small repairs, premixed mortar is affordable; simply add water. Because the exact amount of water required for mortar depends on the humidity, the temperature and the moisture in the sand, there is no recommended water ratio. Follow the guidelines in step 2 below to judge the correct amount of water to add. If the mortar begins to dry out while you are working, retemper it by adding a small amount of water; retemper a batch only once. If the mortar is older than 2 1/2 hours, throw it away and mix a new batch. Use the techniques in steps 3 to 5 on page 118 to mortar uniform masonry units such as bricks and blocks; while the same procedure can be used on uniform, finely-cut stone, stone usually is irregular and must be mortared one unit at a time.

MORTAR	USES	DRY INGREDIENTS
TYPE N	Used for outdoor, above-ground masonry subjected to severe weathering	1 part portland cement*, 1 part hydrated lime and 6 parts sand
		1 part type II masonry cement and 3 parts sand
TYPE M	Used for general masonry and below-ground masonry in contact with soil, e.g. foundations, retaining walls, walkways	1 part portland cement*, 1/4 part hydrated lime and 3 parts sand
		1 part portland cement*, 1 part type II masonry cement and 6 parts sand
TYPE S	Used for masonry subjected to lateral force, e.g. walls designed to resist strong winds	1 part portland cement*, 1/2 part hydrated lime and 4 1/2 parts sand
		1/2 part portland cement*, 1 part type II masonry cement and 4 1/2 parts sand
FIRECLAY	Used for interior fireplace work where resistance to heat is required	1 part fireclay mortar (available premixed) and 3 parts sand

*White portland cement is recommended for light and colored mortar.

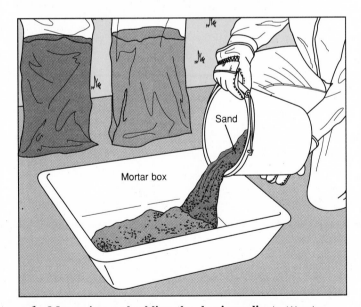

1 **Measuring and adding the dry ingredients.** Wearing work gloves, follow one of the recipes above, measuring the dry ingredients in a bucket or other container; for most home repairs, a mortar box is a convenient size for mixing. First, measure and pour the sand into the mortar box *(above)*, then measure and add the cement. Mix the sand and cement thoroughly with a mason's hoe or a trowel. If hydrated lime is called for in the recipe, measure and add it to the other dry ingredients.

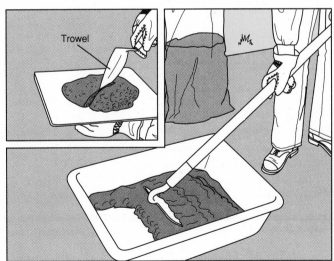

2 **Mixing in water and testing the mortar.** Wearing work gloves, use a mason's hoe to make a depression in the dry ingredients. Add clean water, a little at a time, mixing it in thoroughly with the hoe *(above)*. When the mortar keeps its shape, test its consistency: Place a small rectangular mound on a hawk and slice down the center of it with a trowel *(inset)*. Properly mixed mortar will hold its shape. If the mix collapses, it is too wet; add more dry ingredients in the correct proportions. If the the mix crumbles or is stiff, add more water, a little at a time. To mortar a course of bricks, blocks or uniform stones, go to step 3.

WORKING WITH MORTAR (CONTINUED)

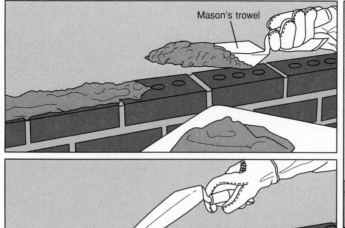

3 **Throwing and smoothing the mortar.** Wearing work gloves, load a
small amount of the mortar batch onto a mason's hawk. Holding a mason's trowel
between your thumb and forefinger, scoop up mortar onto it and position it with the
tip of its blade at the end of the mortar bed *(above, left top)*. Then, flip the trowel over,
rolling the mortar off it and into a straight line *(above, left bottom)*, forming a bed 3/4 to
1 inch thick. With practice, you should be able to form a straight-lined mortar bed 3 to 4
bricks long. If the mortar bed is straight and evenly distributed, go to step 4. If the mortar
bed is spread unevenly, smooth it out with the bottom of the trowel *(above, right)*.

4 **Furrowing the mortar bed.** Wearing work gloves, use
a mason's trowel to furrow the mortar bed: Run the tip of the
trowel blade down the center of the mortar bed, carving a
shallow furrow in it *(above)*. (This spreads out the mortar slightly,
allowing it to be distributed evenly when a brick is pressed down
into position on it.) Lay the first brick on the mortar bed, overlapping
the joint between the bricks in the course below it, and tap it into
the mortar using the end of the trowel handle until the joint is 3/8 to
3/4 inch thick. Use the trowel to butter the end of the second brick
and butt it against the end of the first brick, using the same procedure to form a 3/8- to 3/4-inch joint under it, and between it and the
first brick. Lay other bricks in the row, or course, the same way.

5 **Scraping off excess mortar.** After laying the bricks for
the course, wear work gloves and use the edge of a mason's
trowel to scrape off excess mortar forced out of the joints
(above). Use a wet piece of burlap or rough cloth to wipe mortar
off the face of the bricks. Repeat the procedure from step 3 to lay
another course of bricks, if necessary. Keep the mortar damp until
it cures for 3 days: Mist occasionally with the fine spray of a garden
hose or use duct tape to tape plastic over the surface. Use a jointer
to strike the joints *(page 119)*.

MATCHING MORTAR COLOR

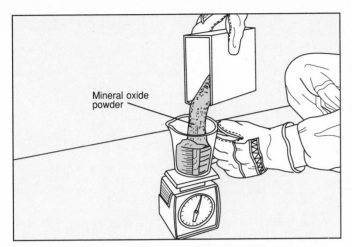

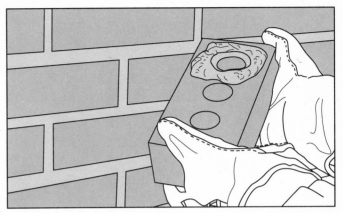

1 **Weighing the mortar ingredients.** To match the color of existing mortar, buy mineral oxide powder at a building supply center; a number of trials are likely to be required. Wearing work gloves, measure the dry ingredients for a small test batch of mortar *(page 117)*; before adding the cement, weigh it on a kitchen scale in a preweighed container. Weigh *(above)* and add mineral oxide powder following the label instructions, using no more than 10 per cent of the weight of the cement. Record the proportion of each ingredient used and mix them together thoroughly.

2 **Comparing the mortar colors.** Add water, a little at a time, and stir throroughly until the mortar is the proper consistency *(page 117)* and without color streaks; the mortar will lighten as it dries. Use a pointing trowel to spread a small amount of the test batch on a brick, concrete block or stone. Allow the mortar to set for 2 days, then compare its color with the color of the existing mortar *(above)*. If the colors are a close match, use the proportions recorded in step 1 to mix enough mortar for your repair. Otherwise, make another test batch: If the first test batch was too dark, add more dry mortar ingredients; if the first test batch was too light, add more mineral oxide powder.

STRIKING MORTAR JOINTS

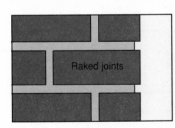
Raked joints

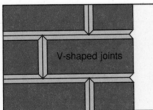
V-shaped joints

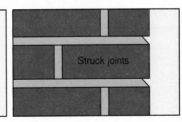
Struck joints

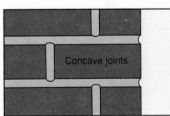
Concave joints

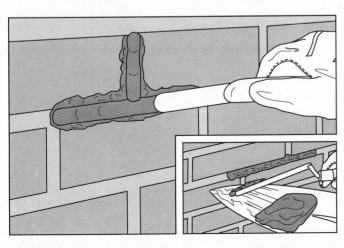

Finishing mortar joints. Examine the existing mortar joints to determine the tool to use: For raked joints *(above, far left)*, use a square-edged jointer, or raking tool. Make V-shaped joints *(above, center left)* with a V-shaped jointer. Struck joints *(above, center right)* are the least water-resistant type; they can be made with the tip of a trowel blade. For concave joints *(above, far right)*, the most common type, use a convex jointer or a piece of 3/8- or 1/2-inch pipe.

Check that each joint is filled with mortar; add mortar, if necessary, using a pointing trowel or a joint filler *(inset)*. Scrape off excess mortar and use a wet piece of burlap or rough cloth to wipe off the face of the masonry units. Before finishing, or striking, the joints, wait 30 minutes or until the mortar sets enough to hold a thumbprint. Use a jointer with a shape that matches the original joints to strike the joints, pressing the mortar into them. *(above)*. Wet the jointer and strike the vertical joints first, then the horizontal joints: Drag the jointer smoothly along each joint *(left)*, leaving its impression in the mortar.

CUTTING WOOD

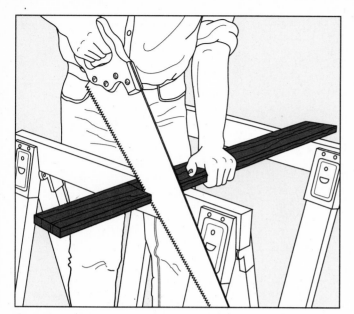

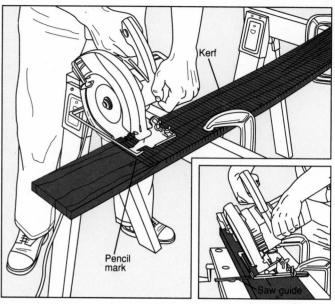

Using a crosscut saw for straight cuts. For quick, rough cuts across the grain, in a form board, for example, use a crosscut saw with about 8 teeth per inch. Measure and mark the wood piece for the cut. Wearing goggles, start the cut holding the saw almost perpendicular to the piece, aligning your shoulder and arm with the sawcut mark. Draw the blade slowly through the piece and toward you a few times; if you cannot grip the piece firmly with one hand, as shown, secure it with C clamps. Lower the angle of the saw to about 45 degrees and cut through the piece on the downstroke *(above)* until the blade is about 1 inch from the end of the cut. To finish the cut, grip the waste end with one hand, hold the saw perpendicular to the piece and use short up-and-down strokes.

Using a circular saw for straight or angled cuts. Measure and mark the wood piece: for kerfs, across it at 1/4- to 1-inch intervals with a try square; for bevels in a key, along it with a straight edge. Set the blade depth: for kerfs, about 1/3 of the wood thickness; for a standard or bevel cut about 1/2 inch more than the wood thickness. Set the baseplate at the desired cutting angle: 90 degrees for kerfs, 20 to 30 degrees for beveling a key. Secure the wood piece with C clamps; nail a key to be beveled to a scrap wood piece first and use a saw guide while cutting it. Wearing goggles, align the baseplate notch with the cutting mark, turn on the saw and push it slowly forward: across the piece for a kerf *(above)*; along the piece for a bevel *(inset)*.

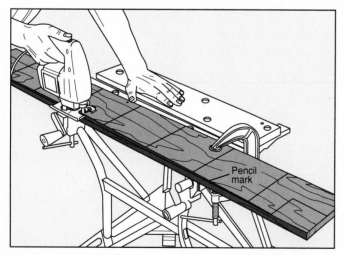

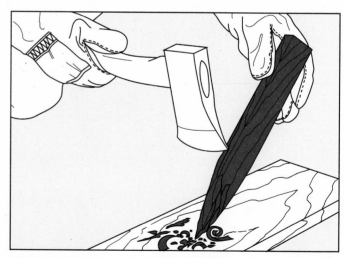

Using a saber saw for curved cuts. Use a saber saw with a blade of 8 to 10 teeth per inch for cutting curves—for example, in a wood piece to be used as a screed for crowning a sand bed. Measure and mark the piece; secure it with C clamps. Wearing goggles, align the baseplate notch with the cutting mark, turn on the saw and push it slowly forward, following the curve *(above)* and keeping the baseplate flat against the piece.

Using a hatchet to sharpen a stake. Cut wood for a stake 12 to 18 inches long using a crosscut saw or a circular saw *(steps above)*. To sharpen the bottom into a point, use a hatchet. Wearing work gloves and goggles, use one hand to hold the top of the stake, positioning it at a 45-degree angle. Grip the hatchet firmly with the other hand and chop the bottom of the stake *(above)*; work upward from the bottom, one side at a time, as shown, until the stake has a point sharp enough to be driven into the ground.

MAKING A TAMPER AND A SCREED

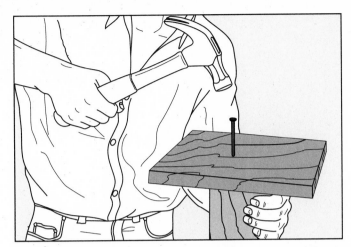

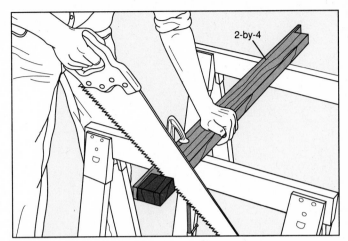

Constructing a tamper. To construct a tamper, use a 2-by-4 or a 2-by-6 for the handle and a 1-by- or 2-by-8 or 10 for the foot. Using a crosscut or a circular saw *(page 120)*, cut the handle chest-height and the foot 8 or 10 inches square. Center the foot on the bottom of the handle, as shown, and drive 3 or 4 common nails through it into the handle with a hammer *(above)*.

Sawing a screed. To make a screed for leveling a sand bed at the proper depth from the top of wood edging, use a crosscut or a circular saw *(page 120)* to cut a 2-by-4 6 inches longer than the width of the sand bed. At each end of the 2-by-4, mark lines for the notches: 3 inches from the end of the 2-by-4, draw a line across it equal in length to the thickness of the paving; draw a second line perpendicular to the first line from it to the end of the 2-by-4. Following the cutting lines, cut out the notches *(above)*.

BUILDING A CHIMNEY CAP FORM

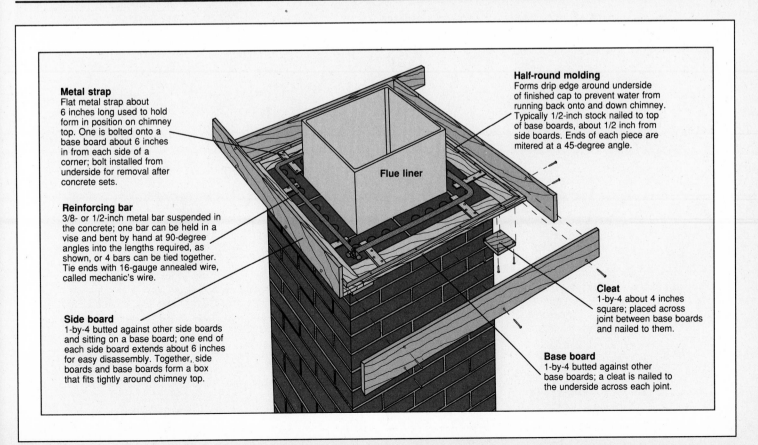

Metal strap
Flat metal strap about 6 inches long used to hold form in position on chimney top. One is bolted onto a base board about 6 inches in from each side of a corner; bolt installed from underside for removal after concrete sets.

Reinforcing bar
3/8- or 1/2-inch metal bar suspended in the concrete; one bar can be held in a vise and bent by hand at 90-degree angles into the lengths required, as shown, or 4 bars can be tied together. Tie ends with 16-gauge annealed wire, called mechanic's wire.

Side board
1-by-4 butted against other side boards and sitting on a base board; one end of each side board extends about 6 inches for easy disassembly. Together, side boards and base boards form a box that fits tightly around chimney top.

Half-round molding
Forms drip edge around underside of finished cap to prevent water from running back onto and down chimney. Typically 1/2-inch stock nailed to top of base boards, about 1/2 inch from side boards. Ends of each piece are mitered at a 45-degree angle.

Flue liner

Cleat
1-by-4 about 4 inches square; placed across joint between base boards and nailed to them.

Base board
1-by-4 butted against other base boards; a cleat is nailed to the underside across each joint.

BUILDING A CHIMNEY CAP FORM (continued)

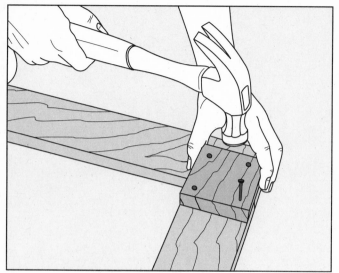

1 Making the base. Prepare to work safely on the roof *(page 114)*. Referring to page 121, use a tape measure to measure the sides of the chimney top and calculate your lumber needs; allow for extra length to make butt joints at the corners and to extend the sides. Build the form indoors or on the ground. Using a crosscut saw or a circular saw *(page 120)*, cut 1-by-4s for the base, the cleats and the sides. Position the base boards flat, butting the ends together. Center a cleat over each corner and use a hammer to drive 1 1/2-inch common nails into it *(above)*.

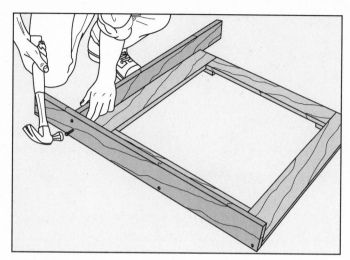

2 Adding the sides. Turn over the base and add the sides. Position a side board against the edge of a base board, one end flush with the corner, the other end extending beyond the corner, as shown. Use a hammer to drive 1 1/2-inch common nails every 8 to 10 inches along the bottom of the side board into the base board. Use the same procedure to add each other side board, butting one end to make a corner and driving at least two nails through the joint *(above)*.

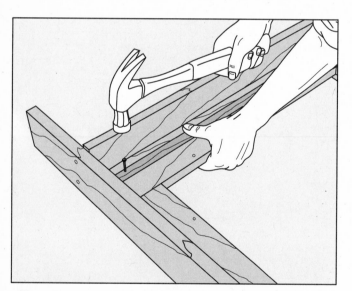

3 Nailing the molding. Draw a line along the top of each base board about 1/2 inch from the side board. Use a crosscut saw or a circular saw *(page 120)* to cut lengths of 1/2-inch half round molding equal to the distance between the points where the lines intersect. With a backsaw and a miter box, cut the ends of each length of molding at a 45-degree angle for mitered corners. Position each length of molding using the lines drawn as reference and use a hammer to drive 1-inch finishing nails into it every 8 to 10 inches along it.

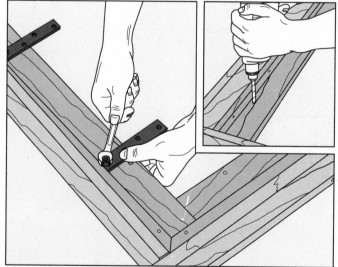

4 Installing the metal straps. Place two 6-inch metal straps on each base board, each strap about 6 inches from a corner; half of each strap should extend over the inside edge of the base board. Mark the fastener holes in each strap on the base board and remove the strap. Wearing goggles, bore holes for bolts using a power drill fitted with a wood bit of the same diameter as the bolts *(inset)*. Reposition each strap and install the bolts from the underside of the base boards and tighten the nuts with a wrench *(above)*. Use masking tape to seal any cracks or holes in the form so that placed concrete cannot escape.

CLEANING THE CHIMNEY FLUE

Unburned carbon particles collect in the chimney flue in the form of soot; chemical vapors condense and collect as creosote. Both soot and creosote are natural products of wood combustion, but can cause serious chimney fires if they are allowed to build up in the flue. **Caution:** Never burn garbage or plastic in a fireplace; plastic can emit caustic acids and garbage fires can burn out of control.

Once a year, have each chimney flue in your home professionally cleaned, or clean it yourself. Chimney cleaning kits are available in various sizes at a building supply center, and include a flue brush and extension poles, available in different lengths; measure the flue before buying a cleaning kit *(step 1)*. Before working on the roof, prepare to work safely *(page 114)*.

1 Measuring the flue. Prepare to work safely on the roof *(page 114)*. Before buying a chimney cleaning kit, use a tape measure to measure the flue size *(above)*; a flue may be round, square or rectangular. Buy a flue brush slightly larger than the flue; if it is of prefabricated metal, use a plastic brush designed for it. Estimate the distance from the chimney top to the damper and buy enough extension poles to reach it.

2 Sealing off the fireplace. To protect the area around the hearth from dislodged soot and creosote, seal off the fireplace entire opening indoors with plastic. Use duct tape to hold the plastic securely *(above)*; be sure to overlap the tape at any joint. After sealing off the chimney opening, open the damper.

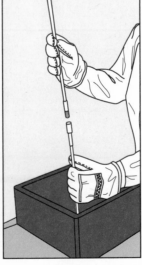

3 Cleaning the chimney flue. Prepare to work safely on the roof *(page 114)*. Wearing work gloves, goggles and a dust mask, attach the brush to the first extension pole. Push the brush into the flue liner and pull it up again, scrubbing off the surface *(above, left)*. Screw on another extension pole *(above, right)* and repeat the procedure. Continue scrubbing and adding extension poles until the brush reaches all the way to the damper. Withdraw the brush from the flue, unscrewing the extension poles as you raise it. Place the chimney brush in a large plastic bag and lower it to the ground. Climb safely off the roof.

4 Vacuuming the fireplace. Soot and creosote dislodged by the cleaning will accumulate in the fireplace; wait for 1 hour before removing the plastic from the fireplace to give the soot and creosote a chance to settle. Then, use a vacuum fitted with an edge-cleaning nozzle to suck up the accumulated soot and creosote *(above)*.

MASONRY HANGERS AND FASTENERS

Hangers and fasteners used on masonry must be suited both to the construction of the masonry and the weight placed on it. Some common types of masonry hangers and fasteners are shown below; unless otherwise noted, they may be used on brick, block, concrete, sandstone and limestone—consult a professional for those appropriate on other stone. Follow the weight guidelines listed on the hanger or fastener package, or ask for sales assistance.

Most hangers and fasteners require holes drilled into the masonry with a power drill or a hammer drill fitted with a masonry bit. The bit gauge needed is usually stamped on the hanger or fastener, or printed on its package; when in doubt, use a small bit and work up to a large one. When drilling, wear goggles and a dust mask. Drill perpendicular to the surface; a slight angle can reduce the holding power of a hanger or fastener.

Masonry nail
Position object and drive nail through it.

Self-furring nail
Used to fasten metal lath 1/4 inch from wall for stucco. Position plug behind lath and against wall, and drive nail through it and into wall.

Steel pin
Position object and drive steel pin through it with stud driver *(page 125)*; do not use on stone.

Plastic nail anchor
Drill hole of same diameter as anchor. Fit anchor through object and drive in nail.

Metal nail anchor
Drill hole of same diameter as anchor. Fit anchor through object and drive in nail.

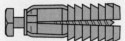

Toggle
Used on hollow concrete blocks. Drill hole to fit folded toggle, fit bolt through object into toggle, push toggle into hole, and tighten bolt.

Lag shield
Drill hole of same diameter as shield. Fit shield into hole, position object, and drive bolt through it and into shield.

Expansion bolt anchor
Drill hole of same diameter as anchor. Fit anchor into hole, position object, and drive bolt through it and into anchor.

Masonry screw
Drill hole about 1/16 inch smaller in diameter than screw, position object, and drive screw through it.

Fiber screw anchor
Drill hole about 1/16 inch larger than anchor. Fit anchor into hole, position object, and drive screw through it and into anchor.

Screw anchor
Drill hole of same diameter as anchor. Fit anchor into hole, position object, and drive screw through it and into anchor.

Hammer-set anchor
Drill hole of same diameter as anchor. Seat anchor in hole with setting tool, position object, and drive bolt through it and into anchor.

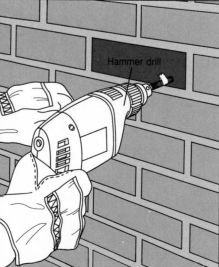

Drill holes for hangers and fasteners.
Holes for hangers and fasteners can be drilled into masonry using a power drill *(far left)* or a hammer drill *(near left)* fitted with a masonry bit; for maximum holding power, drill holes for hangers and fasteners into the masonry unit rather than into a mortar joint. Always use a masonry drill bit of the proper size—the gauge required is usually stamped onto the hanger or fastener. Make sure the bit is loaded correctly and seated tightly in the chuck; wrap masking tape around it, as shown, to know when to stop drilling. Wearing work gloves, goggles and a dust mask, position the bit against the masonry surface and squeeze the drill trigger. Stop drilling periodically to blow out masonry dust, and allow the bit and drill motor to cool.

Using a stud driver. A stud driver, commonly used to fasten furring strips, 2-by-4s, shutters and awnings to masonry, is a gunpowder-actuated tool that fires a steel pin; its use on stone is not recommended. On the hammer-driven type, a blow by a ball-peen hammer activates a charge that forces a steel pin through the object and into the masonry. **Caution:** Never use a stud driver without completely reading the instructions that come with it. When using a stud driver, always wear work gloves, goggles, ear protection, and long sleeves to protect against flying particles. To use the stud driver, load a pin into it following the instructions of the manufacturer. Position the stud driver against the object to be fastened and perpendicular to the masonry surface. Then, strike the firing pin on the end of the stud driver sharply with the ball-peen hammer *(left)*.

REPLACING A LOOSE OR DAMAGED MASONRY ANCHOR

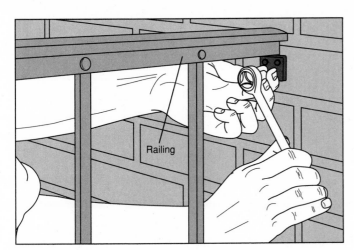

1 Removing the old anchor. If a masonry anchor is loose or damaged, replace it. Take the fastener out of the anchor, using a socket wrench to remove a bolt *(above)*. If you are removing a nail, the anchor may come out with it. If you removed a screw or a bolt, set the object aside to reach the anchor; if necessary, first remove all the fasteners securing it in place. Pull out the damaged anchor using pliers. Install a new anchor and fastener larger than the original using the information on page 124, or install a replacement anchor and fastener the same size as the original *(step 2)*; buy a replacement anchor and fastener, along with epoxy, at a building supply center.

2 Installing a replacement anchor. Blow loose particles out of the hole. Wearing rubber gloves, use a putty knife to fill the hole with epoxy *(above)*, following the instructions on the label. Allow the epoxy to set, but not to stiffen completely. To install a nail and anchor, reposition the object, fit the anchor into the hole in it, and drive the nail into the anchor. To install a screw or a bolt and anchor, fit the anchor into the hole, reposition the object, and drive the screw or the bolt through the hole in it and into the anchor. Scrape off excess epoxy with the edge of the putty knife blade. Wipe epoxy off the face of the masonry using a damp piece of burlap or rough cloth. Let the epoxy cure.

INDEX

Page references in *italics* indicate an illustration of the subject mentioned. Page references in **bold** indicate a Troubleshooting Guide for the subject mentioned.

ACKNOWLEDGMENTS

The editors wish to thank the following:
D. Atwill-Morin & Son Inc., St. Bruno, Que.; Barre Granite Association, Barre, Vt.; Bob Zider and Bob Hilferty, Beck & Beck Inc., Barre, Vt.; Colin Ball, Bondex International, Bramalea, Ont.; Brent Gabby, Brick Institute of America, Reston, Va.; Robert T. Young, Ceramic Tile and Marble Consultants, Inc., Oklahoma City, Okla.; Doug Friedman, Delaware Quarries, Lumberville, Pa.; John Maynard, Dimensional Stone magazine, Woodland Hills, Ca.; Du-For Scaffolding, Montreal, Que.; Joe Donatelli, Jr., Eastern Marble Supply Co., Scotch Plains, N.J.; Maurice Gagnon, Service Gagnon, Montreal, Que.; Gaetan Pelletier and Marcel Lebeau, Graybec, Betcon Division, Longueuil, Que.; Leonard T. McCann, M.A. Henry Ltd., Dundas, Ont.; Dinu Bumbaru, Heritage Montreal, Montreal, Que.; William McDonald, Indiana Limestone Institute, Bedford, Ind.; Bernie Hamilton, Kango Wolf International, Montreal, Que.; Alec MacLeod, Montreal, Que.; Marble Institute of America, Farmington, Mich.; Michel Deraiche, Montreal Brick and Stone, Montreal, Que.; William L. Casteel, National Precast Concrete Association, Indianapolis, Ind.; New York State Department of Environmental Conservation, Albany, NY; Brian Costello, Oakville Fire Department, Oakville, Ont.; J. Pace, Montreal, Que.; Lucien Nantais and Eric Milot, Permacon Group Inc., Montreal, Que.; Bruce McIntosh and William Panarese, Portland Cement Association, Chicago, Illinois; Sandy Rassenti, Montreal, Que.; Robert Scharff, Scharff Associates, New Ringgold, Pa.; Mark Talbot, Talbot Equipment Ltd., Quebec City, Que.; Bob VanLaningham, National Concrete Masonry Association, Herndon, Va. Andris Vitins, Toronto, Ont.; Dr. David Walker, Division of Emergency Medicine, Queen's University, Kingston, Ont.; Barry Coates, Westmount Fire Department, Westmount, Que.

The following persons also assisted in the preparation of this book:
Daniel Bazinet, Arlene Case and Natalie Watanabe.